# Finding Jackie

# Finding Jackie

## A LIFE REINVENTED

## Oline Eaton

DIVERSION
BOOKS

*For Jessica, and for Burvil*

*With endless love to my parents*

DONOVAN WAS HERE

For more information, email info@diversionbooks.com
Diversion Books
A division of Diversion Publishing Corp.
www.diversionbooks.com

First Diversion Books edition, January 2023
Hardcover ISBN: 9781635767933
eBook ISBN: 9781635768220

Printed in the United States of America
10 9 8 7 6 5 4 3 2 1

# CONTENTS

Jacqueline (she doesn't like "Jackie" but everyone calls her that) . . .

—*Tucson Daily Citizen*, October 18, 1960

•

"We always use Jackie," explains [Myron] Fass [ . . . ] "Jacqueline is not American. If anyone saw her on the street, they wouldn't say, there's Jacqueline, they'd say, there's Jackie."

—*Boston Globe*, May 15, 1966

•

"I just saw Jackie," she breathes into my phone. "She looks fabulous!" I do not ask, Jackie Who? I know. Everybody knows.

—Ellen Goodman, *San Bernardino County Sun*, July 29, 1989

•

DAVID LETTERMAN: How did she pronounce her name?
CAROLINE KENNEDY: You wouldn't believe what a big deal this has become, really . . . I should have just left it alone, but I opened my mouth and now, and nobody can pronounce it and everyone's confused . . .
DAVID LETTERMAN: What is, as you understand it, your mother liked to be referred to as . . .
CAROLINE KENNEDY: *Jack-leen* Kennedy.

—*Late Night with David Letterman*, October 6, 2011

# PROLOGUE

I was twelve—two weeks from turning thirteen. I'd not really known who she was though I'd known she was ill.

When she died, this is what struck me: how very much she was loved. I'd been watching the First Lady for years, and it didn't seem to me that she was even liked, much less loved. But that was Hillary. This was Jackie. Jackie, it seemed, was different.

Why?

I'd encountered her the year before during Women's History Month. The teacher miscalculated the weeks in February and so, via a hurriedly Xeroxed handout, Jacqueline Kennedy Onassis eked her way into the classroom pantheon of powerful American women. In this illustration, her enormous '70s earrings and feathered hair presented a startling contrast to the severe buns and furrowed brows of Susan B. Anthony and Sojourner Truth. She appeared alarmingly modern, unhistorical, alive.

I saw her then, but I did not care. Hearing she had died, witnessing the response, I cared completely, inexplicably. And I wanted to know more.

People praised her extraordinary beauty but, looking at photographs, all I saw was an odd-looking woman with strangely spaced eyes. She was eulogized as dignified, classy, a superior wife, mother, decorator, and hostess. The more I read, those prissy adjectives fell away and a far more interesting, substantive woman began to emerge. She climbed pyramids and held interesting jobs and married a foreigner and lived abroad. She consciously stepped outside the rarefied world she'd been born into and saw things, did things,

things that I—a girl trying and failing to be a proper lady, growing up in a white evangelical community in the American South—
longed to see and do.

I wanted to get out, to go somewhere. Where, I didn't know
exactly, much less how, and there were very few women around
to show the way. Mary Richards and Rhoda Morgenstern and Dr.
Michaela Quinn, yes, but they were fictional characters who lived
fictional lives. Jackie was the best example I found of someone real.
Someone who had done this. Jackie offered a way out. Jackie was
my escape.

The summer of 1994, I read every available word written on the
life of Jacqueline Kennedy Onassis. When I began writing about
her a decade later, when I was twenty-two, I imagined I knew her
story. What I learned a decade after that, newly transplanted to
London and writing the story of her life again, is that I knew next
to nothing. Now I know that we maybe only ever know next to
nothing. From there, we just imagine.

We tell ourselves stories in order to live, to cope with life's inher-
ent uncertainties and the fact that we will one day die. We tell them
again and again because, while lives and books end, stories do not.
They go on and on.

●

As a little girl, she was often alone. She wrote poetry and rode
horses and had skinned knees. They said her independence and
courage were extraordinary for someone so young.

As a teenager, she foresaw herself as "the circus queen." It was,
at the time, a joke. In retrospect, it reads as prophesy.

Her ambition, printed in her high school yearbook, was "not to
be a housewife." Later she wrote a boyfriend at Harvard, "Can you
think of anything worse?" She was sure she could not.

Years later, she will confess, "I'm an outsider—and that's uncomfortable in American life." But this wasn't such a bad thing, and
during the 1960 campaign it was the very element of her personality that so vividly set her apart. As *Time* observed of the future First

Lady on the eve of her husband's inauguration in January 1961: "In the larger bear hug of the Kennedy family, Jackie flatly refused to be smothered."

To do so was to exert her own individuality, and it created the sense that beneath the poise and elegance of the First Lady lurked "a beatnik," the word Washington society maven Pearl Mesta used when denouncing her audacity in going bare-legged. Yet another detail that reinforced the sense she was a renegade.

America was gaga for royalty, and so, too, it loved rebels. With her loner tendencies, she perfectly fit the bill: a watered-down, female, First Lady equivalent of Marlon Brando or James Dean. "They took their identities from their husbands," civil rights activist June Murray Wall Williams later remembered of other First Ladies, "whereas Jackie Kennedy, she spoke French, she spoke Spanish, she'd traveled, she'd been abroad."

A fiercely independent woman, Jackie "carv[ed] out her own existence," observed Laura Bergquist, a reporter for *Look* magazine. Jackie did this by putting aside time every afternoon for painting and reading, a self-imposed period of solitude she sternly enforced and during which she read everything. Reading was a palliative, woven into her life to provide imaginative relief from the complications therein. It was a way out: "the magic carpet" she called it in a letter to a friend, leading to anything you could dream of—"escape, adventure, power! everything." She was always eager to get away.

She liked calm and control and she lived in an environment in which both were difficult to achieve due to the intrusions of photographers and journalists, but most especially because of her husband's career and infidelities. "The 'other woman' business was foremost in her mind," said one friend. "She couldn't accept her own frailties," recalled another, an assessment that pulls into focus a picture of a woman struggling with her own shortcomings: a woman who felt constitutionally ill-equipped for the type of life she nonetheless longed for.

In the summer of 1960, a newspaper profile titled "'Jackie' Kennedy, Possible First Lady, Woman of Contrasts," written by Marie Ridder, characterized her as "a many-sided woman." Similarly, in a profile published in *Esquire* four months after his near-fatal stabbing of his wife, Norman Mailer identified Jacqueline Kennedy as "a lady with delicate and exacerbated nerves . . . detached . . . moody and abstracted." These condescending, casually sexist portrayals coalesced into a portrait of a woman who appears in the press and subsequent biographies as almost pathologically unruly and unpredictable when she was, more likely, shy, a classic introvert, and, later, living with PTSD.

She wanted adventure, always had. And yet, when she got a job at a newspaper after college, a colleague observed, "In the real world of the Great Adventure, she found it difficult to approach strangers." She could have been an artist, a writer. Had she not married John Kennedy, friends thought, she would have excelled at both. Either she didn't trust herself or didn't have the nerve to face the public attention. At an exhibition of Peter Beard's work in the early '70s, she pulled the artist aside and told him, "I wish I could do what you're doing—but I can't." Beard noted her frustration with herself.

But she did what she could. She was quick to travel, always exploring, always curious; archeology, ruins especially, remained a lifelong fascination. "The most exciting thing to me," she wrote in a 1962 memo to her husband regarding the discovery of a new site in Sudan, "was that I thought everything had been explored in the world—Troy, Carthage, Babylon, Aztec, etc. There wasn't much left for archeologists. . . . But, now, if I were a young man, I would be an archeologist and go."

*If I were a young man.* How that smarts: The ache of wanting to go. The restrictions, both societal and seemingly self-imposed, that somehow kept her—the American First Lady, one of the most visible women in the world and the most powerful wife in the United States—from seeing for herself the newly opened sites in Egypt and Sudan, that left her stuck at home dreaming about what "Nobody dreamed . . . had ever existed."

There was a transience to her life—in her youth, her marriage to John Kennedy, and later, to Aristotle Onassis—a listlessness that fit well with the rhythms of the jet set: the newly mobile rich with their yachts and planes, always at someone's villa, sipping wine midday. But it's maybe too much to call her a member. Though she liked to dip in and out of this scene, to swim in their pools and relax in their company, she was an outsider there as well. For all that Americans believed she was a symbol of society, she did not quite belong. Always, she felt herself to be outside of things.

We cannot really know her. All we know is she was there. She was real. Once upon a time, as Andy Warhol said, the name *Jackie* seemed to float electric on the air.

No book can capture the totality of a life. It's just a torrent of words in the place where a person once was. The myth is so engrained now that we must almost reimagine or reinvent her if we're to see anything at all: an adventurer, a wanderer, a woman in whom many Americans, for over half a century, have deeply, fiercely wanted to believe.

This is the story of that Jackie and her alarming life.

Some day one of those fashionable biographers who specializes, with a graceful touch, on female personalities with a bravura of their own will piece together the pattern of this one—

where the episode belongs—not in the history of changing American manners and morals, but in that of the fantasy life of Americans.

Max Lerner
Monday, February 23, 1970—THE JANESVILLE GAZETTE—Page 7

# THE NIGHT LIZ & BURTON DESTROYED EDDIE FISHER!

# PHOTOPLAY

Jacqueline Kennedy vs Elizabeth Taylor

## AMERICA'S 2 QUEENS!

A comparison of their days and nights!

How they raise their children! How they treat their men!

BEGINNING AT WHAT SEEMED THE END:

## FRIDAY, NOVEMBER 22, 1963

And then it was over. "I want them to see what they have done," she said. Across the years, she demands we look.

•

The First Lady is looking away when the first shot rings out in Dealey Plaza. By the time she turns, her attention caught by the sound she mistakes for motorcycle backfire crackling through the dense Dallas air, her husband has already been hit once. Texas governor John Connolly, also in the car, is wounded by the same bullet and screaming, "My God, they're going to kill us all!"

The First Lady turns. Alarmed by the expression on the president's face, she leans toward him, trying to figure out what has happened, what is happening. And then, just as she leans in, another bullet enters the rear of his head and explodes out an oval-shaped hole from his skull's right side, so that the president's brain blows open, coming apart mere inches from the First Lady's face. After hours of interviews with her, over countless daiquiris, author William Manchester will reconstruct the moment based on her memories: "Now, in a gesture of infinite grace, he raised his right hand, as though to brush back his tousled chestnut hair. But the motion faltered. The hand fell back limply. He had been reaching for the top of his head. But it wasn't there any more."

•

In his hastily typed notes from a conversation on November 29, 1963, journalist Theodore H. White offers a less stylized account. She tells him what she remembers:

> I saw Connolly grabbing his arms and saying no no no-nonono, with his fist beating—then Jack turned and I turned—all I remember was a blue gray building up ahead; then Jack turned back so neatly; his last expression was soneat; he had his hand out, I asee a piece of his skull coming off; it was flesch colors not white—he was holding out his hand—and I can see this perfectly clean piece detachin itself from his head; then he slumped in my lap; his blood and his brains were in my lap . . . we all lay down in the dor and I kept saying Jack, Jack, Jack  and someone was yelling hes dead hes dead. All the ride to the hospital I kept bending over him saying Jack, Jack can yourhe ar me, I love you Jack. I kept holding the top of his head down trying to keep the [ . . . ] my legs my hands were covered with his brains . . . [ . . . ] I'd tried to hold the top of his head down, maybe I could keep it in . . . I knew he was dead . . . [ . . . ] and I said to myself, 'I thought I'll take care of him every day of . . . I'll make him happy, but I knew he was dead' . . .

•

"She nudged me with her left elbow," remembered a doctor on duty at Parkland Hospital that day. "And then with her right hand handed me a good-sized chunk of the President's brain."

Another physician urged the former First Lady to leave the operating room. She asked, "How can I see anything worse than what I've seen?"

Repeatedly, it was suggested by different people that she change her clothes. Repeatedly, she refused. She said: "I want them to see what they have done."

Her husband has been dead an hour. Already, the Secret Service know about a 26.6-second home movie taken by Abraham Zapruder, a women's clothing manufacturer who was watching the motorcade go through Dealey Plaza during his lunch break. The film contains footage of the fatal bullet's impact. But the president's widow, unaware of its existence, believes she is the only proof of what happened in Dallas.

A week later, she tells Theodore White she should've left the blood and hair on her face. Before she was brought in to witness the new president taking the oath of office, she washed off the evidence, instantly regretting it: "I should have left it there, let them see what they've done. If I'd just had the blood and caked hair when they took the picture . . ." She sensed that no one wanted her in the picture as she was and relented. She's angry at herself because already the image was distorted, the atrocity lessened.

"I saw myself in the mirror," she said, "my whole face splattered with blood and hair. I wiped it off with a Kleenex. History! I thought, no one really wants me there."

# PART I

# Before

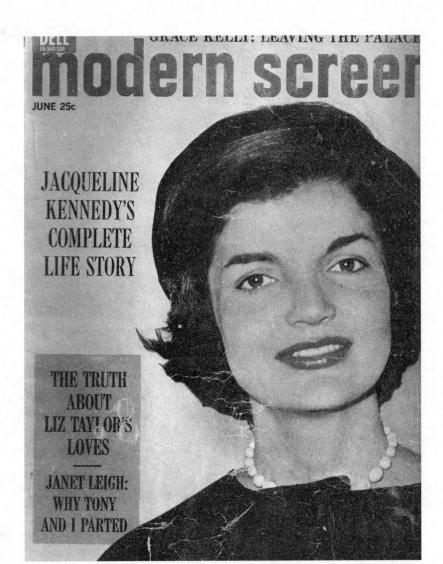

DELL
05-540-206

GRACE KELLY: LEAVING THE PALACE

# modern screen

JUNE 25c

## JACQUELINE KENNEDY'S COMPLETE LIFE STORY

## THE TRUTH ABOUT LIZ TAYLOR'S LOVES

## JANET LEIGH: WHY TONY AND I PARTED

SHE DOES NOT KNOW WHAT WILL HAPPEN TO HER. NO ONE does.

July 28, 1929: she's born in Southampton, New York, six weeks late. She'll spend much of her life wishing people would correctly pronounce her name.

·

A socialite once said of the marriage of Jack and Janet Bouvier, her parents: "Janet married him because his name appeared in the [Social] Register. He married her because her father operated a bank. She was a bitch and he was a bastard, and in the end both were disillusioned." The elements that later defined the public story of the Bouviers' eldest daughter already appear in this brief assessment. This is what she was born into: a world wherein, particularly for white women, the attainment and keeping of social status, money, power, and a man were one's *raison d'etre*.

She adored her father, Black Jack, a charismatic man who looked like Clark Gable, and whose racially charged nickname stemmed from his perpetual deep tan. Her sister, Lee, born two years later, adored him, too, later recalling, "To be with him when we were children, meant joy, excitement, and love. He brought gaiety to everything."

But his gaiety had a dark side. *Rake* was the term used then; *predator* is likely the word we'd use now. "He was an absolute lecher, absolute ravening, ravenous lecher," remembered a school friend. "And Jackie, of course, knew it, and it amused her, but I don't think she was aware—she might have been, she didn't miss anything—of the extent to which we were teasing her father and making fun of him. . . . This man was decidedly repulsive."

In his heyday, Black Jack was sexy; he was also obsessed with the superficial and profligately spent money he did not have. His eldest daughter inherited his widely spaced eyes and an indefatigable love of sexual gossip. As a friend of hers later admitted, "She had all the wrong standards, all the wrong standards, and yet she became something very special in spite of this." "Black Jack was really a very unfortunate man and Jacqueline tried to live him down most of her life," one of John Kennedy's old Harvard roommates later remembered. "There was a sense of buried drama about him, brewing clouds."

Black Jack lavished her with praise and compliments, which came in stark contrast to the feedback she got from her mother. Janet was admittedly in a tight spot. With two young children, she found herself married to an impecunious, flagrantly unfaithful alcoholic. In June 1934, when a society journo photographed Black Jack holding hands with another woman while his wife stood beaming in front of them, unaware of what was literally going on behind her back, Janet was humiliated. The Bouviers spent the next three years separating and reuniting.

In July 1940, in Nevada, Janet finally filed for divorce. The divorce—an ostracizing act for anyone at the time, but one for which women paid a steeper social price than men—forced Janet to solicit financial help from her parents. It was a mortifying ask for a woman known for her implacable pride.

Meticulously mannered and socially ambitious, Janet demanded perfection from her daughters. Lee later mused: "I don't think Jackie ever disliked my mother as you've heard. I think that she was always grateful to her because she felt that she had intentionally enlarged her world—our world—for our sake." If Black Jack failed Janet, Janet was determined she wouldn't fail their daughters. She knew the pressures they faced as society girls and she tried, in her own way, to equip them to meet those challenges, instilling by word and example a belief that underpinned their thinking: a woman needed security, stability, and protection.

In the end, however, each Bouvier girl grew up feeling that she could never measure up. Lee later recounted how Janet always said, "Jacqueline is the intellectual one, and Lee will have twelve children and live in a rose-covered cottage." Likewise, Jackie wistfully told a friend, "Lee was always the pretty one. I guess I was supposed to be the smart one."

With her mother's remarriage in June 1942 to the fabulously wealthy Hugh D. "Hughdie" Auchincloss—a gentle, rather dull man who owned multiple enormous homes and was, reportedly, an "avid" collector of pornography—Jackie's circumstances were cast in stark relief. She was not wealthy herself, but she now moved between Hughdie's homes in Newport, Rhode Island, and the Washington, D.C., suburbs. "She was gorgeous, electrifyingly attractive, and as with electrifying people she had one basic terrible flaw," a friend recalled: "she was absolutely obsessed with poverty, absolutely obsessed . . . she was living in what she considered to be this big house in Washington and she knew that one day she'd be out in the cold. What could she do? How was she going to live?"

To add to her anxieties, the big house in Washington—Hughdie's mansion, Merrywood—wasn't peaceful. Rhode Island was no better. A relative recollected a visit to the Auchincloss's Newport home, Hammersmith Farm, in the early 1950s as, "Nothing but the sound of slamming doors, great feet thundering up and down the stairs, slapping across faces, vile oaths, with Hughdie sitting sort of slumped in the middle of it."

BY THE TIME SHE WAS A TEENAGER, THE YOUNG MISS BOUVIER exhibited the tensions that would come to define her image in later life: sensuality versus stability, a love of luxury fed by financial insecurity, the toughness of an athlete tempered by the sensitivity of an artist. She had established a rigid, protective distance from the world. A friend with whom she traveled recalled her as "probably the most private person I've ever met. I always felt she was living in a dream world." There were, and would always be, pieces of herself she would not share, retreating into what another acquaintance characterized as "a world of manufactured dreams."

At boarding school, she did drama and wrote poetry and short stories. Her writing was lively and clever; she had an eye for details. "I honestly think you could write a book on your travels," her father wrote her in the late 1940s, when she was roaming around Europe. "All you have to do is take the time and you could get out a book that would be a bestseller."

"Don't laugh this off," he cautioned. In time, she seems to have taken her own talents more seriously.

She liked the idea of having a job that would liberate her from musty old Newport—all those mansions and Republicans and everybody you'd known all your life. She wanted to get out, do something different, see something new. "Being a reporter seems a ticket out of the world," she said. A friend of her stepfather's called up the editor of the *Washington Times-Herald* and asked, "Are you still hiring little girls?" Jackie got the gig of the Inquiring Photographer. It paid $42.50 per week.

She did well in journalism, a field in which she had virtually no practical experience other than some lessons at the photography school run by Robert Scurlock—of the pioneering Scurlock photography family, and already famous for his own photographs of African American life in the nation's capital. Soon, aged twenty-two, she earned a pay bump to $56.75. "Some were proud that a girl was doing so well," remembered her dressmaker, Mini Rhea, who read her column religiously. Many of Rhea's clients did too. "A few, who knew her wealthy background, complained that she was taking a job away from some man who needed it, and others, I suspected were jealous. But for the most part, [they] gave her credit for steering away from the easy life she could have had with its round of pleasant parties and no exertion."

It may sound small, but this was a daring route for a white woman of her era and upbringing. "We were supposed to do what we were told," a girlfriend recalled. "In the 1950s, one was practically considered an old maid to marry at twenty-two, but Jackie wanted a college education, to live in Europe, and to get a job as a writer."

She wanted to work, to challenge herself and feel she was a part of an adventure, but she wanted a husband and a family too. It was revolutionary to go to college and hold a job. She didn't necessarily want to be a revolutionary.

This was the late 1940s, early 1950s. The author Brenda Maddox later observed of the culture Jackie Bouvier grew up in: "Goals for girls were as universal as the laws of physics. Girls were supposed to be sexy. The reward for sexiness was virility. Proof of virility was to be on the football team. A girl's rating was measured by the rank of player she could snare." Race is invisible here, but it's white girls Maddox was writing about. Outside of the Black press (newspapers like the *Chicago Defender*, and magazines like *Ebony* and *Jet*), the experiences of Black women and girls were rarely represented or accounted for in the archetypal womanhood of the mid-twentieth-century public sphere.

For the many white women who did have careers, their work was often viewed by others as a short interlude, "the brief interval before their sex betrayed them and they had to put aside ambition for marriage." The role of the housewife was deified. A 1948 General Mills ad in *Life* declared this career "the most important one a woman can choose." A housewife combined "the skills of 15 to 20 trades and professions"; she is, at once, a "purchasing agent and nurse, spiritual advisor and seamstress, interior decorator and teacher, carpenter—and keeper of the cookie jar," and "she knows how to be a glamour girl too."

Jackie didn't want to be a housewife and said so repeatedly. As a teenager at boarding school, she wrote a boyfriend, asking, "Can you think of anything worse than living in a small town like this all your life and competing to see which housewife can bake the best cake?" But for a girl in the 1930s and '40s, there were few independent women in view; her options seemed limited. "[M]any of us knew that we did not want to be like our mothers," Betty Friedan wrote of this generation of women in *The Feminine Mystique*, while also noting the lack of alternatives.

Unmarried at twenty-one, twenty-two, and twenty-three, the young Miss Bouvier felt she was floundering. "The restlessness of her search was evident," recalled an acquaintance of her hopes for marriage. "She wasn't desperate, she wasn't undone, but she was always drily observant and aware of her dilemma." It was a dilemma complicated by her height (5'7"), her intelligence, and the sense that, as he put it, "She was not just every young man's cup of tea."

"I didn't want to marry any of the young men I grew up with," she later admitted, "not because of them but because of their life." But in lieu of that life, she didn't know what she wanted. And such reflections belied the increasing pressure to marry and marry well, for she had no money of her own.

IN LATE 1951, SHE MET JOHN HUSTED, AN INVESTMENT BANKER from New York. When he proposed in January 1952, she accepted. The haste of Husted's proposal suggested an appealing impetuosity and her mother's disapproval may have added to his allure. In a letter to friends, she bragged of how she'd found someone who wasn't "the sensible boy next door" type that her mother thought she should marry.

On January 21, 1952, Miss Bouvier's engagement was announced, but she already had doubts and had begun distancing herself; the termination of their engagement by "mutual consent" was announced in late March.

"I'm ashamed that we both went into it so quickly and gaily but I think . . . we both need something of a shock to make us grow up," she wrote Father Leonard, an Irish priest with whom she'd struck up a correspondence. The whole thing had, she said, "grown me up and it's about time! The next time will be ALL RIGHT and have a happy ending!"

In the end there seemed but one path. "I had the feeling," remembered a former suitor, "that she felt with a little more guts she might take off for Paris or some such place and become totally independent, but instead she settled for security." Still, as evidenced by the broken engagement to Husted, she wouldn't settle for the world she'd been raised in, and marrying a stockbroker from New York wasn't a bold enough leap. She wanted excitement and adventure, and she'd already set her sights on someone else.

Charles Bartlett, D.C. correspondent for the *Chattanooga Times*, had been trying to introduce her to a congressman from Massachusetts for a couple of years. While she was still seeing Husted, Bartlett and his wife finally managed to make the introduction. In many ways, John Kennedy—called Jack by family and friends—was a radical choice. Both the Bouviers and the Lees, Jackie's maternal and paternal family, respectively, didn't have the fanciest of family trees but they flattered themselves that they were old money. Though the Kennedy social stature had been improved by a decade of civic duty, theirs was still a fortune tainted by the *nouveau riche* entrepreneurial stink of bootlegging and Hollywood. Thus, marriage to this Irish Catholic politician would have been seen by someone like Jackie's mother—ironically, also Irish, but erroneously convinced by family lore that she was descended from "the Lees of Virginia"—as a decided step down.

And perhaps, to Jackie, that made it all the more appealing. "My mother used to bring around all these beaus for me," she said, "but he was different." He was, she observed to Father Leonard, "brighter than me."

Neither naïve nor even particularly idealistic, she knew what marriage to a man like this meant. "Maybe it will end very happily," she supposed, "or maybe since he's this old and set in his ways and cares so desperately about his career he just won't want to give up that much time to extra-curricular things like marrying me!"

To a friend, she wrote a pragmatic jingle:

Watch yo' step honey on that path
of roses,
There's more thorns 'neath them thar
leaves than you Knowses.


A shrewd judge of character, she wrote Father Leonard, "He's like my father in a way—loves the chase and is bored with the conquest—and once married needs proof he's still attractive, so flirts with other women and resents you. I saw how that nearly killed Mummy."

She saw and was undeterred.

When they married in September 1953, newspapers around the country identified her as an "Heiress," writing the fairy tale in real time.



THE SUPPOSED FAIRY TALE CONCEALED A COMPLEX REALITY. Strong-willed, tightly wound, and intelligent, both Jack and Jackie were emotionally guarded in the extreme. He was, she thought, "a simple man, yet so complex that he would frustrate anyone trying to understand him . . . he didn't want to reveal himself at all."

She later attributed her husband's emotional reticence to his position in the Kennedy family, between the adored eldest child, Joe, and his younger sister, Rosemary, who was intellectually disabled. Jackie believed that, because Jack's father's attention was so focused on Joe and his mother's on Rosemary, "Jack didn't really get any love there. He was lost . . . he suffered terribly . . . just wasn't loved or paid attention to." He was also often in considerable pain and ill health due to back injuries and Addison's disease, a chronic condition resulting from failure of the adrenal glands. In response to his upbringing and his health, he approached life at a remove and with an insouciance so single-minded that, often, he appeared detached, cold, and uncaring.

"It was difficult," Jack Kennedy said. "I was thirty-six, she was twenty-four. We didn't fully understand each other."

According to her, "It was all wrong."

It hadn't helped that within months of their wedding the couple were beset by difficulties sure to test the most solid relationship: John Kennedy's eight-month incapacitation from back surgery in 1954, a series of miscarriages, a stillbirth in 1956, a subsequent brief separation, and the sudden death of Jackie's father, who'd spiraled into a tailspin of debt and alcoholism. Lacking a permanent home, they relocated with such regularity that a friend observed of Jackie that "every house she had ever lived in was like a one-night stand." The 1957 birth of their daughter, Caroline, helped solidify the Kennedys' shaky bond, but their relationship remained fraught.

A friend of Jack Kennedy's thought they were "the two most isolated, most *alone* people I ever met," and, rather than bringing each other solace, they remained alone together, as another friend put it, like "two cocoons reaching for each other." Jackie once characterized herself and her husband as icebergs, with most of their lives invisible, and said she felt they knew this about each other and that it bonded them. But it was an obstacle as well.

"I think I'm in love," she'd told Father Leonard, but she allowed for the possibility that "Maybe I'm just dazzled and picture myself in a glittering world of crowned heads and Men of Destiny— and not just a sad little housewife." And she confessed that Jack Kennedy's emotions remained a mystery to her, though she imagined "he was as much in love with me as he could be with anyone."

One of Kennedy's female confidantes remembered her impression of the couple around the mid-1950s: "He just couldn't stand her. That's all I got. I mean he couldn't understand or stand her at all at that stage." Later, newspaper columnist Betty Beale observed of the president: "He was an attractive, sexy guy. But he never put her first."

His wife made a joke of this, laughing with a reporter during the 1960 campaign that her husband "had the nerve once to give me an original letter by John Quincy Adams," which he put "Framed, and on HIS study wall." When he gave her a letter by Byron, it was an improvement. "At least I like Byron," she said.

If he wasn't wildly infatuated with her, he was by no means indif-
ferent; he seemed to bask in her intelligence and *je ne sais quoi*. At a
Washington birthday party, Kennedy bragged to the woman sitting
next to him that he only got married because, if he remained a
bachelor, people would think he was "queer." The woman recalled:

> He was saying this to me *sotto voce* all through dinner . . . and
> across the table was Jackie, being a perfect spellbinder as
> always, and he was eyeing her the whole time. . . . And I
> think the impression I got that night—and I think it was the
> first time he overtly made a play for me—was that because of
> her extreme attractiveness that he didn't compete with it, he
> assimilated it and it made him more refulgent . . . she some-
> how enhanced him and made him more of a sun god.

Throughout their marriage, they struggled to overcome what
Jackie once referred to as "an emotional block" between them, a
block that arose because, in the words of a mutual friend, "His love
had certain reservations and hers was total."

Jack Kennedy had seen modeled, in the private life of his father,
an Irish Catholic approach where the wife was idolized, other
women were available as sexual playthings, and forgiveness was
expected in the confessional. One historian dubbed it a familial
"competitive discipline of lust." It was an approach he copied.

She tolerated the pathological philandering, but sometimes the
frustration spilled out. "Jackie is superb in her private life, but do
you think she'll ever amount to anything in her political life?" Jack
Kennedy asked a friend in her presence. Her reply was teasing but
also barbed. "Jack is superb in his political life, but do you think
he'll ever amount to anything in his personal life?"

In 1958, she confided to a neighbor of her mother's, "I don't
know if I can stay with him, he's so unfaithful." The neighbor
pointed out that such an action would destroy her husband's career
and warned, "I doubt you want that mark on your life." She didn't.
She stuck it out, telling a reporter: "What I try to do is make things

as simple and easy for Jack as possible, so that his life is just a bit better for my being around."

In this, Jackie was doing what a good wife did. "More and more these days," a newspaper article informed readers, "the decision on whether a husband gets that new job or a terrific promotion hinges on what the boss-to-be thinks of the man's wife." A "good wife" was, therefore, one who "is capable and does not ask her husband to do her job, but leaves him free to do his own . . . is adaptable and can settle anywhere if necessary . . . [her] primary interest is her husband, home, and children."

1960. SO MUCH HAS NOT YET HAPPENED. WE KNOW HOW it'll go. They do not.

Many Americans expect to experience a nuclear attack during their lifetime. Schoolchildren watch a nine-minute film instructing them:

> The flash of an atomic bomb can come at any time . . . without any warning . . . Sundays, holidays, vacation time, we must be ready every day, all the time. . . . No matter where we live—in the city or the country—we must be ready ALL THE TIME for the atomic bomb.

Schools hold atomic bomb drills, their purpose so unambiguous that Joan Didion later writes, "It never occurred to me that I would not sooner or later—most probably certainly before I ever grew up or got married or went to college—endure the moment of its happening": the dropping of the bomb and her own death.

Television shows like *The Twilight Zone* and *Alfred Hitchcock Presents* explore the anxieties of American life while *The Andy Griffith Show*, *The Flintstones*, and *Bonanza* offer escape. The U.S. Census Bureau reports that 88 percent of American homes have TVs—up from 12 percent in 1950. There are the three network channels—ABC, CBS, and NBC. Depending upon where you live, the strength of your broadcast signal, and the vagaries of the weather, perhaps you can access one or two additional local channels. In May 1961, the head of the Federal Communications Commission denounces American TV as "a vast wasteland": "a procession of game shows, formula comedies about totally unbelievable families, blood and thunder, mayhem, violence, sadism . . . more violence, and cartoons."

The nightly news is fifteen minutes long. *CBS Evening News with Walter Cronkite* won't expand to a full thirty minutes until September 1963.

Newspapers seem more reliable. "Do you know anybody who doesn't read one?" a columnist asks. "Probably not because every literate adult reads one every day." Most cities have multiple papers with morning and evening editions, though the columnist Drew Pearson worries. "In recent years there have become fewer and fewer newspapers," he laments, so that in twenty years, by the 1980s, "you may find that in most American cities there will be only one."

It is the heyday of the magazine and the twilight of the white lady beauty shop. The shops are, of course, segregated—legally in some parts of the country and unofficially in others. The standard medium-sized shop serving white women boasts big mirrors, pink walls, four washbasins, four hair dryers, single copies of *Vogue, Seventeen, Harper's Bazaar*, and *Mademoiselle*, and a mountain of movie magazines.

Sounding like everyone who's ever hated going to the gym, one woman tells a reporter: "I'm always so tired, I dread going to the beauty shop, but I'm always so glad I went." She says it helps her to get out of the house and hear about other people; otherwise her whole world is limited to her husband and kids. According to another, the beauty shop appointment is the only time she has for uninterrupted reading, the only time in the week when she can put her mind to whatever she wants.

For fancy events, the stylist might do an in-house call. Otherwise, Jackie—excepting when she was First Lady—and her Kennedy sisters-in-law got their hair done in beauty shops, too, as did many women of their milieu. For women around the country, of varying means and status, the beauty shop provided a sanctuary; a place to engage in the maintenance required in a patriarchal society, but also a place to escape their home lives, even if only for an hour, and find community together. That quiet time under the hair-dryer— reading, thinking, being—was an essential, nourishing ritual in the broader rhythm of the week.

In New York, thanks to lobbying by the female secretary of state, vending machines are allowed in beauty parlors. It's now legal for those women under the hairdryers to drink sodas and eat sandwiches while they wait. The victory is celebrated as "recognition of a necessary convenience for the busy life women now lead."

1960. It is a different world, and an election year. Kennedy versus Nixon. The New Frontier versus the old guard.

SHE CAMPAIGNED HARD FOR HIM BEFORE HER PREGNANCY in the summer of 1960, but those in charge of the campaign initially underestimated her. They believed she was a liability, presenting as much of a problem with the general electorate as Kennedy's Catholicism. An aide remembered how a number of Kennedy's advisors wanted to sideline her during the campaign, because "they thought the American people's idea of a First Lady was Bess Truman—nice, matronly, dowdy, Midwestern American mother—and that someone like Jackie would turn people off." In Wisconsin, in 1959, a Democratic Party official observed of the Kennedy campaign organizers' attitude toward the candidate's wife: "They were unnecessarily frightened."

In the press, a vast, intriguing array of characterizations emerged: Was she a "socialite heiress who looks like a fashion model" or "a linguist, a seasoned traveler and a former newspaper woman" or a sly woman who "could con the toughest delegate with one melting glance"? It was a far greater range of questions than those asked about the usual candidate's spouse. She "doesn't fit the Madison Avenue image of a presidential wife," an article distributed by the news agency United Press International (UPI) admitted in September 1960, and "It's doubtful that she will try to mold herself to fit any accepted pattern. But she's natural, honest, and thinks that love of art and literature is no sin." She was different but not radical, reporters assured readers: "Her idea of the most desirable life is not a career, 20th century woman style, but the quiet background role of a wife, who can help her husband to success by organizing a pleasant home."

"Obviously, a Jacqueline Kennedy regime in the White House could open up refreshing possibilities," a reporter noted in the summer of 1960. The same went for her husband, whose campaign rhetoric directly positioned him as the man of the future. Kennedy's greatest appeal, a Canadian observer commented prior to the election, was "to the American ego—to [the] American hunger to be first in everything, to avoid the shame of being called shabby and second rate."

President Dwight D. Eisenhower, a man born in the nineteenth century, appeared elderly and old-fashioned, and Vice President Richard Nixon—who made the mistake of continually linking his own appeal to Eisenhower's—vacillated between the vibe of a banker and a thug. In contrast, Kennedy appeared dapper, calm, and dazzling on television. He looked like a movie star. And in real life, at his rallies, people said he looked even better.

Much was made of his Catholicism. The country had never had a Catholic president and the fear lingered that, were a Catholic elected, the Church would have undue influence. "The religious issue," they called it. Jackie thought it nonsense. "I think it's so unfair of people to be against Jack because he's a Catholic," she laughed. "He's such a poor Catholic."

Much was made of her youth too, and to the public, she said that was nonsense. "I'm thirty-one, but please remember," she told a reporter, "I've been married seven years to a man who leads one of the most active lives in the United States, a life in which I've participated." Privately, though, she worried about how her life was changing, writing the couturier Oleg Cassini, "I seem so mercilessly exposed."

Still, for all her reserve, she was refreshingly candid. "I think Jack has a sense of history and the past of his country," she told another reporter. "Someone has to talk to the Russians. If my country were in Jack's hands, to give the decade a start, I'd feel safe."

Regarding criticism that her hair looked like a "floor-mop," she said, "They're beginning to snipe at me about as often as they attack Jack on Catholicism." In retaliation, she offered a gentle dig at Patricia Nixon. It's a dispute summarized by a reporter as such:

> Mrs. John F. Kennedy, a housewife of Hyannis Port, Mass., says she couldn't spend $30,000 a year on clothes unless she wore sable underwear. . . . Mrs. Kennedy says she is convinced she spends less for her raiment than Mrs. Richard M. Nixon, another homemaker. . . . Mrs. Nixon has volunteered no information about the material of which her underthings are fashioned.

ON WEDNESDAY, NOVEMBER 9, 1960, AROUND 12:30 P.M., America received confirmation that the forty-three-year-old John F. Kennedy was to be the youngest elected president in the country's history. His wife would be the third youngest First Lady, and the first to be born in the twentieth century.

A little over two weeks later, the day after Thanksgiving, the Kennedys' son John F. Kennedy Jr. was born three weeks premature.

"I am of so much more fashion interest than other first ladies," Jackie writes Oleg Cassini from her hospital bed. "I refuse to be the Marie Antoinette or Josephine of the 1960s." But, even before the inauguration, the obsession with her looks and her clothes and the way she's living her life is like nothing anyone has ever seen.

The new First Lady's social secretary, Letitia Baldrige, declares: "John Kennedy is our president, but she's our movie star." A few days into her reign, the choreographer George Balanchine coos, "She's like a fairy queen."

"Jacquelines Are Busting Out All Over" read the headlines, as "Every woman under 50" tries to look like the new First Lady. "She will live as a cynosure," *Time* predicts. "Her every public act will cause comment, her chance remarks will raise controversy, and the way she raises her children will bring criticism. . . . Whether she wants to or not, she will influence taste and style. Hers will be a difficult, demanding and often thankless role, and no one knows it better than Jackie."

"I'll just get pregnant and stay pregnant," she says. "It's the only way out."

•

"I was never any different once I was in the White House than I was before, but the press made you different," she later recalls. "Suddenly, everything that'd been a liability before—your hair, that you spoke French, that you just didn't adore to campaign, and you didn't bake bread with flour up to your arms." Now that was part of her appeal, and she was celebrated for it. It was an unnerving shift.

To set the record straight, she authorized a biography, written by her mother's friend, journalist Mary Van Rensselaer Thayer. Reportedly, she wrote huge chunks of it herself while recuperating from the birth of John Jr. in Palm Beach. Her secretary later refers to Thayer's *Jacqueline Bouvier Kennedy* as "the only definitive book about her life."

In it, she is characterized as "an outlaw" and "a tomboy," with what her grandfather called a "French temperament"; teachers remember her as "the prettiest little girl, very clever, very artistic, and full of the devil." "I always knew Jacqueline would make a name for herself someday," one says. "But I really thought it would be by writing a book."

Jackie's early impressions of Jack Kennedy are rendered as high melodrama, but there's also surprising candor, giving insight to her feelings regarding her marriage. Upon meeting her future husband, according to Thayer's 1961 writing, Jackie "realized that here was a man who did not want to marry" and she "knew instantly that he would have a profound, perhaps a disturbing influence on her life." This is how she tells the story in 1960—setting it up as a decision she made, and a decision involving significant emotional compromise for her. "She was frightened," Thayer writes, and she "envisaged heartbreak;" but, "just as swiftly," Jackie "determined such heartbreak would be worth the pain."

1961. THE YEAR "MRS. JFK CAPTURED HEADLINES," Marilyn Monroe and Arthur Miller divorced, and Elizabeth Taylor won the Academy Award for *Butterfield 8*. The year "Princess Margaret's first child pleased everyone by being a boy."

What of the 91 million American women? A misleading figure, because it was only white women and their experience that the newspapers took into account. Some of those women "marched for peace, some learned the Twist, some planned fall-out shelters. They kept their skirts short and debated the seemliness of low-slung pants that bared the navel. Many went on diets—again." And they watched her, "the much-traveled, much-admired First Lady."

In 1961, "Little that Mrs. John F. Kennedy wore, read, attended, said or declined to say, liked or disliked escaped notice . . . she was observed as closely as perhaps any other President's wife has ever been." Perhaps because, according to one American polled by George Gallup, "She does people good in getting their minds off Khrushchev for awhile."

She was a cypher, anything you wanted her to be. "If you looked at her one way," a columnist analyzed, "you saw a charming young woman who would bring modernity to the White House. If you looked at her another way, you saw a flibbertigibbet . . . destined to give middle class ladies of this nation screaming fits."

Everything she did—wearing Lilly Pulitzer shift dresses, dancing the Twist at a private party, drinking daiquiris before dinner—wound up in the papers. "Men: If you want to know what your wife is going to look like during the next few years," a columnist suggested, "take a good look at Jackie Kennedy. . . . Mrs. American en masse is going to be following in her fashion footsteps." But it wasn't just America, and it wasn't just about fashion.

Her international appeal was unparalleled. In Paris in May of 1961, the president introduced himself as "the man who accompanied Jacqueline Kennedy to Paris." Days later in Vienna, the papers reported, "Her youth and beauty . . . [drew] people to her automatically, like a movie star." In a dispatch back to the U.S., a reporter on the ground observed, "Many people in Paris and Vienna looked on her as a link between the New Frontier and the Old World . . . her handsome, 44-year-old husband as the leader of a great nation in a frightening nuclear age."

When he was asked to shake the president's hand for a photograph, Soviet premier Nikita Khrushchev winked and told the newspaperman, "I'd like to shake *her* hand first."

THE TRANSITION INTO THE ROLE OF FIRST LADY WAS DIFficult. Given the complications of her private life, her whole new lifestyle, the family dynamics, and occasional bouts of depression and ill health, on top of the humiliation of her husband's pathological philandering (Truman Capote: "All those Kennedy men are the same—they're like dogs. They have to stop and pee on every fire hydrant"), she was determined to barricade her family against the intrusions of press coverage and public interest. "I just wanted to save some normal life for Jack and the children and me," she later wrote her mother-in-law, Rose Kennedy. "My first fight was to fight for a sane life for my babies and their father."

Outwardly, her contributions appeared confined to appropriately feminine realms—fashion, decorating, and gardening. Determined that the interiors of the White House reflect the grandness and the sweep of American history, she carried on much-publicized work with a committee to locate the treasures prior presidents had let slip away, saying, "I would write fifty letters to fifty museum curators if I could bring Andrew Jackson's inkwell home." In September 1961, *Life* magazine snuck a peek into her "dusty but fascinating adventure." It was a project that "she has assigned herself as the major task of her career as First Lady" with, *Life* noted, the president's "husbandly encouragement."

"How could I help wanting to do it?" she asked the reporter, in a rambling and confused reply that was both revealing and typical of how she spoke in interviews. "I don't know . . . is it a reverence for beauty or for history? I guess both. I've always cared. My best friends are people who care. I don't know . . . when you read Proust or listen to Jack talk about history or go to Mount Vernon, you understand." In private, she was more concise about the work of scholarship she was pulling off: "When it is done, de Gaulle would be ashamed at Versailles."

"All the art here is going to be American," she informed *Life*. "There is wonderful American art and I want to display it." This was to be a huge part of her contribution as First Lady—not just "restoring" the White House to a grandeur it had never known, but also showing Americans they had a history of which they could be proud.

Not yet 200 years old, a sense of the nation's newness lingered and its reputation as a rugged land of wild frontiers, hot tempers, and cowboys—all of which were a key component of the American self-image—implied a certain lack of cultural tradition. This wasn't the reality, but the perception, one the First Lady played an instrumental role in changing.

On February 14, 1962, her tour of the newly restored White House aired simultaneously on NBC and CBS. An "excellent hour of television" during which the First Lady "made some history come alive" and struck "a blow for freedom" by wearing low-heeled shoes. "She looked charming, spoke in a soft, breathy voice, was poised, dignified—and she was a definite TV hit." When he joined her at the program's conclusion, the president noted that his wife's project had made American history a far more compelling drama by telling it through the president's home. He imagined that some of the people who visited the restored house "may want to some day live here themselves—which I think would be very good—even the girls."

For many Americans, the White House tour was the first opportunity they'd had to hear the First Lady's voice. To many, it came as a revelation—low and slow and as though she were slightly out of breath. Not everyone was impressed. "Why would a married woman with two children wish to dress and talk in a 13-year-old 'kittenish' manner?" one viewer complained to the *El Paso Herald-Post*. "To do so, as an average housewife, would be ridiculous; however, to do so in the White House is disgusting."

But on the whole, she received raves. One critic marveled that she offered "revealing evidence that our literature and arts rank with the best in the world." A writer at the Associated Press (AP) suggested that of all the Kennedys, "none has been a greater surprise than the President's wife, Jacqueline," who "looked so young, so fragile, so chic" but "really shone" during her trips abroad. When she returned from a foreign visit, a columnist observed, "Jackie is back from her tour, safe and sound, and I'm glad to have her home. The country's a nicer place when she is here."

At the White House, letters arrived for her addressed to "Your Majesty."

Letitia Baldrige called it "a great failure" that the image projected of her to the public was so empty, and so at odds with who she was. The public conceived of her only as "a wonderful wife and mother . . . a beautiful, poised, young woman of artistic talent . . . someone who hates politics and hates politicians," where there was actually "such a bright, intelligent person . . . interested in issues," a woman who "interrogated [the president] as to what was going on."

She was extremely good at reading people, calling out pho-
nies, and identifying those who would be loyal and had the president's best interests at heart. "She wouldn't advise his staff,"
observed Major General Chester Clifton, "she would advise
him—that's why nobody knew about it." She was "working with
him upstairs," according to Baldrige, "seeing how she could help
in her way to further the political gains of the United States of
America and its foreign policy." Behind the scenes, she quietly,
powerfully intervened with a phone call or a letter, particularly
with foreign leaders.

When the First Lady visited India in March 1962, accompanied
by her sister, it was a trip fraught with diplomatic complications.
She was going to Pakistan immediately after, and as the nations
were rivals, she had to appear to enjoy both equally to avoid offend-
ing either. It was a diplomatic mission, always, and she took pains
to stress that. Annoyed by the journalists reporting on the trip as
though it were a fashion show, on her first day in India, a statement
was released clarifying that her trip was "purely political." While she
was away, both CBS and NBC dedicated their 10:30–11:00 p.m.
EST slot to special political analysis of her trip.

In India, they called her "Amriki Rani," Queen of America. In
Pakistan, 100,000 people lined the six-mile route from the airport
and she rode into town amid a flurry of flags and flower petals.

But hers was a power she wielded on her own terms and, invariably, there was criticism. Penelope Laingen, wife of a political offi-
cer in Pakistan, remembered how the First Lady's staff kept revising
the itinerary while the ambassador set up the program for the visit,
saying "she won't do this, she won't shake hands, she won't give
gifts, she wants to take a nap at such and such a time." At one
point, the ambassador, frustrated, exclaimed, "Well, if she's a basket
case, why doesn't she stay home?"

Nonetheless, when it was all over, Drew Pearson reported that she
proved herself "a great saleswoman for the USA." She had successfully
been the caring, culturally sensitive face of the Kennedy administration

abroad, a role that had tremendous impact and strengthened what India's prime minister Nehru characterized as his country's "psychological pull" toward the United States. The president reportedly confided to the editor of *Newsweek*, "Jackie took all the bitterness out of our relations with India . . . Jackie did a helluva job."

PARTS OF THIS STORY ARE ESPECIALLY DIFFICULT TO capture because it is hard, in retrospect—knowing what we know now—to inhabit the terror these events provoked at the time.

The Cuban Missile Crisis, October 1962: for thirteen days, everything hangs in the balance. All around the world, people believe that the future is over, mutually assured destruction looms, and they are going to die.

Jack Kennedy calls his wife at their rented home in Virginia and asks her to return to the White House. "From then on, it seemed there was no waking or sleeping," she later remembered. When he asks her to take the children to a bunker, she says she told him: "If anything happens, we're all going to stay right here with you. I just want to be with you, and I want to die with you, and the children do, too—than live without you."

• 

October 24: The *Irving Daily News Texan*, page one. "Showdown Looms as Red Ships Near US Blockade." On page eight: A television producer announces, "No matter your politics, the fact is that the No. 1 star in America today is Jacqueline Kennedy."

"Mrs. Jacqueline Kennedy faces a new White House routine as a result of President Kennedy's hard work with the job of handling the Cuban and Berlin problems," the UPI reports. "All Washington is now being geared to the job ahead, one of making the United States safe from Commies."

•

On October 28 it's all over. She takes the children back to the retreat in Virginia.

•

On the other side of the country, in midterm elections the following week, Richard Nixon runs for governor of California. If he loses, the papers note, "it will probably mean political curtains for Nixon, at the age of 49."

Richard Nixon does not win.

AS FIRST LADY, SHE IS SET ON being HERSELF AND WARY OF being boxed in by a cause. August Heckscher, the Special Consultant to the President on the Arts, found her an "ambivalent figure": "Sometimes she seemed to draw back as if she didn't want to get too much involved with this." But she quietly supported people and organizations with which she felt a connection.

Appalled by the poverty she'd seen in West Virginia during the campaign, as First Lady, she orders all the White House glassware from West Virginia's Morgantown Glassware Guild. When a different manufacturer offers to donate an expensive set of crystal to the White House, Mrs. Kennedy writes her decorator: "—the whole problem is still West Virginia—it still is NO— . . . I would practically break all the glasses & order new ones each week—it's the only way I have to help them."

Down in Durham, North Carolina, a Black, gay kid named André Leon Talley is living with his grandmother and watching Jackie. Hearing her talk about the simple glasses she'd found in West Virginia, the State Dining Room linens, and the portraiture held in the White House's collection, Talley is transfixed.

Later, he attributes his own love of antiques and history to her and calls her "my heroine in all things that mattered." He'll remember how the women around him followed her example, his aunts and grandmother reinterpreting Jackie's style for themselves and their own budgets, wearing pillbox hats and chain-strapped hand-bags and gloves to church.

"Jackie Kennedy seemed more like a film star than the wife of the president," Talley recalls. "She had more impact on me than any actress."

1963, EDGING UP ON AN ELECTION YEAR. STILL, THE WOR-ries of 1960 persist; still the campaign people fear she's a liability.

March: "One of the burning topics ad nauseum is Mrs. John F. Kennedy [. . . and] a pattern of conversation is developing: the crux of which is the validity of Mrs. Kennedy's behavior pat-tern, or, to put it bluntly, is Jacqueline Kennedy the President's Achilles heel? Is she losing votes which will count in 1964? Is her star waning?"

The following month, just after Easter weekend, the White House announces the First Lady is expecting a baby in August.

"I'm taking the veil," she'd told Letitia Baldrige earlier in the year, ordering her social secretary to reduce her obligations. In late May, Baldrige decides to leave her position at the White House—not because of friction with the First Lady but because, as she writes a friend, of her "desire to STOP BEING POOR." Jackie asks her friend Nancy Tuckerman to come in as Baldrige's replacement.

The pair had been roommates at boarding school and friends ever since (and their friendship will endure the rest of Jackie's life). Baldrige thinks Jackie had Nancy under her thumb, but Tuckerman's greatest asset, as the White House Chief Usher observed, was that "She knew all the First Lady's foibles, and how she wanted to operate. She knew exactly what to send upstairs [for her review], when to send it, what to discuss with her, and what subjects to avoid."

They're close friends. Jackie trusts Nancy, and, from this point forward, she will depend upon Nancy enormously—for protection and security. When she pitches the job to her, she says, "It's mostly fun."

IN EARLY AUGUST 1963, JACK KENNEDY CONFIDES TO A friend: "I'd known a lot of attractive women in my lifetime before I got married, but of all of them there was only one I could have married—and I married her." When asked by another friend if he's ever been in love, Jack Kennedy tells her, "No, but I've been *very* interested once or twice."

The following weekend, Jackie goes into labor and their son Patrick is born prematurely. He dies three days later.

When their daughter Arabella was stillborn in 1956, Jack Kennedy was away vacationing in France, and, as Rose Kennedy wrote one of her daughters at the time, "we all agreed that on Bobby's advice it would be better for him not to be told as he would want to go home immediately, and Jackie is so depressed that it would be very tragic for both of them." And so Jack Kennedy was kept away, and she endured that first loss alone. In contrast, Patrick's death is a blow they sustain together.

She tells the nurses: "I'm coming back here next year to have another baby. So you better be ready for me." She and her husband leave the hospital hand in hand. She tells him, "There's just one thing I couldn't stand—if I ever lost you."

SHE'S GRIEVING AND, AS WITH HER EARLIER PREGNANCIES, probably suffering from postnatal depression. In October 1963, she embarks on what is described as a "wholly private" trip to Greece and a cruise aboard the yacht of a man named Aristotle "Ari" Onassis. The cruise is intended to lift her spirits.

She's not always gotten along with her sister—Lee is four years younger, which felt like a lifetime now and then—but they were close during this period. With their kids all around the same age and her life so hectic, Jackie often needed Lee and she tried to bring her sister along into this glittering world. She knows it's difficult, being the sister of the First Lady. They lean on each other, and Lee is concerned about her now.

Lee had only just annulled her first marriage and already she and Ari are rumored to be sleeping together. It was kept quiet for the most part; Lee's second husband, Stas Radziwill, accompanied them. Ari's official mistress, Maria Callas, was in the picture if not on the boat.

Lee thought him "magnetic," this exotic man, like a character out of myth or a foreign film. "He walked like a potentate," she later wrote, "noticing and wanting to be noticed. He enjoyed observing, with a habitual cigar in his hand. His hair was thick with brilliantine and his olive skin was smooth. His voice sounded like soft gravel—raspy, but low." Lee was enamored of Ari and Ari enjoyed her company, but he seems to have been thoroughly beguiled by her sister. One of his friends remembered him, after the cruise, saying of Jackie: "One day, she and I will meet again, and this time, nothing will stand in my way."

He intrigued her, too, as a colorful and interesting figure and as a friend, but her mind was elsewhere. Since she couldn't get a workable phone connection aboard Onassis's yacht, the *Christina*, she wrote her husband long letters every night.

The cruise was "strictly private," the papers said, the itinerary "shrouded in secrecy." Onassis was reportedly not planning to be onboard, but then he was—supposedly at the First Lady's insistence—present at "a festive shipboard midnight party," during which "Strains of continental dance music" were heard ashore. The First Lady wore a "short formal evening dress." An eyewitness characterized her as "very happy, very charming and very conversational." This mourning woman, laughing and bearing her knees.

She extends her stay. Not quite ready to go back to her job and the White House and all those dreary responsibilities, she is still melancholy. She stays away, she'll later admit, a little too long, but she needed the fun and the freedom and release.

•

She's still away when the criticism begins. In a press release, Representative Oliver P. Bolton, the Republican congressman from Ohio, declares it improper for the First Lady to accept "the lavish hospitality of a foreign individual whose shipping interests . . . received favored treatment from the U.S. government."

Quickly, the press turns on Bolton for "jump[ing] into the gray area of what can be considered fair comment" by speaking badly about the president's wife. But Bolton's criticism hits a nerve and, because of Onassis's controversial dealings with the U.S. Maritime Administration, it isn't entirely unwarranted. From 1948 to 1951, Onassis's companies had purchased surplus ships from the U.S. government, violating a law that restricted the sale of such ships to U.S. citizens. In 1955, the United States charged both Onassis and his shipping industry archrival, Stavros Niarchos, with conspiracy to defraud the government through illegal purchase of these ships. Companies under their control were fined. Though both Onassis and Niarchos were personally cleared of the charges, the incident marred their reputations in the U.S. and cemented their public images as maritime criminals.

Given this, the presence of the newly appointed undersecretary of commerce, Franklin Roosevelt Jr., on Onassis's yacht along with Jackie, Stas, and Lee looked wrong.

A few days after the First Lady's return, columnist Drew Pearson adds a new angle to the story, reporting that Jackie was dispatched on the cruise to dissuade Lee from divorcing Stas and marrying Ari; he would be an embarrassing brother-in-law for the president.

In late October 1963, rumors are still swirling and Barry Goldwater, the presumed Republican candidate for 1964, wades into the fray. While no one could begrudge the First Lady her pleasure after her recent bereavement, Goldwater acknowledges, the presence of Franklin Roosevelt Jr., a government official, on this "pleasure junket" was a clear political conflict.

It's a blistering round of press but a valid critique, one to which the president is sensitive. Again, there are whispers she is a liability.

•

But she returns refreshed and ready to go back to work, and they appear easier in one another's company that autumn. A close friend observes that, by that point, "Jack was about as faithful as he was ever going to be. It was more than Jackie had hoped for, but less than she deserved." Reporters were surprised to see the traditionally reticent Kennedys embracing and holding hands in public. Laura Bergquist felt Jackie had become "his haven, his refuge, his separate world."

At dinner one night, he teases her. He knows she feels guilty about the political furor her holiday has caused and he uses that, says she has to accompany him on a campaign trip the next month to make it up. There's bickering among the Democrats in Texas and the president is scheduled for a two-day fence-mending trip. It'll be a lot of smiling and hand shaking and barbecue dinners. She says she'll go anywhere with him.

ON NOVEMBER 5—ONE YEAR OUT FROM ELECTION DAY—THE UPI's White House reporter, Helen Thomas, complains that as First Lady, Jackie has "attended only one major political fundraising dinner . . . shied away from anything that smacks of political duty," and been "absent at all of the out-of-town presidential birthday celebrations held to fatten party coffers." In other words, she isn't being a team player, despite the fact that earlier that year, "she said she would do what her husband wanted her to do." Jackie continues to do only what she wants.

Two weeks later, another columnist identifies this as "the main criticism of the First Lady, Jacqueline Kennedy"—this sense that "she is not 'politically-minded.'" It's a problem that her accompanying the president on an upcoming political trip to Texas—her first visit to that state—will hopefully offset. She is joining the president on "through Texas stopping off at the famous LBJ ranch," a move, in turn, expected to "somewhat offset a criticism aimed at President Kennedy, who, it is rumored, will dump Johnson as his running mate in the 1964 election."

The campaign, the commentators, the White House staff—they didn't know what to do with "the 'Jackie' individuality." Was it an asset or an Achilles' heel? Would it lose votes or gain them? Was she a star or a liability? Could America handle this quiet rebel?

"Texas will be a good testing ground for Mrs. Kennedy's venture into politics," writes another columnist, suggesting that she might be a "secret weapon" in a region noted for a number of violent incidents of political extremism. Most recently, during a visit to Dallas in late October, the United Nations ambassador Adlai Stevenson had been "cursed, booed, beat and spat on" by a mob of protesters from the ultra-conservative John Birch Society.

"I regret the violent behavior of the few and I realize it was only a few," Stevenson said the following day, but he noted that "Such behavior after a speech on peace gives the Soviets and the rest of the world an unfortunate impression."

•

Thursday, November 21. San Antonio . . . Houston . . . Fort Worth . . .

The response to her is staggering. "Jackie Kennedy was driven through cheering throngs of Texans," a Texas paper observed of her arrival in Houston, briefly noting: "Her husband came too."

"Presidents seldom serve as spear carriers, but John F. Kennedy was one in San Antonio and Houston," the *Chicago Daily News* reported on the morning of November 22. "[T]here may be a few disapproving voices, but the ayes of Texas are for her—overwhelmingly. . . . From the moment she stepped out of the blue-nosed presidential jet . . . Mrs. Kennedy lit up the state like a gusher on fire." Just that first day in Texas, already she demonstrated "an aptitude for campaigning that could make her a busy woman next year when this business gets serious."

On Friday, at breakfast in Fort Worth, the president jokes that he is again, as he was in Paris, the man who accompanies Jacqueline Kennedy. Dallas . . . then on to Austin . . . then the weekend at the Johnsons' ranch and Thanksgiving in Hyannis and, after that, Christmas, and then the campaign will begin in earnest. She is looking ahead. It's 70° F, sun shining. She's dressed too warmly, anticipating the brief coolness to be had in the shade of the overpass just ahead and then——

## FRIDAY, NOVEMBER 22, 1963

# PART II

# After

THE WOMAN WHO SAVED DICK VAN DYKE'S MARRIAG

# TV RADIO MIRROR

## HOW A MOTHER HIDES HER TEARS...

Jackie's struggle
to teach the children
why Kennedys don't cry

NOVEMBER 29, 1963: ONE WEEK AFTER THE MURDER; THE day after Thanksgiving. She calls Theodore H. White, a writer for *Life* magazine; there is something she wanted the readers of *Life* to know.

White writes the final essay in forty-five minutes, then dictates it to his editors over a telephone hanging on the kitchen wall at Joe and Rose Kennedy's house in Hyannis. Just as his editors suggest there's "too much Camelot," she enters the kitchen and overhears. Feeling her thoughts have already been over-edited, she insists they keep the Camelot stuff.

Published in the December 6 issue of *Life*, White's two-page essay begins with Jackie's memories of November 22. It isn't until the second page that she says Jack Kennedy often quoted "classical" things, and she's "so ashamed" she keeps thinking of a line from a musical, how "At night, before we'd go to sleep, Jack liked to play some records; and the song he loved most came at the very end of this record. The lines he loved to hear were: *Don't let it be forgot, that once there was a spot, for one brief shining moment that was known as Camelot.*" In the final published interview, she repeats this lyric four times.

This wouldn't be her only recasting. In the coming years, to historians, she will repeatedly push the idea of John F. Kennedy as a Greek figure. But the metaphor she gives the readers of *Life* is Camelot: a far more immediate and accessible image. It was her refrain, "the idea that transfixed her." That lyric. "She said . . . she does not want [people] to forget John F. Kennedy or read of him only in dusty or bitter histories," White wrote. She wants them to remember "For one brief shining moment there was Camelot," and also, that "it will never be that way again."

It's a conceit that the Kennedy court historian Arthur Schlesinger Jr. believes would have "provoked John Kennedy to profane disclaimer."

•

The appearance of this essay in *Life* magazine, its placement within the December 6 issue and its serialization in newspapers throughout the United States, crucially established the myth that gradually surrounded President Kennedy's administration and his entire family—a myth in which many Americans were already emotionally invested but which, up to that moment, lacked a name. The fact that it was President Kennedy's widow who named it, and so soon after the murder, played a fundamental role in their attachment to it, their belief in it, and also their connection to her from this point on.

It was *Life*'s second week of assassination coverage. The previous issue featured a portrait of JFK: young, tanned, gazing into an unknown future with a look of confident concern. The following week, attention turned to his widow and the cover featured her standing on the White House steps, holding the hands of her two children. Inside, readers were reminded that John Jr. turned three on the day of his father's burial, and Caroline turned six two days later. The assassination coverage was extensive and vivid, and it provided a dramatic recounting of scenes with which readers were already familiar, having just watched them on TV the week before.

A strange and awful weekend, unlike any other they'd ever known. On Friday, President Kennedy was killed. An unimaginable act committed by a man named Lee Harvey Oswald—a twenty-four-year-old, married to a Russian woman and, the papers reported, "a self-styled Communist." On Sunday, in advance of coverage of JFK's funeral due to begin in D.C., both NBC and CBS cut away to the Dallas jail as Oswald was brought out for transfer to a different facility. And so, when local nightclub owner Jack Ruby stepped forward and shot Oswald, he did so on live TV.

It was, the papers noted, "the first time in history that the nation's television viewers watched a murder being committed."

Through gazes fixed upon the television, during those four long days when the country's three television networks ran nearly continuous coverage, Americans were united in a way taken for granted now—but which they experienced then as something startling and new. Forty-one million American television sets were tuned to the funeral coverage. Meetings were canceled, events postponed, a thirty-day mourning period announced, and many activities of daily life suspended, opening a period of time in which there was literally nothing to do but watch TV, mourn, and get through the holidays, one after the other, first Thanksgiving then Christmas then New Year's.

But they had to do something. Many wrote letters to Jackie. "When we heard of 'our President's' assassination," a junior at Junipero Memorial High in Monterey, California, wrote on behalf of her Religion III class, "the whole school seemed to die with him. Girls cryed [*sic*] and some went into hysteria. Our minds became completely blank." There was one spot of hope, however: "We, as voters of tomorrow, would love to see Robert Kennedy run for President." "Our only hope now," concurred another writer, "is that Robert F. Kennedy will run for President." The day after John Kennedy's burial, a high school senior wrote the former First Lady: "I read a quoted sentence by Mr. Kennedy in a recent article. It stated that if something happened to him today, Robert would take his place, and if something happened to Robert, Ted would take Robert's place. I pray this is true."

For many Americans, there was a dire need for an intellectual framework to cope with the overwhelming grief triggered by losing this person they didn't even know. Why did they feel the way they did? He was "with his young and beautiful wife, the symbol of America as he and most of us like to think of America: itself young, itself always hopeful, believing." Without John Kennedy, after "one of the most reprehensible deeds of all time," what was America now?

While he was elected by 49.7 percent of the voting public, after his death, 65 percent of Americans claimed to have voted for him. This was the national mood just a week and a half after the murder in Dallas, when the December 6 issue of *Life* magazine landed in mailboxes and Jackie's memories were excerpted in newspapers. America, bereft, was primed for the consolation of magic.

JACK KENNEDY'S WIDOW DOES NOT KNOW THIS; SHE IS OPER-ating in an entirely different world. A world where, she fears, her husband is being forgotten and America is moving on.

She worries his memory will be in the keep of writers critical of his administration. According to Teddy White, she specifically name-checks veteran reporters Arthur Krock and Merriman Smith, and she worries that "all those people are going to write about him [JFK] as history." She has a very specific idea of how he should be written about, and she doesn't want his legacy left to these "bitter old men."

In her grief, she tries to control the story that appears most vulnerable, the story she's most at risk of losing, a story that already, in fact, no longer belongs to her: that of her life with her husband. Her husband had been taken away from her, and now she sees his legacy being taken away from him. That's what she is fighting against. He "loved Camelot," she said. Significantly, it wasn't the Arthurian myth in its purest form. She wasn't saying the witty and urbane John F. Kennedy went to bed with a gilt-edged volume of Malory's *Le Morte d'Arthur*.

No. He was listening to a cast recording of Lerner and Lowe's blockbuster Broadway musical. A production based on T. H. White's popular novel *The Once and Future King* and starring Richard Burton, Julie Andrews, and Robert Goulet. *Camelot* was a piece of popular culture with which many Americans were familiar. The cast recording Jack Kennedy's widow said he loved, with the lyric she couldn't get out of her head, was in its 148th week on *Billboard*'s Top 100 LPs chart.

Through a reference to a popular record, in an interview for publication in the country's most widely read popular news magazine, she bypassed the historians to tell Americans herself that John F. Kennedy was a lot like them but that he was also magic, as was the America he led. She could not possibly have imagined how fervently the people would believe.

Years later, she acknowledged this metaphor had maybe been a bad idea; it was, perhaps, "overly sentimental." What she really wanted, the author William Manchester eventually realized, was "just one big blank page for November 22, 1963."

# 1964

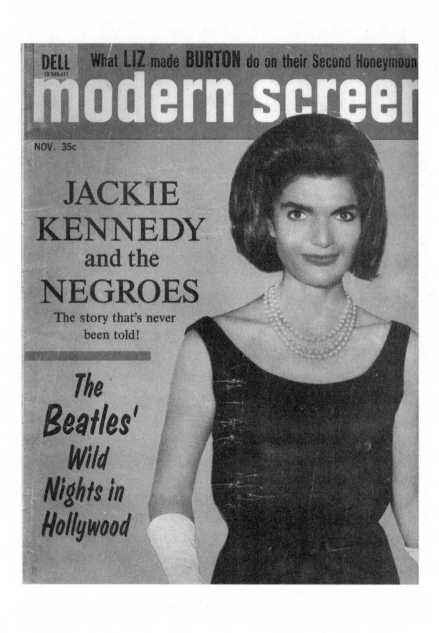

DELL
20-540-411

What **LIZ** made **BURTON** do on their Second Honeymoon

# modern screen

NOV. 35c

## JACKIE KENNEDY
### and the
## NEGROES

The story that's never
been told!

*The
Beatles'
Wild
Nights in
Hollywood*

LATER, SHE WILL DESCRIBE HERSELF DURING THIS TIME AS "a living wound."

·

The family whispers she is unstable. Her godfather reports back to a cousin, "Both the clarity of her thinking and the stability of her emotions had been temporarily undermined." It is a wonder, they marvel, that she remains sane.

Her friend, Secretary of Defense Robert McNamara, presents her with two portraits of the late president. When her three-year-old son John kisses them and says, "Good night, Daddy," she returns them to McNamara, saying, "It's simply more than I can stand."

A friend from her debutante days reports that she's suffering "deep depressions, suicidal feelings."

Through the spring, she conducts interviews. She testifies before the President's Commission on the Assassination of President Kennedy. She recalls her life with Jack Kennedy to Arthur Schlesinger Jr., as part of a major oral history initiative for the future JFK Library. Simultaneously, she recounts the circumstances of her husband's murder to the author William Manchester, who has been authorized by the Kennedy family to produce an account of the president's death. She is doing this for history, she says, talking for history; in her grief, telling the story of the worst day of her life—"the story from hell," her sister-in-law, Ethel, calls it—again and again.

She experiences recurring nightmares. To Joan Kennedy, Teddy's wife, she confides: "I've heard that gun go off 10,000 times."

In his diaries, a Washington priest records a meeting where she asks, if she were to commit suicide, would she be separated from her husband in heaven?

In a letter to the bishop who delivered her husband's eulogy, she worries: "It will be so long before I am dead and even then I don't know if I will be reunited with him."

To Father Leonard, the Irish priest with whom she'd been corresponding for years, she writes: "God will have a bit of explaining to do to me."

Responding to a condolence letter from former vice president Richard Nixon, she cautions him to be grateful for what he has.

> I know how you must feel—so long on the path—so closely missing the greatest prize— . . . please be consoled by what you already have—your life and your family—We never value life enough when we have it—and I would not have had Jack live his life any other way—though I know his death could have been prevented, and I will never cease to torture myself with that—But if you do not win—please think of all that you have.

She's sorting through her husband's things, pulling papers and organizing his personal belongings for the library she is going to build in his name. Every night she's working, and drinking quite a lot.

"It's so much easier doing it while you're here than at night when I'm alone," she tells her assistant Mary Barelli Gallagher. "I just drown my sorrows in vodka."

During a religious training class, Caroline Kennedy interrupts the lesson to tell her teacher, "My mother cries all the time."

•

She does not know what to do with herself; suddenly she is without a husband, a home, and a job. Magazine editors pitch writing assignments and publishers offer editorships. The AP suggests a weekly column, CBS News invites her to narrate a documentary, *Vogue* wants a feature article on child-rearing, and Harper & Row suggests a children's book. She rejects these offers but doesn't completely shut the door.

When Bobby Kennedy mentions to a *Ladies' Home Journal* reporter that Jackie might be open to the possibility of an editorship, she takes a meeting with the magazine's editor. She also meets with *McCall's* and *Good Housekeeping* then sends her assistant Pam Turnure to follow-up lunches with both. In response to the offer of an editorship from *Town & Country*, she writes a note to Turnure instructing her to "Write a very nice no," because "who knows—later on I might want to do something."

She reportedly tells a magazine editor, "What I really would like to do is keep President Kennedy's ideas alive. But the only way I know is to work through some man. Maybe I could do it somehow through Robert Kennedy."

For now, she sees her greatest obligation as raising her children. They are, she writes a friend, going to be her "vengeance on the world." She's also committed to ensuring that her husband's memory endures. "She thought—wrongly," an acquaintance observed, that "she had failed her husband in his life," and she will, she says, commit the rest of her life to commemorating his. But how to live like that? How to move forward with this anchor to the past?

She cuts back on the drinking, gradually ramps up her social life, but she is still too often alone. Always, she'd been a woman who needed solitude—but this is too much. There is, at the very core of things, a lack. Never has she felt so vulnerable, so exposed.

She's trying to keep her kids safe in a house in Georgetown that has become D.C.'s number one tourist attraction. The spectators are so relentless in their quest for mementoes that one of the five policemen guarding the place comments, "If you didn't have a policeman here, you wouldn't have a house there."

Sometimes she'll go out with interesting people. There's a dinner with Marlon Brando, a brief romance with architect John Carl Warnecke, the designer of President Kennedy's grave site. That one's serious enough that they vacation in Hawaii together and reportedly talk marriage, but nothing comes of it.

She goes out with men she can flirt with, only to come back to the stillness of her house, which is both a reminder and a reproach.

"How awful," she writes a friend, "when the best in you is not called upon anymore—by your husband—or by your President—and you have no one to love and live for and are just left to be your miserable self that you were trying to escape all your life."

Increasingly, she travels because it's easier to be constantly in search of the new than to confront what has happened and all she has lost.

"When I go on a trip," she says, "it's all right, but it's so empty and depressing to come home."

She is constantly on the go, both with and without her kids.

Colorado, Acapulco, Vermont, England, Hawaii. A month in Hyannis, back to Newport, skiing in Sun Valley. Switzerland, Italy, Argentina, Spain, Hawaii again, and an escape to Antigua. Even for someone affiliated with the so-called jet set, this is a lot. As the columnist Liz Smith observes: "Jackie Kennedy has discovered that one way to make life bearable as a public monument is to move her base hither and yon."

On and on she goes, trying to make life bearable, trying to escape her miserable self.

SHE'D ALWAYS BEEN CLOSE TO HER BROTHER-IN-LAW ROBERT Kennedy and she leans heavily upon him during this time. Seemingly the favorite of his mother, Bobby Kennedy was a slight, scrappy man, to whom, ever since his brother's first campaign, the adjective "ruthless" fiercely clung. As John Kennedy's attorney general, he defied government rules and brought his dog to the office, where he conducted business with his shirtsleeves rolled up and his feet on the desk—much to the disgust of J. Edgar Hoover, his nemesis at the FBI.

He excited extremes in people, most often either implacable hate (President Lyndon Johnson: "I won't bother answering that grandstanding little runt") or devotion (Jackie: Bobby is "the one I would put my hand in the fire for"). His own career revolved around that of his brother and, with John Kennedy's death, this man, whose reputation for ruthlessness belied a gentle soul, was shattered seemingly beyond repair.

In their sadness, the widow and brother grew closer. Bobby would "get on the phone and say, 'Jackie, get yourself feeling up! Don't just sit around there and mope!'" recalled Roswell Gilpatric, her longtime friend and, later, sometimes beau. "He was very good in keeping up her morale and spirits when she might get into a depression." Bobby tried to buck her up, but he was just as debilitated by grief, in a "haze of pain," according to one friend. One of Bobby's secretaries felt he and Jackie "needed each other, both trying to recuperate."

That fall, seeking to escape the frenzy that surrounds her in Washington, she relocates to New York City, where her sister and sisters-in-law have homes. That same year, Bobby takes up residence in New York, in preparation for his run for the state's open Senate seat. Solange Batsell, an old friend and neighbor who saw Jackie often during this period, remembers how Bobby "was right there helping her in every way possible. . . . She was very, very stoic and would give these dinner parties . . . and he'd be there at those dinners." He insisted she host these parties because he wanted her surrounded by friends and family and good conversation, not just sitting home alone. But she always wore the same yellow shantung dress, and Solange felt she didn't care much about herself or things like pretty dresses then.

But people were talking. In autumn 1964, gossip columnist Suzy—the pen name for Aileen Mehle, whose daily column appeared in ninety papers across the U.S.—wrote a number of items implying they were lovers. In 1970, the columnist Rowland Evans noted in an oral history for the JFK Library that "a lot of people thought there was something going on there that wasn't." An employee of Ethel Kennedy remembered a buzz and a lot of downstairs whispers among the staff, but noted there was never any hard proof. She said it was "more a feeling in the air than anything that anybody actually saw."

Some folks said they saw things and heard things, and they recounted those things to biographers. "The two of them carried on like a pair of lovesick teenagers," Franklin Roosevelt Jr. contended. "People used to see them at Le Club, their torsos stuck together as they danced the night away." But Roosevelt hadn't actually seen them himself: other people had seen them, and he heard it after. This is much like the film producer's friend who stayed in a hotel suite opposite Jackie's at the Carlyle, saw her leaving with Bobby, and swore they were having an affair because, according to the film producer, "you can look at people and tell if they've been intimate . . . my friend could tell."

"Though there was no affair," contended Senator George Smathers, "I believe Bobby's wife thought there was one." A friend of Ethel's asserted, "Her suspicions were well founded. I'm ninety-nine percent certain they were involved, and I'm sure Ethel caught on at some point. . . . And you could see how it might have all started, and how, after JFK's death, they could have had a mad, morbid attraction to each other, and how this initial attachment continued to grow."

"Rubbish," Robert Kennedy's spokesman, Frank Mankiewicz, declared, but even he admitted it was a story that nicely aligned with "people's fantasy world of what the Kennedys were like."

When I asked in 2014 about the possibility of an affair between Jackie and Bobby, Ambassador William vanden Heuvel told me:

> There's no evidence of any kind about it. I mean, I can't even imagine it. No. And I was very close to Robert Kennedy. I was his assistant when he was Attorney General and traveled with him often and I was with him in his campaign in 1968 . . . who knows what people do but, I mean, I think I was close enough to get a sense of their own life and attitudes towards one another. So I would not have said that.

He paused, chuckled, and then said: "It's a good story though! Nobody's going to dispel it because nobody can either prove or disprove."

SO MANY STORIES ARE SWIRLING THROUGH AMERICA, AND so much violence. In August, Jackie writes a friend: "Disenchantment is setting in . . . we know the world will be much worse."

Not yet a year since her husband's murder, just two weeks after she moves to her new apartment in New York at 1040 Fifth Avenue, there's a bomb scare. For over two hours, police, firemen, Secret Service, and FBI agents check the building from roof to cellar.

She's panicked, talking to Bobby, crying into the phone about how she and her kids are going to be blown up, what has she done to deserve this, why is this happening to her. The police won't let the family evacuate because the caller says there are snipers in the street, ready to shoot her if she tries to flee. And so she and her children—ages three and six—wait in their new home and wonder if they will die.

"She was a prisoner in that place," said Ken O'Donnell, a Kennedy aide who heard the story from Bobby. "She was trapped like a caged animal."

•

After an election interpreted as a landslide victory for liberalism, President Lyndon Johnson declares, "These are the most hopeful times in all the years since Christ was born."

## SUNDAY, NOVEMBER 22, 1964

She is in her shell of grief. She writes the poet Robert Lowell: "I wish that President Kennedy was alive and that you would be reading at his Inauguration."

# 1965

# HOLLYWOOD'S HOTTEST INTERRACIAL AFFAIRS

# MOVIE MIRROR

ONLY **25**c OCT.

**JACKIE
DATES LIZ'
BEST FRIEND!**
*the Full Story*

**DAVID McCALLUM
talks about
SEX
and the
MARRIED
MAN!**

**JULIE ANDREWS:
THEY DON'T
CALL HER
A NICE
GIRL NOW!**

BARBARA PARKINS: **PEYTON PLACE RUINED MY REPUTATION**

**SYBIL'S NEW BABY — How Her Two Husbands Feel**

PAGE ONE OF THE *NEW YORK TIMES* ON MARCH 7: "WHITE Alabamians Stage Selma March to Support Negroes." Five columns over: "3,500 U.S. Marines Going to Vietnam."

It is not yet a "war," but rather American involvement in a conflict arising out of the end of French colonial rule and a partitioning of the country at the Geneva Convention in 1954, which resulted in political tumult and, in the North, the rise of communist regimes. In the *New York Times*, the 23,500 "American military men" already serving in South Vietnam are billed as "advisors to the country's army, navy and air force." These additional 3,500 Marines are then identified as "the first United States ground combat troops committed to help in the fight against the Vietcong insurgency."

Two weeks later, in Detroit, eighty-two-year-old Alice Herz—a pacifist Quaker who fled the Nazis—stands on a street corner. Herz pours cleaning fluid over herself and lights a match, immolating herself "to protest the arms race all over the world." In a letter she left behind, she writes, "I wanted to call attention to this problem by choosing the illuminating death of a Buddhist."

The following month, at a press conference, the president says the bombing of North Vietnam will continue and vows to pursue a policy of firmness.

On July 28—the former First Lady's thirty-sixth birthday—LBJ announces that the number of troops in South Vietnam will be increased from 75,000 to 125,000, and the draft will gradually be raised from 17,000 men a month to 35,000. Hanoi, the *New York Times* notes, is preparing its people for an American war.

Slowly, America moves into Southeast Asia. Suddenly, it seems a war is breaking out at home.

•

That August, in Watts—a high-density, low-income, largely African American section of Los Angeles—a twenty-one-year-old Black man is pulled over by a white cop who suspects him of driving drunk. Tensions escalate. Rumors spread. Word on the street is that police have kicked a pregnant woman. Los Angeles television station KTLA reports: "With the suddenness of a lightning bolt and all the fury of an infernal holocaust, there was HELL in the City of Angels!"

Two days later, the *New York Times* reports: "Officials were at a loss to explain the cause of the rioting, which started last night after a routine drunken driving arrest. The unusually hot, smoggy weather was doubtless a contributing factor. Many Negroes at the scene complained about alleged police brutality but few cited specific instances to support their charges." Note the skepticism, the inability to believe such an "alleged" thing could even be possible. Also the requirement for those on the receiving end of the brutality to provide compelling evidence of their own harm.

•

In New York, on November 1, 1965, Jackie and the children are leaving an All Saints' Day service when a woman jumps out of the crowd around the church and grabs Caroline. She screams at the eight-year-old child: "YOUR MOTHER IS A WICKED WOMAN WHO HAS KILLED THREE PEOPLE." Jackie pries the woman loose.

The next day in Washington, Norman Morrison, another Quaker upset by the Johnson administration's policy on Vietnam, burns himself to death within view of Defense Secretary Robert McNamara's office. In a follow-up profile a few days later, the *New York Times* reveals that a scrap of charred paper in Morrison's notebook included an indictment of modern American life: "The richer we get materially, the poorer we get spiritually."

The following Tuesday at dawn in New York, twenty-two-year-old Roger LaPorte stands in front of the Dag Hammarskjöld

Library in the United Nations complex and sets himself on fire. "I'm antiwar, all wars, I did this as a religious action," he tells the paramedics.

The chief United States delegate to the UN worries. "Perhaps we are not sufficiently communicating to the people of the world our dedication," he says, "our attachment and complete commitment to the idea that peace is the only way for mankind in this nuclear age."

That night, one of the largest power failures in history blacks out a stretch of 80,000 square miles—nearly all of New York City, sections of nine northeastern states, and two Canadian provinces. It affects over 25 million people. The *New York Times* headline the following day: "CITY GROPES IN DARK."

Jackie is with Caroline at a ballet class. The Secret Service bundles them into a car and they drive uptown in the pitch-black night, back to 1040 Fifth.

·

At a dinner party, she discusses the problems of widowhood—the sense that people now perceive her as somehow altered, impaired. "[I]t was such an extraordinary reaction—she had this horror as if she herself had done something wrong," remembers a woman present. "She felt blighted by this state."

## MONDAY, NOVEMBER 22, 1965 ●

Robert Lowell, who has bipolar disorder, is now hospitalized at McLean, a psychiatric facility in Belmont, Massachusetts. On December 30, 1965, Jackie writes him: "I think of you so often— and hope that you do not suffer— . . . I think you were lucky to be away over Christmas. If I were you I would never come back—but you are braver than me."

# 1966

SHE'S IN HER SHELL OF GRIEF, AND ON THE GO: Switzerland, Italy, Portugal, Argentina, Spain, England, then summer in Hawaii.

•

There are approximately thirty-five movie magazines a month, and it's the movie magazines that take much of the blame for the press coverage of her. These are the magazines piled high by the hairdryers at the beauty shop, passed back and forth between neighbors, then kept in boxes in the downstairs hall closet. "[A]ll those trashy movie magazines" that pre-teen boomer girls, like the future feminist media scholar Susan J. Douglas, will later remember they used to "gorge on," with their stories of Jackie and Elizabeth Taylor and Patty Duke and the Lennon Sisters. Magazines first developed by the Hollywood studios in the 1910s as publicity vehicles for their screen stars. Since the 1960s—with the collapse of the studio system and the advent of TV—the mags have cast their eyes beyond Tinsel Town and started covering the stars of life.

Precisely who qualified for stardom was somewhat of a gray area then, as *TV Radio Mirror Album* noted when justifying its naming of Jackie as "Star of the Year" in January 1963:

> Can the First Lady properly be called a "star?" The word is used in show business to describe a personality so warm and vital that we forget we know it only as a picture on a TV screen or a name in newsprint. We feel that we know the actual person, as someone close to us. And certainly Jacqueline Kennedy is all that!

The coverage was hesitant at first, often pitting the First Lady against naughty celebs—Liz Taylor was her most frequent foil—and upholding Jackie as the ideal of refined, controlled American womanhood. But after the president's death, all bets are off. There are months where Jackie's face features on every single movie magazine at the newsstand.

But it isn't just the movie magazines: *Life, Look, Esquire,* the *Saturday Evening Post* . . . they all cover her. The photographer Ron Galella notices her name is now regularly appearing on the request sheets he gets from *Time* and *Newsweek*. "I began to realize that the media paid big money for good pictures of Jackie," he remembers. He begins tracking her, photographing her.

The book publishers are catching on too. There's a new biography by Dawn Langley Simmons (née Gordon Langley Hall) and Ann Pinchot, available in hardback for sixty cents. It "doesn't reveal anything racy," a reviewer from the *Northwest Arkansas Times* notes, this "well-organized collection of pertinent information strung together by a narrative which provides a sympathetic closeup." But it goes beyond what one can find in the movie magazines and, the reviewer observes, "The principal merit the book has is that a variety of such information is collected between the covers of a single book."

There seems to be no end to the interest in her, but pondering the phenomenon, another editor imagines: "If Jackie married an older man, she would dwindle."

ON JULY 30, APPROXIMATELY 2,000 SPECTATORS LINE THE narrow main street when she attends her half-sister's wedding in Newport, Rhode Island. During the service, the shouting beyond the doors drowns out the couple's vows. After the bridal party exits, people rush the church, pilfering flowers from the altar, taking home as relics pieces of the white cloth carpet that lines the aisle and the canvas canopy at the church entrance.

In the convent across the street, nuns watch. Disturbed by the frenzy, they kneel and pray for peace.

At a dinner party the following night, Bobby Kennedy tells Jackie that William Manchester has sold serial rights to *The Death of a President* to *Look* magazine.

•

This is a story that begins in that awful winter of 1964, with the Kennedys' selection of William Manchester to write the definitive, authorized account of the assassination. Manchester's "sole concern," he said at the time, was "that it be a genuine contribution to history," and that the book come out before the author Jim Bishop's *The Day Kennedy Was Shot*.

She's no fan of Bishop, who was prepping his book, *A Day in the Life of President Kennedy*, for publication when the president was killed. It was, she believed, "a stupid book and not true," so when Bishop wrote her in early 1964 asking for an interview, she demurred and asked him to desist. "She's trying to copyright the assassination," Bishop complained.

In a letter, she told Bishop she knew "all sorts of different and never ending, conflicting, and sometimes sensational things would be written about President Kennedy's death," and this was why she "hired William Manchester"—specifically "to protect President Kennedy and truth . . . and if I decide the book should never be published—then Mr. Manchester will be reimbursed for his time." Though, she admitted, "I suppose I must let it appear—for I have no right to suppress history, which people have a right to know, for reasons of private pain."

She dispatched a copy of this letter to William Manchester. He bristled at her use of the word "hired."

And so, on July 31, when Bobby tells her Manchester sold the serial rights to *Look* magazine for $665,000, she's livid—appalled by the price, the highest paid for such rights at that time, and the broadened exposure serialization ensures. It's particularly upsetting since she has yet to read or approve the book.

In response, her secretary Pam Turnure reads the manuscript and supplies Manchester with a list of revisions. According to Manchester, Turnure's requests were combined with the requests of Bobby's people and they were all submitted under Jackie's name. While Jackie's excisions were "largely trivial"—references to the children, family letters, the cigarettes in her purse, which a scene where the president appears in a state of undress—Bobby's aides proposed over 75 percent of the requested deletions, which constituted, in Manchester's view, "a rewriting of history" and "outright distortion." Much of this material had to do with the book's unflattering depiction of current president Lyndon Johnson, who appeared, according to an early reader, "almost in the role of [Camelot's] Mordred."

Her concern is that the whole project appears to be moving forward without her consent and beyond her control. She summons the publisher of *Look* and his attorney to Hyannis. They agree to reduce the number of installments and run them in January 1967 rather than at the anniversary in November. A small victory.

She asks Manchester to come to Hyannis, where she hopes to woo him to her way of seeing things and turn him against *Look*.

She feels he is betraying her trust by incorporating into his account elements of the ten-hour "frightfully emotional interview" she gave him and then denying the cuts she requests. Every effort she makes to stymie this book is thwarted, but she thinks that if she can get him to agree to the spin that there was never a Kennedy-approved manuscript, *Look* will be forced to cancel the serialization and the book will receive far less publicity. The Kennedy camp, in turn, would compensate Manchester with a higher percentage of the book's royalties.

The serialization is her primary concern, which Manchester seems not to understand: that she doesn't want this story spread across four weeks, with photos, in a glossy magazine, next to advertisements for tires and pantyhose and breakfast cereals.

Manchester is unmoved. He doesn't seem sympathetic to how this experience might reactivate the trauma of her husband's murder and he mostly portrays her as a bitch. Jackie, Manchester claims, "blazed high as a bonfire," as she declared defiantly, "Unless I run off with Eddie Fisher, the people will think anyone who is in the fight with me is a rat."

She feels violated that this cruel man has, as she writes President Johnson, "twisted everything" in his history.

The death of the president isn't just history. It's the day her husband was murdered in front of her eyes, the day in which she could not save him, the day she almost died herself.

## Tuesday November 22 1966

She picks up John from school. John stays silent, slips his hand into his mother's, and the pair of them walk back to 1040 Fifth. As they walk the four blocks home from St. David's, back down Fifth Avenue, a group of children follows them, chanting: "Your father's dead . . . Your father's dead."

THE FOLLOWING MONTH, SHE SUES *LOOK*, SETTING IN motion what *Time* declares "the biggest brouhaha over a book that the nation has ever known." The brouhaha is short-lived, as *Look*—hoping to avoid a costly court battle—quickly capitulates, slicing out 1,600 words that its editor-in-chief reassures the *New York Post* are only "slush."

It is a hollow victory. The passages she objected to had long since filtered into the press, a slip for which her fight with Manchester was largely responsible. She's also under serious media attack for having tried to control and censor history.

There is a sense that this story of the president's death is *owned* by the press and the American people, and there's a marked lack of empathy for how her husband's murder affects her.

This backlash is occurring well before the development of a post-traumatic stress disorder (PTSD) diagnosis in the 1980s. Even

Jackie lacked a framework for her own experiences. Understandings of trauma were far less sophisticated then than they are today, though the responses to it probably haven't changed as much as we would like.

So, after the passage of a certain reasonable amount of time devoted to grieving widowhood—one year, let's say—there seems to have been an assumption that she be over it. There would, from then on, be less leeway given her, in the press and by the public, for the fact that she had suffered both a cataclysmic loss and a horrifying trauma.

A syndicated columnist, with the best intentions and a heap of casual sexism, defends her as "a fine and lovely lady, in the sort of emotional bind all women are capable of, flaying away at a small tight group of dominant males." She is vulnerable, a widow, with a "right to determine the extent of sorrow she is willing to share with the world" and, in her efforts to stop the book, simply displaying "intensely human characteristics."

"No good wife would do otherwise," another editorialist allows, "but she is holding her hand to the avalanche."

The story was no longer hers.

# 1967

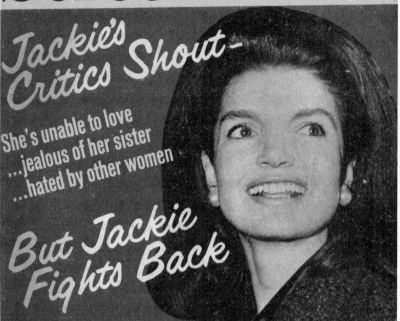

DEC.

# Screen Stars

*Jackie's Critics Shout –*

She's unable to love
...jealous of her sister
...hated by other women

*But Jackie Fights Back*

**Warning To The Monkees:**
**STAY AWAY FROM LSD**

**Bustline Beauty:**
SEXIEST STARS REVEAL THEIR SECRETS

MIA AND NANCY SINATRA CONFESS:
"We Can Never
Go To Church Again"

**The Woman's Weapon**
**Julie Andrews**
**Dares Not Use**

ALL ABOUT ELVIS' BABY, PAUL NEWMAN'S MARRIAGE BLUES, HAYLEY MILLS' LOVE AFFAIR WITH A MARRIED MAN

SHE MEETS UP WITH DOROTHY SCHIFF, THE *NEW YORK POST*
publisher. Schiff wasn't so much a friend as someone with whom
Jackie occasionally had quasi-revealing lunches, presumably aware
that some of the details might eventually inform what was printed
in the press. Over lunch, she confides: "The board is moved and all
the little pieces change places."

•

President Johnson insists the war is being won, a war about which
some Americans begin to think he is lying. The carnage slips into
homes, airing on TV news during the dinner hour, printed in wom-
en's magazines.

In its January 1967 issue, *Ladies' Home Journal*—a mild-
mannered publication with the motto "The Magazine Women
Believe In"—runs an article by Martha Gelhorn. In it, the reporter
quotes a New Jersey housewife who's adopted two Vietnamese
children and recently returned from the war zone: "Before I went
to Saigon, I had heard and read that napalm melts the flesh, and I
thought that's nonsense, because I can put a roast in the oven and
the fat will melt but the meat stays there. Well, I went and saw these
children burned by napalm and it is absolutely true."

•

Two months later, the *Saturday Evening Post* features a story titled
"Jackie Kennedy: A View from the Crowd," which analyzes the
"The National Sport of Watching Jackie Kennedy." It includes a
map of "Jackie Kennedy's Manhattan."

She's angry enough to consent to an interview with a pair of journalists. "Why a map," she asks them, "a detailed diagram showing

just where my children are at various times of the day? Why is it so important to a story to give our address, or the name of the children's schools, times of classes. Why?"

•

That month, Dr. Benjamin Spock—the nation's leading expert on parenting, who'd literally written the book on child rearing by which baby boomers were raised, and who supported JFK in 1960 ("Dr. Spock is for my husband," Jackie said, "and I am for Dr. Spock.")—appears arm-in-arm with Dr. Martin Luther King Jr. at an anti-war march. Walking down Chicago's State Street, he wears a three-piece suit and stands behind a little boy carrying a sign that reads: CHILDREN ARE NOT BORN TO BURN.

The "tragic adventure in Vietnam," Dr. King calls it. There's a rumor that Dr. King might run for president in '68, with Dr. Spock as his running mate.

RUMORS ABOUT HER AND BOBBY KENNEDY REMAIN A GENtle hum in the growing cacophony of stories about other beaux. It's hard to tell what was romantic and what wasn't among her public friendships with successful, erudite men. Every man sparked wedding rumors; every outing was a major news event.

On May 26, 1967, she goes for a walk with the dancer Rudolph Nureyev. She smiles. In some syndicated newspapers, this is a page-one story.

But the walk with Nureyev is nothing compared to the hysteria excited by her friendship with David Ormsby-Gore, Lord Harlech. Almost immediately after Ormsby-Gore's wife died in an automobile accident in May 1967, the media launched a full-scale campaign lobbying on his behalf. "When I was writing Sybil Ormsby-Gore's obituary, I predicted he would have a romance with Jackie," one society reporter recalled. *Esquire* decreed it: "The greatest romantic cliff-hanger since Taylor and Burton."

It isn't just the media. In her diary, her former mother-in-law, Rose Kennedy, observes: "David Harlech seemed to be almost an ideal choice." On board his yacht, the *Christina*, Aristotle Onassis—who was seeing her whenever he was in New York—appeared concerned. "He kept pumping me about Jackie," remembered Joan Thring, Nureyev's manager, of a cruise she accompanied Onassis on in 1967. "Especially about her and David Harlech. Did I think they had been lovers?"

The hysteria reached such proportions that by September 1967, just four months after Lady Harlech's death, this idea was enough a part of the cultural conversation that a reader wrote in to *Parade*—one of the country's most widely read magazines, which was included as a weekly supplement in many American newspapers on Sundays—asking: "Who is this David Ormsby-Gore everyone wants Jackie Kennedy to marry?" *Parade* characterized him as "tall, slender, smooth, balding, wealthy, educated, considered at the moment one of Britain's greatest 'catches'" and noted that marriage to Ormsby-Gore would net her a title and "remove her and her children from the U.S. publicity spotlight." Problem solved.

Throughout this period, in reality she remains largely detached. Joe Kennedy's nurse, Rita Dallas, sees her with Ormsby-Gore during a visit to Hyannis Port, and notes, "Whenever they were together, she always looked as if she were alone."

WITH ARISTOTLE ONASSIS, THOUGH, EVERYTHING IS DIFferent. From the beginning of their friendship in 1963, he welcomed her into his world and encouraged her to express her emotions.

After the president's death, Onassis slid back into the picture. He was compassionate, kind, a good listener and friend. He gave her and her children his attention and his time—attending school plays, meeting her mother, and joining the family at horse shows despite his distaste for them. The lengths he went to made an impression.

In contrast to Jack Kennedy, Ari appeared emotionally open, and he showered her with attention. But he, too, was a wild choice.

He'd always held great appeal for the women of the jet set, who found him charismatic, cosmopolitan, and sensual—a tantalizing contrast to the droll prep school boys of their debutante youths. He was sexy, swaggering with new money, and capable of great kindness. He spoke Greek, Spanish, French, and English, and his conversation provided a welcome relief from the staid country club chat.

But the society grand dames, the matrons of Newport—women like her mother, Janet Auchincloss, and her mother's friends—were nonplused. They deplored his brazenness, his manners, his otherness. And so, though he was unfailingly polite to important, powerful men and attentive to beautiful, interesting women, he never entirely escaped the stigma of being unlike them.

He appeared not to give a damn. Many a sunbathing Newport matron averted her eyes when he showed up at the beach in tiny, woolen swim shorts while all the other men were wearing Bermuda-length madras swim trunks. "He had very good legs," Solange Herter remembered nearly fifty years later, laughing as she told me. "He wore short shorts with very good legs."

Solange once asked him how he was always so poised and attractive though he wasn't particularly good looking. He told her, "I always look suntanned; that way people think I'm successful."

But no matter how successful he was or how he longed to be respected by the aristocracy, he refused to cater to their notions of respectability. To Jackie, Ari appeared a rebel—someone who wouldn't kowtow to other people's expectations. It was a trait that Jackie, herself rebellious in this way, found compelling.

Like her, he remained an isolated, itinerant figure, an outsider. Never quite comfortable on solid ground, he circled the earth aboard his yacht. He was a romantic figure, and for her, he held mythic appeal. He spoke of Odysseus and took her to Ithaca. And gradually, over the years, he came to represent a daring alternative to her American life.

But, for now, she continued to travel, and he continued to work. "For him, life was a chess game," Lee Radziwill later wrote. "His patience was enduring; time was unimportant."

"Like Richard Nixon, he would never do things spontaneously," remembered one of his relatives. "He would sit back and think and have the vision to see what was happening and why. He was very perceptive." He made it clear he would wait for her until she was ready to get away, until she was ready to leave America for good.

SHE IS APPALLED BY WHAT IS HAPPENING IN VIETNAM. IN A LETter to Secretary of Defense Robert McNamara, she calls the situation "more complex than any dark hell that Shakespeare ever looked into."

When she goes to Cambodia in November 1967, she's criticized for her indifference, for being so near the fighting in Vietnam, only ninety miles away, and not visiting troops. But the war appears to have been part of her motivation in going and it played a role in her trip.

She initially planned to visit in February 1967, but when Prince Norodom Sihanouk of Cambodia tells her he is going to be away, she reschedules for November. She wants to see Sihanouk because she plans to petition him to intervene with the North Vietnamese for the release of American prisoners of war.

Getting her into Cambodia is complicated. Due to the severance of United States–Cambodian diplomatic relations in 1965, she needs a military plane to get in. The State Department has to go through the Australian ambassador to arrange her trip. But her friends Robert McNamara and the ambassador-at-large Averell Harriman know that if they can get her there, it could be a significant gesture of rapprochement.

The Cambodian government is eager, producing an itinerary that she declares "the most backbreaking schedule ever proposed." In a letter, she reminds Harriman that "traveling is twice as exhausting for a woman as for a man—you are expected to look nice, at State Dinners, in steaming daytime heat—and you have to sacrifice time you could be taking a nap to get your hair fixed." She chides him: "I am not the Queen. I am not campaigning. I refused to be pushed around."

Daniel Oliver Newberry—special assistant to Harriman— is responsible for working out most of the details of her trip. According to Newberry, she wanted to go to Angkor because "Some famous French scholar had told her that she should see it," and she insisted that she be allowed "to go NOW." The unimpressed Newberry overheard Ambassador Harriman talking to Defense Secretary McNamara and felt they both "dreaded having to talk to Mrs. Kennedy." In a State Department oral history, he contends that she wanted to go to Cambodia so badly that the State Department "had to 'cook up' a mission for her," so that U.S. military transport could be used to get her from Bangkok into Phnom Penh.

Newberry portrays her as a pushy woman, one whom everyone at the State Department dreads having to deal with—an assessment that doesn't jive with the reality: the people dealing with her were close, personal friends. More likely, Newberry didn't understand the dynamics at play.

And so, when she jokes with Harriman—in response to Newberry's having opened Prince Sihanouk's invitation to her, teasing, "Averell, suppose that that letter had been a 'tender' avowal"—Newberry is stunned. He cites this as the beginning of his "disillusionment with the 'Camelot' image of the widow Kennedy." He expects her to be a quiet princess without a sense of humor. Turns out she isn't the Jackie he imagined, and his testimony is colored with the bitterness of someone deceived.

•

October 27. Averell Harriman, memo to General Ellsworth Bunker (U.S. ambassador to South Vietnam) and General William Westmoreland (Commander, Military Assistance Command,

Vietnam): "Mrs. Kennedy plans to raise, on humanitarian basis, subject of American prisoners held by Viet Cong with Prince Sihanouk. There is of course no assurance that anything useful will result, but to preserve any possibility of success this should be very closely held."

•

"Fairytale Trip for Jackie," the headlines gasp. She receives an "almost unprecedented warm welcome," equaled only "by that given last year to French President Charles de Gaulle"—a distinction significant not simply because of de Gaulle's status as a world leader, but also because Sihanouk considered him "Cambodia's greatest friend."

The following evening, at Angkor, she walks barefoot through ruins, lit by torches and starlight. At the temple, "She ran her fingers wonderingly over stone friezes depicting mythical creatures and legendary battles between gods, men and monkeys." In close-up photographs, she appears serene. According to the British press, at Angkor, she is "mobbed and jostled as American press and television men crawled over the temple like ants at a bag of sugar."

Part of the press excitement is due to the fact that David Ormsby-Gore is with her. His presence is interpreted as tacit proof of an impending wedding. However, as the former British ambassador to the United States, he's actually accompanying her in a diplomatic capacity rather than a romantic one.

She's trying to avoid saying anything to upset the delicate détente being finagled. She also must contend with Prince Sihanouk, who seems enamored of her but is something of a loose cannon. Earlier in the day that she went to Angkor, the prince held a press conference in which he described Cambodia's relationship with Communist China as "very close" and declared to a room of American reporters that his country would continue to support North Vietnam "in their fight against you."

In the car on the way to the airport, she reminds the prince of how, the evening before, she spoke of the conditions under which the prisoners were held in North Vietnam and how he had agreed with her that they were deplorable and that this was a humanitarian issue. She speaks of two civilian POWs, Gustav Hertz and Douglas Ramsey, whose families she and the Kennedys had been in communication with; deeply shaken by the news of Mr. Hertz's recent death from malaria, she connects it to the imprisonment of Mr. Ramsey. She asks the prince to intervene against the horrifying treatment of innocent civilians.

Her sense is that Sihanouk wants to avoid a serious discussion, but the prince does tell her to have Mrs. Ramsey write him a letter asking for his intercession in light of Mr. Hertz's tragic death.

She leaves, the press notes, "looking a bit tired."

•

November 8. Mike Forrestal's memo to Ambassador Harriman and Secretary McNamara: "Trip has had no adverse consequences up to present other than thoroughly to exhaust Mrs. Kennedy."

•

She takes flak for this trip: for (in one commentator's words) giving "both social and diplomatic status to the curious [Prince] Sihanouk" and dining with a "dictator" while committing "a snub, by omission, to the American effort in Vietnam." She's disparaged for being "within a few miles of South Vietnam" and giving "no thought to visiting American fighting men." The ghost of JFK is evoked, alongside the suggestion that he surely wouldn't approve of his wife bungling into diplomatic relations. (Only later would it be reported Bobby and Teddy Kennedy had encouraged her to go.)

But, despite the critics, the trip is a success. "It took the chill out of Cambodian-American relations," observed a reporter of her visit, "and by doing so, opened the door to an improvement." The *Times of London* noted after her departure that, in Cambodia, "there is no doubt now about a new warmth towards the Americans."

## WEDNESDAY, NOVEMBER 22, 1967

IN DECEMBER, LIZ SMITH'S FIVE-PART PROFILE OF ORMSBY-Gore as "The Man Most Likely to Succeed with Jackie Kennedy" runs in papers throughout the country.

Then amid the promotional tour for his book, which assesses the conditions of twentieth-century Western civilization, Ormsby-Gore is repeatedly asked about the state of his love life. He refutes the rumors, telling reporters, "I've said it in Seattle. I've said it in San Francisco. I've said it in Norfolk. I've said it in Charleston, and now I'm saying it in Washington, D.C. There is no truth whatsoever to the story."

But that wasn't entirely true. Ormsby-Gore later admitted to a biographer that the pair had slept together, but he said it wasn't serious—Jackie remained ambivalent, and she continued seeing other men. One of Ormsby-Gore's daughters remembered them as "two wounded birds together." Ormsby-Gore's second wife, Pamela, whom he married in 1969, later said she thought they "fell on each other to commiserate together"; that Jackie thought Ormsby-Gore was attractive and could have had him if she wanted him, but she did not want to be pinned down.

•

She feels hemmed in. She's with a friend at a show, who suggests at the intermission that they go get refreshments once the theater has cleared. "I can't," she says. "I can't do that." And then a voice in the distance exclaims, "There's Jackie Kennedy!" and there's a thunderous rush as people who've moved out into the lobby for drinks come rushing back into the theater, running down both aisles, filing through the row in front of hers, gawping.

Another night: A friend accompanies her to the ballet. Some woman from the crowd comes up and screams in her face, screaming that she had killed the president. Ghastly, the friend remembered, such an awful way to live.

When Dorothy Schiff tells her she's very brave to go to Cambodia, she replies, tartly, "It's safer there than here."

August 1968, Photoplay

# 1968

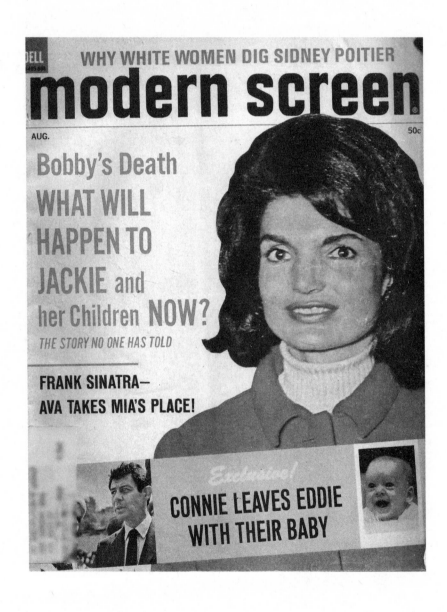

SHE'S ON EDGE. AT A PERFORMANCE, REVOLVER SHOTS GO off onstage and, according to photographer Cecil Beaton, who's sitting next to her, "Jackie nearly jumped out of her chair, and over the rail in the dress circle."

Robert McNamara—who, as secretary of defense, has played a critical role in the war's escalation—sees her at a dinner party. They're chatting when she abruptly goes off on him about Vietnam. Hitting her fists against his chest, she begs, "Stop the killing, stop the killing!"

At a family gathering where Bobby announces he's going to run in '68, she exclaims, "Won't it be wonderful when we get back in the White House?"

When Bobby's wife, Ethel, replies, "What do you mean, *we?*" Jackie flees the room.

Her position, both in the Kennedy family and in America, is increasingly awkward.

•

The press and the public remain doggedly focused on David Ormsby-Gore, Lord Harlech. In March, when she goes to Mexico with her friend Roswell Gilpatric to tour Mayan ruins, reporters call out, "Will you marry Lord Harlech?" This inquiry earns them nothing but "a tight smile and dead silence." Gilpatric is married and D.C. gossips are whispering that she must have colluded with him on this vacation solely "to throw the Harlech prophets off the track."

•

That spring, Bobby Kennedy is running in the Democratic primary for president and drawing massive crowds—a racially, generationally, economically diverse coalition, some of whom he is, inevitably, bound to disappoint, but who now strain to touch him, to make contact, as though he is a god or a messiah or young Elvis.

"You've just got to give yourself to the people," he says. "And to trust them, and from then on . . . either [luck is] with you or it isn't."

He rides around in a convertible and leaps into frenzied crowds. He doesn't worry. Warned of the danger, he says, "These are my kind of people."

An aide asks Jackie to convince Bobby to reinstate his Secret Service protection. She says she's tried, but he won't do it.

The papers avoid grim prophecies but, behind the scenes, people talk. "He has the stuff to go all the way," a reporter at *Newsweek* informs the author George Plimpton. "But he's not going to go all the way . . . somebody is going to shoot him. . . . He's out there now waiting for him."

"You know, of course, that your guy will be killed," the French writer Romain Gary says to Pierre Salinger, John Kennedy's former press secretary.

"I know there will be another assassination attempt sooner or later," Kennedy himself reportedly tells Gary.

On Tuesday, April 2, she draws Arthur Schlesinger aside at a dinner party in New York. "Do you know what I think will happen to Bobby?" she asks. "The same thing that happened to Jack. There is so much hatred in this country, and more people hate Bobby than hated Jack."

There is so much hatred. Two days later, in Memphis, Martin Luther King Jr. is murdered. Hearing the news, in New York, she jots down notes on a yellow legal pad, writing about "this senseless, senseless act of hate which took away a man who preached love and hope."

"When will our country learn that to live by the sword is to perish by the sword?" she wonders. "In the agonizing months that lie ahead I pray that everyone will look into his heart and try to find more room for love and justice there. And for the people Dr. King led, who have suffered so much and who have so much still to hope for, I pray that his sacrifice will help to bring to them all that they deserve."

But in the public record, her feelings toward King are very much frozen in 1964: the result of all the intelligence FBI director J. Edgar Hoover fed to the Kennedy brothers to discredit King. The brothers, in turn, repeated it to her in that autumn of 1963. And so, in a 1964 oral history, she tells Arthur Schlesinger, "I just can't see a picture of Martin Luther King without thinking . . . that man's terrible," because Jack had told her there was "a tape that the FBI had of Martin Luther King when he was here [in Washington] for the freedom march . . . [where] he was calling up all these girls and arranging for a party . . . sort of an orgy in the hotel." And, later, Bobby told her Hoover told him that, at the president's funeral, Dr. King "made fun of Cardinal Cushing and said that he was drunk at [the funeral]. And things about [how] they almost dropped the coffin." None of this has been proven true.

Hoover hated King and "did everything possible to make Dr. King look like somebody from another planet," remembered Representative John Lewis, who believed King "admired, he loved . . . the Kennedy family" and he would never have said such a thing at John Kennedy's funeral.

"Obviously J. Edgar Hoover had passed on something that Martin Luther King said about my father's funeral, to Uncle Bobby and to Mommy. And obviously, she was upset about that," Caroline Kennedy later maintained. "It shows you the poisonous . . . activities of J. Edgar Hoover, and the idea that this is going on at the highest levels of government is really twisted."

Hoover was adept at "spinning webs," and it's possible the orgy tape was faked and intended as a warning to Jack Kennedy that his own extramarital activities were known to the director. But, knowing nothing of Hoover's schemes, Jackie knew only that she'd received this information from two men she trusted, and so she repeated it to Schlesinger and concluded, "Martin Luther King is really a tricky person."

Four years later, everything looks different. Bobby Kennedy learns about the killing en route to a campaign event in Indianapolis. That evening, he speaks to a predominantly Black audience that has not yet heard the news. When he tells them, there are screams. And then, standing on the back of a flatbed truck, Bobby speaks off-the-cuff for nearly five minutes, giving what will later be viewed as one of the most significant speeches of the modern era.

Speaking publicly about the death of John Kennedy for the first time, he tells the crowd:

> For those of you who are Black and are tempted to fill with hatred and mistrust of the injustice of such an act, against all white people, I would only say that I can also feel in my own heart the same kind of feeling. I had a member of my family killed, but he was killed by a white man. . . . What we need in the United States is not division; what we need in the United States is not hatred; what we need in the United States is not violence and lawlessness, but is love, and wisdom, and compassion toward one another, and a feeling of justice toward those who still suffer within our country, whether they be white or whether they be Black.

On April 9, she goes with Bobby, Ethel, and Ted down to Atlanta. In the guest book at the King home, she writes Coretta Scott King: "I share your grief in this hour of sorrow but his death will help to free us from the violence and tragedy which hate often produces. He will always be remembered as one of our nation's martyred greats."

She seems to think Mrs. King will draw comfort from her husband's martyrdom, that martyrdom will give it meaning—an interesting assumption, as meaning is precisely what she felt was missing from her own husband's death, that he was killed by "a silly little communist" rather than for his civil rights legislation.

When he sees her at the funeral, former vice president Richard Nixon—ever awkward and never one for small talk—blurts, "Mrs. Kennedy, this must bring back many memories." An unhelpful reminder because, no doubt, it does.

Her attendance isn't without controversy and, in the weeks after, there is an active effort by the Kings to head off criticism of her. Later that month, Reverend Martin Luther King Sr. speaks with gossip columnist Maxine Cheshire. He tells her that Mrs. Kennedy was a guest of Mrs. King and that she was personally invited by Mrs. King, who "had gotten word that Mrs. Kennedy was hesitating to come for fear her gesture would be misinterpreted" as a political stunt.

"[Jackie] gave no reason to suspect her motivation as having anything to do with politics," Cheshire concluded, while also noting that at that time, in 1968, the former First Lady was still receiving "critical mail referring harshly" to a photograph that had circulated of her holding four-year-old Bobby Johnson in her lap during a 1965 Christmas party in the Bronx.

The day after the funeral, she calls Dorothy Schiff, the *New York Post* reporter/acquaintance she occasionally speaks with. "Think how they must feel today," she says of the Kings.

When Schiff sees her for lunch a few days later, she talks about writing, about work, saying the only thing she'd be interested in doing would be on the Yucatan. She's just returned from a trip there and thinks she might write something, then use the profits to help the impoverished people in that area. Schiff notes she's lost a lot of weight and appears depressed. She is, Schiff feels, "much less the queen than when she first came to New York."

"She talked about [her Polish brother-in-law] Stash [sic] Radziwill," Schiff recalls. "She said when you speak another language you assume a different personality; imagine being married to someone not of your country; There would be things you would never understand or know about him."

To Bobby she is alleged to have said: "America's going to the dogs. I don't know why you want to be president."

SHE'S SEEING A LOT OF ARI. SHE IS, PERHAPS, ALREADY imagining marriage to a foreigner.

In early April, she and Ari lunch together at Orsini. At Easter, a photographer catches them in Palm Beach. An April 25 gossip column notes they popped into P.J. Clarke's in New York with Rudolph Nureyev and Margot Fonteyn; it was, however, Nureyev's "tight pants and boots, cap and short fur jacket" that "monopolized the stares." Come late May, she reportedly enjoys "an unusually secretive" holiday in the Caribbean, supposedly aboard Ari's yacht, possibly accompanied by Elizabeth Taylor and Richard Burton. The gossip columnist Suzy mentions in her column that Ari was in Hyannis over the summer and that he let the Kennedy kids bury him in the sand.

Still, Ari is identified only as "a close friend of Mrs. Kennedy's sister." They are not considered a couple. These are not dates. The gossip columnist Earl Wilson calls them "long-time good friends."

The relationship receives less attention, in part, because David Ormsby-Gore makes such good copy. He wasn't a particularly charismatic, sexy man, but he was British, a widower, and a Lord— elements that, for Americans, made him exotic enough to be an interesting choice and bland enough not to pose a threat to JFK's memory. The Lord and the former First Lady was a fairy tale, yes, but one guaranteed not to eclipse Camelot.

In contrast, Onassis was Mediterranean, an elderly, divorced businessman known to be in a long-term relationship with the opera star Maria Callas. The responses to him were usually couched in terms of his height (short!), his age (old!), and his business practices (crooked!), but they betrayed a white, Anglo-Saxon, American snobbishness as well.

When the gossip writer Doris Lilly appears on The *Merv Griffin Show* and suggests Ari as a possible beau, she's reportedly booed for the suggestion.

•

On May 6, 1968, at a family dinner including Jackie, her mother, Ari, Bobby and Ethel, and Rudolph Nureyev and his agent Joan Thring, Thring sensed that marriage was in the works.

"It had been brought up, in front of the mother, with Bobby," and Thring sensed Bobby's annoyance. But she also felt the relationship was inevitably going to end in marriage, a possibility discussed openly that night.

Jackie feels constricted, tied to the Kennedy family and obligated in ways that make her uneasy. "She basically wanted what she felt she needed when it came to financing," contended George Smathers. "No more. No less. She spent a lot, don't get me wrong [ . . . ] But after his death, she wasn't inconsiderate about it, as has been painted in the past. The Kennedys were pretty cheap."

As a widow, she had to barter herself to gain access to the money she needed for a big purchase, even a practical one. When she needed a new car, a friend remembered "she practically had to bribe Bobby" to get it, by promising that she would publicly support him if he ran for president.

"This cannot go on," Rose Kennedy reportedly warned Janet Auchincloss, suggesting she tell her daughter to cut back on staff and personal expenditures, saying, "Now that Jack isn't here to provide for her, Jackie's going to have to learn to survive on less." Rose was suggesting she overhaul her budget. It seems Jackie was planning to overhaul her life.

ON MONDAY, JUNE 3, BOBBY AND ETHEL ARE RIDING through San Francisco's Chinatown: no armed bodyguards, no

Secret Service. A round of shots goes off. Bobby flinches once but remains standing. Fearless in the face of what sounds to everyone around him like gunfire, he reaches back into the crowd and continues shaking hands. It was only firecrackers.

In New York, earlier that same day, the pop artist Andy Warhol is shot. When she speaks to Bobby that night, Jackie mentions the shooting, how Warhol was talking on the phone in his office when Valerie Solanas, an actress from his latest film, entered and shot him. His chances of survival are, as of that evening, said to be fifty-fifty. When Bobby gets off the phone, he mentions the Warhol shooting. "This country has gone mad," he says, "absolutely mad."

The following day, June 4, Bobby wins the California primary—a triumph that may lead to his being declared the Democratic candidate for the presidential election later that year.

In Los Angeles, around midnight, after a speech to his supporters, the senator leaves the podium of the Ambassador Hotel's ballroom and is on his way to an adjoining dining room for a brief press conference. He turns, as though scanning the crowd to locate the orange and white of his wife's minidress. A sound reverberates against the steel surfaces of the kitchen. The assistant maître d'hôtel, who's been directing Bobby through the melee by holding his hand, feels it slip from his grasp; loses the grip completely; and, when he looks for the senator, sees him sliding to the concrete floor.

Ecstatic cries of "We want Bobby! We want Bobby!" still emanate from the ballroom as wails of "Oh God, oh Christ, why? WHY?" fill the kitchen corridor.

A crush of photographers, kitchen staff, family, and campaign volunteers press forward as Ethel Kennedy screams at them to get back.

Repeatedly, someone shouts for a doctor.

Bystanders yell, "Get the gun, get the gun," as a director pleads with his cameraman: "Shoot it, shoot it, please shoot it!"

The senator lies on the floor, a puddle of blood beneath him seeping from the wound in his head where the bullet has entered just behind the ear. His lips move, his eyes are open. Someone has unbuttoned his white shirt. A busboy has placed a rosary in his bloodied hand.

·

It's 4:15 a.m. in New York and Jackie is asleep when Stas Radziwill calls from London and asks how Bobby's doing. When she tells Stas that Bobby's won California, he realizes she does not know her brother-in-law has been shot. She'd turned off the TV and gone to bed once she heard he won.

Five minutes later, she's on the phone with the *New York Times*, talking to a reporter on the night desk, trying to get more information. The following morning's paper will include a small report on page thirty-two: "Mrs. John F. Kennedy Calls Times on Shooting."

·

As she heads to California, Roswell Gilpatric finds her "alarmingly distraught." She keeps conflating the murders, imagining she is First Lady and that her husband has died again. At the airport in New York, she keeps repeating that it can't have happened. When she lands in Los Angeles, a Kennedy aide describes her as "slowly withering away from the inside," with what another aide remembers as "a wild, hunted-animal look."

It's clear Bobby won't recover, but everyone else in the family is too traumatized to give the order to remove him from life support. It's reportedly Jackie who speaks with the doctors on June 6, Jackie who stops the machines.

·

There's a pervasive sense of déjà vu. As though this were not a new horror but, rather, a reprise of the old one. On the return flight to New York, she worries the plane carrying Robert Kennedy's casket is the same one that brought her husband home from Dallas. She refuses to board until assured otherwise.

It's so similar: the shooting, the death, the funeral, all those children, all those Kennedys and the whole world watching.

After the funeral train back to D.C. and the candlelight burial, "after this long, long day," back at her mother's house in Georgetown, as everyone else sleeps, she writes a letter to the conductor Leonard Bernstein, to thank him for participating in the funeral. She tells him how much the "sensitive trembling . . . those few soaring moments of Mahler" moved her, how the selected pieces of music were so "appropriate for this Kennedy—my Kaleidoscopic brother-in-law—and his wife who loved him mystically . . . they were something this world will never see again."

"In awful times," she writes, "I think the only thing that comforts you is the goodness of people." But she worries that "when I come home I will be so tired—and I may start thinking about the badness in people."

IT WAS A TIME OF RECKONING. IN THE IMMEDIATE AFTERMATH of the shooting, in the lobby of the Ambassador Hotel, a woman laid her head on a counter, repeating audibly, "My God, my God, what kind of country is this?" On the morning of June 5, as the senator lay dying, New York's WPIX-TV went silent and broadcast nothing but the single word SHAME for two and a half hours. The following day, in a commencement address at City University that he'd rewritten after the shooting, Arthur Schlesinger Jr. declared Americans "the most frightening people on the planet," observing: "We are a violent people with a violent history, and the instinct for violence has seeped into the bloodstream of our national life."

"I hate this country," Jackie reportedly says the day after Bobby dies. "I despise America and I don't want my children to live here anymore. If they're killing Kennedys, my kids are #1 targets. . . . I want to get out of this country." Years later, she expressed it in these terms again: "I wanted to go away. They were killing Kennedys and I didn't want them to harm my children. I wanted to go off." And so she did.

But it would be an oversimplification to pin her motivation for marrying Ari entirely on Bobby's death, because the plan had been in motion for some time. Loss may have heightened the urgency with which events unfolded, but she'd already made up her mind.

Marriage to Ari made sense in many respects. As one of her cousins psychoanalyzed it:

> Those of us who had grown up with Jackie felt that Onassis was precisely the type of man we thought she would marry. She had always liked older men, even as a teenager. And we all knew that her mother and father had relentlessly coached her to marry a very rich man. Furthermore, Onassis was, in many ways, a man very much like Jackie's father, who she had adored. Like Black Jack Bouvier, Onassis was a very masculine, protective type who loved to indulge women. Both men were totally materialistic. Both were very "worldly." And both had a way of making a woman feel very appreciated and secure. Security was what Jackie needed after Bobby's murder.

Depending on who you talked to, this marriage made total sense or was wildly out of character. Even among her acquaintances, the reactions were almost always extreme.

Some saw it as evidence of mental instability and wondered if she had entirely come undone; if she'd married Onassis because, in the wake of Bobby's murder, she had, quite literally, lost her mind. An old friend from Vassar thought so. When asked about it decades later, it seemed she was still trying to make sense of it. "It was so out of character for her, it was mind-boggling," she said. "I will never understand it. . . . I think it was just so awful. . . . She's a woman of great dignity. Even as a young girl she had dignity. And there was something to me so undignified about the marriage to Onassis. It was such an aberration."

But such logic overlooks the reality that emotions don't always square with etiquette. Twice now, in less than five years, the board had moved and all the pieces changed places. Incapable of rearranging the pieces, she was, finally, chucking the board.

On September 8, four days before the fifteenth anniversary of her marriage to Jack Kennedy, she writes a friend that she now realizes grief is "an element one lives in—like sea or sky or earth—but an element one hopes eventually one might escape—never loving, never caring about anyone else—but perhaps grieving less." She had hoped this. But then she writes, "Now I know it is forever————grieving————"

Two weeks later, in a letter to the same friend, she draws a different conclusion: "In the end the only strong thing is love—the only thing that keeps one strong."

•

Thursday, October 17. The *Boston Herald-Traveler* reports "a completely knowledgeable source" claims Jackie intends "to marry the Greek shipping magnate, Aristotle Socrates Onassis . . . one of the world's richest men."

But no one else seems to know anything.

Jackie's former social secretary Nancy Tuckerman tells reporters, "As far as I know Mrs. Kennedy is not planning to get married." Ted Kennedy's office has "no knowledge of Mrs. Kennedy's plans."

Cardinal Richard Cushing—the priest who officiated her wedding to Jack Kennedy and "a longtime family intimate"—seems to possess rather more information but he isn't telling. "No comment . . . my lips are sealed . . . no comment at all," he says before admitting "an official announcement may be coming up tonight."

Within an hour of the cardinal's remarks, Janet Auchincloss announces the engagement.

"JACKIE TO MARRY ONASSIS" screams the front page of the *Des Moines Register* in two-inch type, above "WEDDING NEXT WEEK ON HIS PRIVATE ISLE" and additional headlines announcing that, with her remarriage, she'll be losing her government widow's pension and that she faces excommunication from the Catholic Church for marrying a divorcé.

•

She leaves New York aboard Olympic Airways' regularly scheduled Flight 412, the 8:30 p.m. to Athens.

Legend has it that as she left her apartment building that evening, a middle-aged woman stepped from the mass of people crowding the street to bid her farewell and exclaimed, "Jackie, say it isn't so!"

THE STORY OF HER WEDDING MAKES THE FRONT PAGE OF the *New York Times* for four straight days. The outcry around the world is beyond all reason.

"Jackie! How Could You!" exclaims *Expressen* in Stockholm, where the marriage was seen as "definitely politically interesting." In Copenhagen, "people on the streets debated why Jackie chose Onassis." They were reeling in France, where it was "unbelievable" (*L'Aurore*), the "Most stupefying news of the year" (*Paris Jour*), "the most surprising and unexpected [marriage] of the century" (*France-Soir*). In the Soviet Union, people reportedly surrounded the car of an American mathematician, asking, "Is it true about Jackie? Is she marrying a handsome American millionaire?" Hearing it was Onassis, the American remembered, "The Russians wept real tears."

"She has lost 99.99 per cent of the admiration she once had in the world by this single act," announced an indignant office worker in Madrid.

The following month, the humorist Art Buchwald will write, quite seriously, "Of all the events of 1968, none has had more of an effect on the American people than the marriage of Jackie Kennedy to Greek zillionaire Aristotle Onassis. People who had no opinion on the Vietnamese war, the crisis of the cities or the youth revolution all had something to say about Mrs. Kennedy's nuptials."

In Washington, D.C., where Jackie lived for much of her twenties and thirties, the columnist Isabel Shelton reports that there was, initially, "shocked incredulity . . . [that] the living embodiment of the spirit of Camelot—the beautiful, noble, grieving widow" had allied herself with "an aging, divorced maritime pirate." But then Washingtonians pulled themselves together and decided "they had never believed in Camelot in the first place, because it "was an invention of the romantic, totally non-political mind of Jacqueline Kennedy."

In Boston, according to Mary McGrory, it was "a family tragedy" and Bostonians were "appalled": "They felt for Rose, they felt for Teddy, they felt for Ethel, and they felt for themselves." Everywhere, McGrory noted, "Her selection of Onassis was regarded as a personal affront . . . they feel that Jackie owed them something—exactly what is not known."

Richard Nixon, the Republican presidential candidate, was in Boston that day. The "new Nixon"—then fifty-five, "a much more mature Nixon, made more solid, more confident and more judicious by the ups and downs of the last eight years," a man of "glittering generalities" then believed to be the frontrunner—was lying low, not wanting to appear to intrude upon the nation's grief. Privately, McGrory reports, "Nixon said grimly he thought Mrs. Kennedy had dashed off so she could marry Onassis before the election and draw off the Greek vote that might have gone for his vice presidential candidate, Spiro T. Agnew." An unlikely motivation, because, as Ari reportedly told an employee, "They hate my Greek guts."

Why? "Since the assassination of her husband, President John F. Kennedy, in 1963, so-called friends of the family and social leaders from Cape Cod to Palm Beach and from Switzerland to Cambodia have tried to hunch, speculate or determine what this dynamic thirty-nine-year-old widow and mother of two would do about her future life," observed veteran reporter Merriman Smith. But, in all their imaginings of how her life might go, Americans did not expect this.

It was expected that she'd marry someone like John F. Kennedy. That she chose a second husband describable as "an aging, heavily-featured multimillionaire who in the eyes of the world was too shrewd, overly ambitious and somewhat tarnished by divorce and a flamboyant love affair [with Maria Callas]" was incongruous. As was the fact that he was Greek, characterized as "foreign" and, by prevailing mid-twentieth-century American conceptions of race, "ethnic"—i.e., not white.

They do not understand her choice. It doesn't align with the image. This is not who Jackie is supposed to be, nor who she's supposed to wind up with.

The question everyone is asking: for love or for money? Her few friends who spoke to the press hesitated to say love and instead advanced the idea of companionship. She "has been very lonely." But she was hopeful too: "Jackie used to say that her life was over, that it ended when Jack died. Now she realizes that she still has a life ahead of her."

SHE IS, HER FRIENDS FEAR, JUST ANOTHER COLLECTIBLE FOR him. Supportive in public, they privately warn her he's risky. André Meyer—an elderly, French-born investment banker who's been advising her for years and may be in love with her himself—tells Dorothy Schiff he spent two weeks trying to convince Jackie not to marry Ari, but she wouldn't listen. According to Schiff, "He said she wanted to marry Onassis more than Onassis wanted to marry Jackie."

Before Meyer can negotiate a deal for her, she flies off and marries Ari. She thinks him worth the risk.

•

Ari's son and daughter think he doesn't much care for her. Christina Onassis later recalls her brother saying, "Daddy married Jackie because he was in love with the *idea* of marrying her, not because he loved her."

Always, Aristotle Onassis tried to mold and control the women in his life. His first wife, Tina Livanos, was seventeen when they married, and he was allegedly physically abusive. With Maria Callas—the opera diva who had been his girlfriend for nearly a decade—he often resorted to verbal abuse, sneering that her voice was just a "whistle . . . that no longer works," making clear how he hated her practicing, how he hated everything connected with her work, anything that took her away from him. And yet she left her husband for him, though he refused to commit, telling her, "This is a pay-as-you-go arrangement," a declaration that left her always on edge, always afraid he might leave her—as, ultimately, he did.

People wondered how Maria Callas was faring now. Many Greeks believed they were fated to be together, Onassis and Callas, but, reportedly, his family disapproved: they thought he should marry someone more respectable, a royal or some such. His older sister, Artemis, especially, with whom he was very close, was vehemently against his marrying Maria.

The lovers reportedly argued in the summer of 1968. One of Ari's advisors later imagined,

All of it wouldn't have happened, the marriage to Jackie wouldn't have happened, if Maria hadn't rushed off the *Christina* in a huff in the summer of 1968. It was a catastrophic mistake because it angered Onassis and left the field completely to Jackie. Ari was bound to Maria, and while he liked to have the occasional affair on the side, he wouldn't have been able to leave her and hook up with Jackie if Callas hadn't left him. . . . It was the biggest mistake Maria ever made.

By all accounts, Maria was devastated. "[T]hey'll both pay, I can assure you of that," she'll write a friend a few weeks later. "I think of him as a madman and therefore am putting him out of my mind as such."

With Jackie, it seems he's kinder. This is a woman who's beguiled him for years, this fiercely independent American. So much has happened to her and, with his wealth, he can protect her. It's flattering too: the fact that she has chosen him and the belief that he can protect the most famous woman in the world.

And who is this man she's marrying? He's most often portrayed as a pirate. The image stems from his business success, to which—in America, at least—the stink of ill-gotten gains always clung. He's identified as "The Greek Tycoon," with the emphasis on his Greekness and the implication that his success is the result of foreign and therefore dubious tactics.

Pirates are sometimes romanticized, but this is decidedly unsexy. Italian newsmagazine *L'Espresso* celebrates Ari's marriage to the former Mrs. Kennedy by pronouncing the bridegroom a "grizzled satrap, with his liver-colored skin, thick hair, fleshy nose, the wide horsey grin." Contrast this with the delicacy with which *Parade* handled David Ormsby-Gore's hairline when it first declared him "tall, slender, smooth" before acknowledging his baldness. This Italian screed captures the general vibe worldwide. Lee Radziwill is right on the mark when she figures "blond, young, rich, and Anglo-Saxon" would've met with a better reception.

A pragmatic businessman, he isn't too troubled by the pirate image; any publicity is good publicity, and all that. It seems his wife doesn't mind it much either. She likes calculated risk and adventure. Repeatedly, she finds herself attracted to successful men of dubious repute and questionable character. She's "fascinated by pirates," her stepbrother remembers. "I've always identified Jackie with pirates," a friend reminisces. "Her father looked like a pirate. She married a pirate, Ari Onassis."

"Yeah, he looked like one," Solange Herter admits to me. "A little bandana to the side. He fit the part very well. But I think he thought of himself as a rough diamond, a successful rough diamond."

A kid whose family lost all their money, he left the war-torn world he grew up in and, through a series of canny investments and occasional dumb luck, became, for a time, one of the richest men in the world. He's a beguiling figure, so shrouded in competing layers of myth that it's nearly impossible to get a sense of him.

A man who feels more grounded on the sea, who feels women have their place and should be kept firmly within it, but who none-theless surrounds himself with challenging women who will accommodate and love him but who have strong personalities all their own.

"[A]n alive and vital person who has come up from nowhere," Jackie reportedly said of him after the cruise in 1963.

He likes flirting with women and pleasing them. His secretary keeps a comb and mirror in her desk drawer so, when his wife comes to visit for lunch, he can primp—a surprising bit of vanity from a man known for the ill fit of his suits.

A workaholic, his surrounding atmosphere seems always, no matter the hour, to involve ringing phones. A contrarian who says things simply to be provocative, but who also has a ferocious temper turned off and on like a tap, from which his loved ones are not spared.

"He was a Greek man," people often say, which feels like an evasion.

She's attracted to the Greeks because, as she wrote Arthur Schlesinger Jr. years before her remarriage:

> There is a conflict in the hearts and minds of the Greeks. Greeks have esteem and respect for the gods; yet the Greek was the first to write and proclaim that Man was the measure of all things. This conflict with the gods is the essence of the Greek tragedy and a key to the Greek character. The Greeks are mystics. This mysticism can be traced to the influence of the sea—the boundlessness and mystery of the sea respond to the yearning of the Greeks for a supernatural rapport with divinity. The Greeks are curious and it is this curiosity that inspired a search and a thirst for knowledge and the Socratic contribution to the world that virtue is knowledge.

She writes this years before her remarriage, but already it's as if she's forecasting the themes of her escape: mysticism, the seas, curiosity, and conflict with the gods. All elements of her life with Jack Kennedy, but which now move more fiercely toward the fore, and which prove a through line between her marriages. On the surface, she's attracted to rogues, but it seems that beneath that, the men in her life all share this fundamental longing—her father less so, but certainly Ari and Jack—which suggests, perhaps, that she recognizes this conflict within herself and that is also partly why she seeks solace in Greece.

But just as Jackie comes to us now as a mirage at the end of a hall of whispers, so, too, does her second husband.

A WORLD OF MANUFACTURED DREAMS. IT'S A WELCOME REF-uge from uptight New England and the violence tearing through the country she left behind. A week after the wedding, she hops over to Athens where she smiles and informs the inquiring press, "I am very happy with my marriage and I like everything in Greece." A few days later, she goes swimming off the coast of Skorpios and beams radiantly at photographers, her demeanor bordering on flirtatious.

The fashion tabloid *Women's Wear Daily* dubs her new husband "Daddy-O" two days after the wedding. Ten days later, she's rechristened too. They call her "Jackie O."

She seems to reinvent herself, ignoring autograph seekers who refer to her as "Mrs. Kennedy," indulging only those who call her "Mrs. Onassis" and altering the name on her checks and driver's license to read "Jacqueline Bouvier Onassis," a move interpreted as symbolically erasing her Kennedy past.

A cousin notes, "She seemed a completely new woman. . . . Just lighter, better. . . . She had gotten on with things."

The Kennedys, too, think she's made a success of it. Rose Kennedy notes in her diary that Jackie seems happy, and there is a new lilt to her voice. Her former sister-in-law Pat Kennedy Lawford reports back to Rose: "she is genuinely more relaxed and really devoted to Onassis."

In the process of painting her portrait, the artist Aaron Shikler scraps his initial effort because it no longer captures the woman she is. "The melancholy widow I had been painting was transformed," he recalls. "She became jollier, gayer, much more relaxed and girlish."

The relationship is fiery. Kiki Feroudi Moutsatsos, a Greek woman in her early twenties who'd been working for Onassis as his personal secretary, hears everything. A personal pilot of Ari's recounts to Kiki a fight the pair had aboard a flight to Paris. Swearing, shouting, threats of divorce; then, half an hour later, they're overheard having sex.

There's a strong physical attraction and the newlyweds act, in Kiki's words, "like teenagers, unable to keep their hands and lips off each other's bodies." Shortly after the wedding, in Athens, Ari reportedly boasts to a friend, "Five times a night—she surpasses all the women I have ever known." Whether this is the truth or chauvinistic grandstanding, she reportedly confides to a friend, "He makes me come alive."

But this aliveness isn't just about sex. It's also to do with freedom—not just physical and financial but freedom from fear, from her own image, the freedom of leisure, the freedom to roam. As her stepbrother observes, "In Greece, she had a completely different lifestyle. She wanted to be on her own." She wanted to be free, at peace.

•

But all is not peaceful in Greece. In April 1967, a group of Greek generals had staged a coup d'etat usurping the country's democratic government. After a shaky beginning, by the following year, this right-wing military dictatorship—known as the junta or, more formally, Regime of the Colonels (or, in the parlance of the colonels themselves, Εθνοσωτήριος Επανάστασις, meaning "Revolution to Save the Nation")—transformed itself into what a reporter from the *Chicago Daily News* characterized as "a perfectly organized police state."

Jackie's new husband is decidedly apolitical, throwing his lot in with whoever will do him the most good business-wise. As Ari is one of the most influential men in Greece, the junta is eager for him to invest in the country and wants to woo him to their side. Onassis's holdings are distributed across the globe, but his biggest investment in Greece is Olympic Airways, the airline he leases from the Greek government and operates on its behalf. There are rumors that in return for his support, the junta will favor him with a post, perhaps make him president someday. Jackie may, again, be the First Lady.

A resistance movement numbering 50,000 to 60,000 tries to establish a government in exile. But in late 1968, the fact that many of the movement's leaders see Jackie as "their brightest hope," and are counting on her to counsel Onassis in JFK's ideals, is interpreted as evidence of the movement's weakness.

No one can quite figure out where her allegiance lies.

Through a mutual friend, she appears to have been introduced to Andreas Papandreou—son of Georgios, an anti-monarchist, anti-communist liberal leader who served three terms as prime minister. Andreas claims Jackie as a supporter of the resistance, saying that, during his last visit to the U.S., she gave him a $500 check.

The elder Papandreou's policies were believed to have contributed to the turmoil that sparked the military takeover and, since coming to power, the junta kept him under house arrest. His November 1, 1968, death excites the biggest protest against the dictatorship to date. More than 300,000 people turn up along the funeral route to protest, shouting "We want freedom!"

In an Athens courtroom the following day, a man accused of attempting to assassinate the junta's leader claims he has been tortured. "Medieval tortures are going on," he shouts from the dock. He is immediately silenced and charged with insulting authority. Greece seems a dangerous place.

•

So does America. "As we look at America, we see cities enveloped in smoke and flame. We hear sirens in the night," Richard Nixon told the crowd at the Republican National Convention in August, just three weeks before a police riot at the Democratic National Convention in Chicago seemed to prove everything he said correct. "We see Americans dying on distant battlefields abroad. We see Americans hating each other; fighting each other; killing each other at home. And as we see and hear these things, millions of Americans cry out in anguish. Did we come all this way for this?"

Nixon implores Americans to move forward into the "exciting adventure" of realizing their destiny, an adventure begun "by committing ourselves to the truth—to see it like it is, and tell it like it is—to find the truth, to speak the truth, and to live the truth."

His campaign slogan: NIXON'S THE ONE!

Johnson's on his way out of office and Nixon's coming in, on a 1 percent margin, with promises he'll restore law and order in America's cities and tell Americans the truth.

•

On November 6, there's a bomb threat aboard a flight on Olympic Airways, Onassis's airline. His son, Alexander, is a passenger.

Two days later, two men calling themselves "International Commandos for Greece" use a pistol and a hand grenade to hijack an Olympic flight. Bound for Athens, they force it to return to Paris. Aboard, they distribute pamphlets condemning Onassis for his aid to the Greek government and his support of the junta.

•

If Americans are afraid, how much more intensely must she fear for her safety? In her world, they aren't abstract worries but very real.

In mid-November, the couple visits the Radziwills at their country home outside London. While they're there, a robber enters the house and steals $12,000 worth of jewels. "It was a very cheeky burglary," marvels one of the detectives. "There must have been about 50 newsmen milling around the house all day and there were still plenty of them about for most of the night." The big break in the case comes when, according to the *New York Times*, an Italian photographer —"hoping to take pictures of the Onassis couple"—got a photograph of the robber climbing through a second-floor window.

The presence of security offers little comfort. She's sitting with Ari at a café in Paris when an American tourist approaches and spits in her face.

In "private," they're under constant surveillance by the press and Ari's employees. According to Kiki Moutsatsos: "If Mr. Onassis raised his voice at his wife, I was informed, either immediately or the next morning. Nothing concerning this couple around whose affairs all our lives revolved escaped our careful scrutiny."

And yet, even under such scrutiny, someone could intrude, steal, or kill. Ari has all the security money can buy. Still, people could get in and pilfer his wife's jewelry box.

**FRIDAY, NOVEMBER 22, 1968**

IF JOHN KENNEDY HAD LIVED AND WON IN '64, HE'D BE leaving office. If John Kennedy had lived and lost in '64, perhaps he would have run again, maybe against Nixon, and won again, maybe against Nixon, in '68. He'd left behind so many ifs, so many ways the events of the last five years could have been different, a series of possibilities compounded by Bobby's death a few months before.

Had they lived, Americans wondered, would we still hear sirens in the night?

•

She's flying with the children from New York on December 19 when her flight is delayed as the police check the plane for bombs. She waits in the terminal with Caroline and John until the authorities give the go-ahead four hours later, and they are off to Greece.

•

In Paris, the actor Elizabeth Taylor sits in her dressing room. On a break from filming *The Only Game in Town*, she chats with a reporter from *Life*. "Power," she says, "is being able to do what you want to do."

Some bit of gossip about Jackie and Onassis comes up. Taylor, the reporter sees, visibly bristles.

"The public puts you upon that pedestal," she says. "Then they wait like vultures to tear you down. What would the public rather Jackie do? Have discreet little love affairs? Sneak around corners mentally and physically for the rest of her life? She thought long and hard about it. It must have been agonizing for her. I'm stubborn too, when I believe in something. Stubbornness, pride— they're not particularly attractive attributes, but they are necessary to keep you alive."

# 1969

## DIAHANN CARROLL CONFESSES
What She [...] Tells Her Little Girl about Being Half Black and Half White

# modern screen ®

JAN. 50c

## THE REAL REASONS BEHIND

# JACKIE'S SHOCKING MARRIAGE

- How she decided to marry a man old enough to be her father
- The part Jackie's sister played
- How Caroline, John and the Kennedys feel
- The Church rules on Onassis' Divorce
- THE MAN WHO FOLLOWED JACKIE ON HER HONEYMOON

## GIANT GOSSIP BONU[...]
The Inside Stories Behind the Year's [...]

"69-O!" WOMEN'S WEAR DAILY CALLS IT. AN ASTONISHING amount of information filters into the press. From this, an itinerary is cobbled together.

On Wednesday, January 8, she's all over town in a black mink, black boots, black tights, and black shades. She acquiesces when a cab driver requests an autograph for his daughter. Then she walks to a clothing boutique, where she believes she spots a photographer inside. To avoid him, according to *Women's Wear Daily*, she immediately walks to the back workroom and leaves by a dark back stairway, escorted by one of the shop assistants, who lights matches the whole way down. An unnecessarily dramatic exit, as it turns out, for there was no photographer present.

On February 16, the Os "stopped traffic" at the burger joint P.J. Clarke's.

Mid-March, she's in Bonwit Teller's Safari Room, snapping up a pair of nylon harem pants in purple to be topped off with a red suede vest. Word is she's prepping her closets for a spring trip to the Caribbean.

"She peeked out of the nail salon amid ship and counted the house," reports *Women's Wear Daily* of their arrival in Nassau, capital of the Bahamas. "By this time the tourists had spotted the *Christina* and were standing around in tight little groups, Instamatics at the ready, waiting for her to show."

First, Christina—"a beautiful slim girl . . . Jackie's new step-daughter"—slips off quietly on her own. Next comes John ("somber—unhappy with the way things were going"), with three friends, then Caroline ("shapely in a flowered print"), followed by three of her friends. The children zoom away and, eager for a look at their mother, the *paparazzi* begin circling the yacht. While they're on one side, Jackie and a friend slip out the other, sneaking down the gangplank.

"Look, it's President Kennedy's mother!" someone in the crowd exclaims. It is indeed Rose Kennedy. Nearing eighty, she shows no signs of slowing down. One journalist dubs her "Senior citizen of the Jet-Set," while an impertinent former editor of *Vogue* says of the mother of nine, "She has the bosom of a girl in her teens."

Jackie and Rose go down to the shops. Observers characterize their dynamic as "very chummy."

"This puts an end to all those rumors about Jackie being pregnant," says a local clerk. "She looks so thin."

Rose returns to Palm Beach for Easter, but the Onassises hang around Nassau as the city around them devolves into a circus. A pair of cruise ships arriving out of Miami dock alongside the *Christina* and the passengers forgo tours of Bay Street to Jackie-watch from their deck chairs. For everyone off the ships, a local helicopter service offers rides at a rate of $7.50 per person, with a promise to linger above the *Christina* so customers can snap a few shots.

•

So we know where she is, some of the time, such as when she's photographed going out to dinner or at an event. Thanks to *Women's Wear Daily*—which reports on her movements in such detail that it's dubbed *What Jackie Wears Daily*—we know what she's wearing, where she's shopping, and what she's rumored to have bought. But she isn't always going to plays, lunches, and airports. Some days she stays in and doesn't wash her hair. Some nights, most nights, she turns in early. Sometimes she goes out, hails a cab, sees a movie, and buys a dress—and reporters never know.

"Even if we lived in the best of all possible worlds," the *New York Times* acknowledges, "and even if every item we read about Jackie in our newspapers and magazines were accurate—two very big ifs—these items would give us an inaccurate impression of Jackie's life. A news item is, by definition, an event. . . . Journalism

almost invariably alters the truth if only by withholding nonevents."
Biography does the same.

•

Raising her children in New York and settling into a marriage that
moves all over the map, she continues traveling—Mexico, Paris,
Barbados, Paris again, Rome—but she's often on Skorpios and
aboard the *Christina*. A certain transience comes of living on an
island and a yacht, but she makes considerable efforts to build a
home. Literally and figuratively.

On Skorpios, Ari built his house high on the mountain, but he
prefers the *Christina* and often stays aboard while docked. She likes
the mobility the yacht affords, but prefers solid ground for day-to-
day life, and so begins renovating the island's original home—a
nineteenth-century villa fallen into disrepair.

Skorpios is notably less haunted by the ghosts of Maria Callas
and Tina, Ari's first wife, whose portrait she asks the *Christina*'s
staff to remove from its prominent place in the ship's entryway.
"Seeing her beautiful face in that painting grieves me," she tells
Artemis. Skorpios, in contrast, seems a fresh start, a sanctuary of
her own.

She's always enjoyed decorating, perhaps because her life has felt
so rootless. As a kid she shuffled between her mother and father;
as a teenager, she moved between boarding school and her stepfather's homes in D.C., Newport, and Virginia. Marriage to Jack was
characterized by this same rhythm and it only intensified during
her widowhood. But throughout, she maintained a base—first the
White House, then 1040 Fifth—where she cultivated a comfortable
environment, surrounded by fresh flowers and beautiful objects.
With Ari's permission, she seems to have tried to cultivate such a
space for herself with the Pink House.

Her surroundings are always a work in progress; she's constantly
rearranging and reupholstering furniture, removing and replacing
pieces, trying to perfect the space and the objects in it by adjusting
the scene around her. This puzzles Kiki Moutsatsos, who asks why

she likes to change things so much. "There are so many things in this world that I cannot change, but when it comes to furniture and draperies and flowers and even the roads in Skorpios, I can make the changes I want," Jackie tells her. "That brings me enormous satisfaction and pleasure." It also brings a sense of control.

Skorpios is a beautiful place. On the island, as you go from breakfast to a morning swim to an afternoon of painting and sunbathing, the sun accompanies you on your circuit. Areas to sit and think and eat, beaches on which to swim and paint and play, are strategically placed to be ideal at a particular hour with its particular light. "The sun was everywhere," remembered a visitor, "the setting sun, the rising sun, shining on the other islands in the distance, it was factored into the relationship of these incredible spaces to the whole environment."

Ari travels constantly and so, even on Skorpios, she's often alone. This has usually been the case. She once described her marriage to Jack Kennedy as "renewals of love after . . . separations," a circumstance she tolerated and perhaps even sometimes enjoyed. And so, as she did in Georgetown and the White House and New York, she fills the hours with swimming, reading, and decorating projects, striking a balance of liveliness and solitude. She seems content.

•

Ari is a demanding man, and the *Christina* is his pride and joy. James Mellon, a later guest, is amazed by how well Ari knows the boat and how, if something goes wrong with the engine, he simply goes down and fixes it himself: "There wasn't a thing on that damn boat he couldn't do as well as anybody else on it."

Mellon, of the wealthy Pittsburgh family, knew yachts. This snippet of the ship's history was recounted to him by Ari:

> She was built in Montreal as a Canadian frigate in 1944 and was bought and converted into a yacht by him in 1953. . . . The ship is run by a crew of 55 men, all Greeks except for the steward, Charles, and the chef, who are Frenchmen.

There are 10 guest cabins, my own being the one in which the fat arse of Winston Churchill reposed on many occasions. Knowing the psychology of nouveaux riches, I expected to find a little gold plaque over my bed announcing Churchill's former occupancy. But there is nothing of the kind. There is, however, a fake El Greco hanging in the salon. Original masterpieces cannot be kept on a yacht because of the sea air. Ari built a swimming pool in the after deck of the ship to fill the space where the rear gun had been torn out.

Mellon declares it "the world's poshest yacht," but it's already twenty-five years old at the time. While much has been made of Onassis's opulent hosting and the ship's extravagance—the lapis fireplace, the salon and spa, the medical facility, the barstools covered in a soft leather made from the foreskins of whales—truth is, the *Christina* is getting on in years and starting to show some wear. "He told me that that boat was almost finished," Mellon remembered. "It was beginning to fall apart all over the place."

Jackie reportedly hates the pool and calls it, dismissively, "the bathtub." Whenever the ship is in port, it seems she is always escaping to swim in other people's pools.

Life aboard the ship was bustling when Callas was around, but the dynamic shifts with Ari's remarriage. It's notably quieter, which seems to be Jackie's influence. She's content with small groups of friends and family, people with whom she can relax and for whom she does not have to be on show.

•

They enjoy each other's company. When they're aboard *Christina*, while he works, she sits beside him, sketching satirical portraits. He regales her with epics and myths, and he makes her laugh. He sends notes requesting her company on the deck and, as the crew reports back to Kiki, the pair of them waltz and tango until sunup.

As Rose Kennedy put it, aboard the *Christina* and on Skorpios, "Life [is] pleasant, quiet, uneventful." And it's precisely that uneventfulness—in a world that so often overwhelms with its demands and tragedy—that Jackie enjoys, and that the people who drop in to visit find so appealing. The escape factor: the ability to get away to this lovely little island in the sea, so private it isn't on maps, or to hide out on a yacht where all their needs are met, and they feel free.

He's king and she plays queen. After having been on her own, shouldering all that adulation, the attention of the whole world focused upon her, what a release to slip into a world where every detail is choreographed by someone else—someone she trusts—all for her pleasure, all for her. Here, according to Kiki, the only thing "everyone wanted from her was for her to be happy."

•

Their marriage appears unconventional. It seems they are more often apart than together and there is talk that all is not well. Speaking to a reporter, Ari pooh-poohs reports of a breakup: "Jackie is a little bird that needs its freedom and security—and she gets both from me. She can do exactly as she pleases, visit international fashion shows or go to the theaters. I never question her and she never queries me."

Freedom and security. That is what she wants.

IN AMERICA, THE PUBLIC DRAMA DROPS OFF THE RADAR. Almost as though numbness descends after the horrors of 1968— the killings of King and Kennedy, police brutality at the Democratic National Convention, and Jackie's marriage to Onassis. And so in that summer of 1969, for the generation accustomed to the rhetoric of American World War II victories, it's possible to think things are looking up. Or, at the very least, it's preferable to hope.

Nixon is president. Elvis is opening in Vegas. Twenty-five thousand troops are to be withdrawn from Vietnam. And the Americans

are about to realize John F. Kennedy's dream of putting a man on
the moon.

•

Six days after Jack Kennedy's death, Jackie spent thirty minutes
with his successor. Her one request involved the space program
and renaming the space center after her husband.

> The reason I asked was, I can remember this first speech
> Jack made in Texas was that there would be a rocket one
> day that would go to the moon. I kept thinking, "That's
> going to be forgotten, and his dreams are going to be for-
> gotten." I had this terrible fear then that he'd be forgotten,
> and I thought, "Well, maybe they'll remember some day
> that this man did dream that."

Five and a half years later, in 1969, spacecraft are still launching
from Cape Kennedy in an effort to realize John Kennedy's dream.
He'd called it "the most hazardous and dangerous and greatest
adventure on which man has ever embarked." And it's an adventure
that represents—for a generation terrorized by the fear of Russians
getting there first and pointing their missiles at America—not just
the triumph of American technology, but the protection of the
globe from "the Russian menace."

"Nothing less than *control of the heavens* was at stake," the novelist Tom Wolfe observed in *The Right Stuff* (1979). For, as Lyndon
Johnson once thundered, Americans wouldn't tolerate going "to
bed each night by the light of a Communist moon."

On Friday evening, July 18, the astronauts prepare to swing into
the moon's gravity field and begin their orbit in advance of Sunday's
landing. Three American men, soaring toward their destiny, about
to colonize the moon.

MEANWHILE, THAT FRIDAY NIGHT IN MASSACHUSETTS, ROSE and Joe Kennedy's last remaining son—the presumed Democratic candidate of some future presidential election (if not '72, then surely '76)—is driving his car across the Dike Bridge on Chappaquiddick Island, trying to make the ferry back to Edgartown, Massachusetts.

Following JFK's death, the Kennedys maintained a stoic veneer, accepting that, in Bobby's words, "Bad luck is something you endure." But, with Bobby's death, Ted Kennedy inherited both his brothers' political legacies and their thirteen children almost by default. "I can't let go," he told an aide. "If I let go, Ethel will let go, and my mother will let go, and all my sisters." This responsibility to the family and the nation, to his brothers' legacies, and to their widows was a burden too great for an unhappily married alcoholic man who reportedly had never wanted a political life. Surrounded by elderly parents and fatherless children, he is crumbling. "He has been," *Time* notes, "a different and deeply troubled man."

Jackie provided a more vivid description in a September 1968 letter to Robert McNamara, where she remembered:

> Teddy sailing the sound this summer with this terrible look of not real gaiety, on his face—and his lips cracked with red wine—all his crew's lips cracked with red wine—as he took Bobby's sons and Jack's son to sea—It is Celtic—and you know we will all be annihilated in the end—but we will all go down with Teddy's brave head.

The youngest child, the charming fuckup, always in the shadow of older, stronger, more charismatic men—now here he was, in charge and ruthlessly exposed.

Jackie saw the writing on the wall. "I believe Ted has an unconscious drive to self-destruct," Roswell Gilpatric remembered her telling him. "I think it comes from the fact that he knows he'll never live up to what people expect of him," she said. "He's not

Jack. He's not Bobby. And he believes that what he is, is just not enough."

One reporter declared Senator Ted Kennedy "an accident waiting to happen."

The accident happened around 11:15 p.m. on Friday, July 18. Hearing about it the next day, Norman Mailer interrupts his writing on the moon landing for *Life* magazine to note that this turn of events represents a "blow to the fortunes of the Kennedys" and "also a blow to one hundred interesting possibilities in American life."

"Never, *never* will he be president now," Ros Gilpatric says Jackie said to him.

Ted Kennedy was in Edgartown for the Yacht Club's annual regatta. While there, he attended a party for RFK campaign staff held on Chappaquiddick Island. Racing to make the ferry back, he lost control of his 1967 Oldsmobile and drove it off a wooden bridge. He then swam to safety and returned to his hotel, where he made seventeen phone calls. But he didn't talk to the police until the following morning. At that point, he informed them that he'd left a young woman in the car he abandoned; but, by then, two boys had already discovered the car, the body of Mary Jo Kopechne inside.

On July 20, beneath the headline ASTRONAUTS SWING INTO MOON ORBIT IN PREPARATION FOR TODAY'S LANDING, the story of Chappaquiddick makes its debut on page one of the *New York Times*. The paper blandly declares, as though the senator is in no way responsible, that the "incident was another in a series of violent events that have hounded the Kennedy family ever since it came to prominence in American political life."

"Teddy Escapes, Blonde Drowns" the less restrained *New York Daily News* blares in three-inch type.

That afternoon, at 4:17 p.m. Eastern Daylight Time, Apollo 11 lands in the Sea of Tranquility on the moon's surface. Around the world, people watch. A little over six hours later, Neil Armstrong walks on the moon.

In Houston, Mailer checks in to the press room at NASA head-quarters and observes, "Excitement was now divided between Kennedy and the moon. Or was Kennedy even more interesting?" The stories swirl around one another and in the six hours between the landing and the walk, as Mailer contemplates the marriages of the astronauts for his article, he is distracted: "From time to time, like the memory of a telegram whose news was so awful one kept circling the fact of it, came back the simple unalterable fact that Teddy Kennedy had been in a bad accident and a girl had drowned and he had not reported it until morning."

It's something, observers note, that could derail the Democratic Party and have significant political consequences. Kennedy appears to be the only viable Democratic candidate—the only man who could unify the party and possibly win.

The president's aides fear the hoopla over the moon landing—already a Kennedy victory—will obscure the Chappaquiddick awfulness and render it insufficiently damaging to Kennedy's fortunes for '72. But Nixon scoffs at their worries, telling them, "It'll be hard to hush this one up; too many reporters want to win a Pulitzer Prize."

He's right. And the questions emerging will plague Ted Kennedy for the rest of his career: What happened? Why didn't he report it? What was his relationship with the girl who died? Who was she?

Though the press often refers to her by her hair color rather than her name, Mary Jo Kopechne, as *Time* eulogized her, was "the girl next door . . . [g]irlish and gung-ho . . . bright, blonde, and at least conventionally pretty," and so delicate, according to an RFK aide, that she "almost scowled at hearing a dirty word." It's a prissy portrait. The word "girl" infantilizes a woman who was then twenty-nine.

Mary Jo was ambitious. She started her career in 1963 as a secretary for Senator George Smathers and for the next seven years worked her way up, in Teddy's words, as "one of the most devoted members of the staff of Senator Robert Kennedy" to a coveted position with an agency running Democratic campaigns. She had no interest in marriage; a colleague recalled, "Her total life was politics."

"[The party] was a steak cookout, not a Roman orgy," one attendee protested to *Time*. Which was all well and good, but it looked like an orgy, and that was dire.

A week after the incident, the senator makes an emotional yet cagey appeal to the Massachusetts electorate. It helps him hold his Senate seat, but does little to prove his innocence after a week spent discussing his guilt. Even he admits in his address, "My conduct and conversations . . . to the extent that I can remember them, make no sense."

John Kennedy's philandering wouldn't be common knowledge for a few years yet, so the American public remained largely unaware of that familial atmosphere of competitive lust (and its full extent). There may have been rumors, but this was the first time that a Kennedy man was seen to be, in spectacularly public fashion, cheating on his wife. That might not have been the reality (likely, it wasn't), but that's how it looked.

Americans were left with many questions. All they know for certain is something horrible happened with Teddy. Had he been unfaithful? Had he killed her? Would he run for president in 1972? Only one of these was a question people expected to ask of a Kennedy brother in 1969, and the answer seems clear enough.

"Never," Jackie tells Ros. "*Never* will he be president now."

•

Was she there, then? It's unclear. A number of sources claim she went to Hyannis. Nicholas Stamosis, who worked at Olympic at the time, said that when she got the call and heard what happened, she moved up a previously planned trip and went to the U.S. a week early.

Joe Kennedy's nurse, Rita Dallas, claimed she was there and opened her home for strategy sessions with Kennedy advisors. "These men were all dear friends of hers," said Dallas, "so she was a big part of what was being decided. However, she spent her time with them, not with the family." Which seems odd because, if she was there, it was most likely to support Ted's wife, Joan—thirty-two, then pregnant, and the member of the family with whom she had the most in common and to whom she was closest.

Joan was shy and gentle and, like her husband, terrorized by the thought that he would be *next*. Wearing a white minidress, the exuberance of her blonde bouffant tempered by a black bow, she'd accompanied him to the funeral in Plymouth, Pennsylvania, where she pointedly refrained from holding his hand. As they walked into the church, their collective beauty reportedly excited an incongruous sigh of "Isn't he handsome; isn't she pretty?" from the funeral crowd. Gorgeous they may have been, but they were trapped in a marriage that—due to his philandering and their shared drinking problems—proved a destructive hell for them both.

So it would make sense for Jackie to have gone and been there for the sister-in-law to whom she was closest. It makes less sense for her to have gone and stayed locked up in strategy sessions.

Leo Damore, who wrote a book on the Chappaquiddick scandal, also placed her in Hyannis—though, curiously, he leaves her out of his own account. "She was there because she had a stake in what happened to the family, because of her children," he told a biographer. Damore thought she was ambivalent, reluctant to be there, and that she didn't want word to get out that she was, as she didn't want to appear to be publicly supporting Ted. "I believe that she felt Ted was guilty of something," Damore claimed, "even if she didn't know what it was."

However, in the press, there is no mention of her presence. It's a bizarre blackout, particularly glaring in a life so assiduously documented in the papers. Not a month prior, when she was in Paris, *Women's Wear Daily* diligently reported a moment when her shoe fell off as she dashed into Maxim's. And yet, there are no photos of her airport arrivals or departures during this week, no stories of how she came to save the day or support Ted.

If she was in Hyannis, as these people said, then the press must have known. And yet news of this didn't appear in the papers, suggesting that, in this instance, they protected her. They kept her out of this mess while they could.

But she isn't naïve; she knows the reality. "In the end, they've always been bastards," Joan says Jackie said to her. "Haven't they, these Kennedy men? Nothing has changed, I suppose."

"WE HAVE HAD PLENTY OF POLITICAL SCANDALS IN THE United States," a former member of the Kennedy administration declares. "Men have done deeds, chased women and reeled drunk through the portals of the White House. But we have never had a scandal involving a potential president and a dead person."

Jackie's mother reportedly laments to friends that it's "so ignominious" that the other Kennedy tragedies had "a nobility, a grandeur" wholly lacking here. "If you could see him now," a source tells Liz Smith, "you'd feel sorry for him . . . he was just sitting in the Senate stupefied, glassy-eyed. And the rats all began to desert the sinking ship."

It will have a lasting impact, they imagine. "The lid is off," a former aide of Lyndon Johnson's tells Smith, "the can of worms has been opened . . . you watch now, somebody will write a book about the Kennedy men. To date, [it] was just 'talk' in Washington. . . . But now it is becoming public, being printed."

*Time* calls it "The Kennedy Debacle," and shoves the astronauts off its cover in favor of a picture from Kopechne's funeral: an image of the senator in his neck brace and necktie, hair slicked back and teeth gritted, looking for all the world like the loser in a bar brawl.

But the astronauts' story isn't quite over yet. Once they'd landed on the moon, the Americans had to bring them back—a part of the adventure not without peril. Prior to the space shuttles of the 1980s and their aircraft-like landings, returning spacecraft parachuted into the ocean. And so, to come home, the Apollo 11 astronauts had to jettison the Lunar Module into outer space, then reenter Earth's orbit and steer the Command Module into the Pacific Ocean, abandoning the spacecraft and rendezvousing with a helicopter dispatched from a nearby aircraft carrier.

On the afternoon of July 24, the astronauts bolted out of the blue sky and splashed down in the Pacific—a spectacle aired on national TV and watched by Jackie aboard the *Christina*. Fearing pathogens brought back from the moon, the three men were sent into twenty-one days of quarantine in a mobile home unit. Greeting them through the window, President Richard Nixon declares it "the greatest week in the history of the world since the Creation."

*Time* calls the moon landing "a vindication of some of the traditional strengths and precepts in the American character and experience: perseverance, organizational skill, the willingness to respond to competition—even the belief that the U.S. enjoys a special destiny in the world." But it's an accomplishment that raises the question: "If we can put men on the moon, why can't we build adequate housing? Or feed all citizens equally? Or end social and economic injustices?"

Despite—or, for some, perhaps because of—the inequality and imperialism it represents, many perceive Armstrong's one small step as progress. Both a nod back to JFK and a giant leap into an uncertain future into which Jackie, her first husband often on her mind, must venture without him. As must all Americans.

Within the space of one week, the Americans met John Kennedy's dare to put men on the moon and bring them back, just as Ted Kennedy wrecked his political fortunes in failing to safely return a young woman to her hotel. The drag of the past pulls at the present, and time moves ever on.

JULY 28 IS HER FORTIETH BIRTHDAY. AMONG THE GIFTS HE GIVES her, Ari includes a pair of gold earrings that, according to the *New*

*York Times*, "consist of a sapphire-studded earth at the ear and a larger moon decorated with rubies hanging from a chain. The Apollo ship is attached to a thin gold thread, which circles the earth and drops to the moon."

This description gets pretty much everything wrong. No rubies or emeralds, no spaceship whizzing round the earth and dropping to the moon. Just a solid eighteen-carat gold ball at the ear, toward which four gold cones, in a single file, ascend from a dangling cratered gold sphere.

It's a showy gift steeped in symbolism, one her second husband commissions to commemorate a historic event set in motion by her first. She reportedly tells the Greek actress Katina Paxinou that Ari promised to give her the moon itself in 1970.

She spends the day quietly with family. Somewhere in the midst of all this, a letter arrives for John from McGeorge Bundy—a former member of the Kennedy administration. The letter itself doesn't survive but the replies have. The day after his mother's birthday, from the *Christina*, John scrawls Bundy a thank-you note: "I am very thanful [*sic*] and proud of the letter you gave me. I'm very glad about the astreonauts [*sic*] to [*sic*]."

On August 7, his mother writes her own letter to Bundy:

> I will never be so touched in all my life as I was by your extraordinary letter to my son. . . . There was just a silence— We were all so moved—all the thoughts at those days of going to the moon—and Jack not there to see it—and John who must find his father through long years of searching— Thank you for what you did for him—and for Jack.

The moon, and Jack, must be much on her mind. How extraordinary, how bittersweet, to watch the realization of something Jack Kennedy had only dreamed of; yet another reminder of his absence.

She releases no public statements, there are no photographs. But she's with her children and, like so many others, staring at the moon, watching men walk upon it. She doesn't seem too bothered with getting older, with hitting forty, though there are no grand pronouncements coming from her regarding that either. There are, however, photographs, and a very public party.

Thrown by Ari, it's a banger, beginning with dinner at their villa in Glyfada—Athens' ritziest suburb—then moving on to a nightclub on the coast. "It was her baptism into Athenian night life," a guest blabs to reporters. "She was really thrilled and looked very happy." The AP describes her birthday ensemble as "a pastel print minidress with sandals and gold earrings shaped like miniature spaceships flying to the moon." Her outfit sounds breathtakingly futuristic.

And yet she cannot entirely escape the ugliness in America. Articles on Teddy's unfolding calamity are repeatedly neighbored by stories about her. A photograph of her beaming at her birthday party in her paisley print minidress caps an ominous article entitled "New Inquest Attempt in Drowning Incident." Repeatedly, her face illustrates the possibility that Ted Kennedy may have killed someone.

•

She is, at once, part of the future and of the past. Norman Mailer, in a profile for *Esquire*'s issue on the American woman, had once written of her:

> She is one of us. By which I mean that she has not one face but many, not a true voice but accents, not a past so much as memories which cannot speak to one another. . . . Somewhere in her mute vitality is a wash of our fatigue, of existential fatigue, of the great fatigue which comes from being adventurous in a world where most of the bets are covered cold and statisticians prosper.

This was 1962. Mailer was between wives and writing of an America in which John Kennedy and Marilyn Monroe still lived, where the University of Mississippi remained segregated and there had not yet been a Cuban Missile Crisis. An America of which Mailer observed "our tragedy is that we diverge as countrymen further and further away from one another, like a spaceship broken apart in flight which now drifts mournfully in isolated orbits, satellites to each other, planets none, communication faint." In truth, Jackie's just as broken and mournful, which is probably part of her power, part of why she bewitched.

Anything can happen. These are such scary, tiring times, and still, amid all the uncertainty, there she is: a woman by this point more myth than real, an image—reassuring and familiar—scattered across the everyday so you'd see her name and her face in the morning paper like you'd see the stars in the sky at night. And you'd try to imagine what her life might be like out there in Greece, just as you'd stare up into the dark of the evening, trying to grasp, to believe it's all real: that there really were men up there in all that blackness of space, walking on the moon.

THAT AUTUMN, A LITTLE MORE LIGHT IS LET IN ON THE myth.

For a while now, her former secretary has been shopping a book. Hunting for a collaborator, Mary Barelli Gallagher first approached Angèle "Ginger" de T. Gingras, a journalist who knew Jackie Bouvier from her days at the *Washington Times-Herald*. Of their meeting, Gingras remembers, "I looked at Mrs. Gallagher. I listened to her. I wondered what kind of book was in her. I thought, 'My God, poor Mrs. Kennedy.'"

In November 1968, Frances Spatz Leighton, the cowriter Gallagher settled upon, sent a snappy memo to several New York publishers, listing the book's highlights as such: "Politics. What Jackie would and would not do. How he handled her. How she handled him. The gay times, the grim times. The humor." Soon, Gallagher had a contract.

There'd been a preview in June 1969, when *Ladies' Home Journal* began a two-month serialization of Gallagher's memoir that, according to veteran reporter Vera Glaser, "hit the gossip fan like a raw egg." It was, in the words of one commentator, a portrait "drawn with a pen dipped in sheer venom."

Gallagher was unrepentant. "People kept asking, what is Jackie like," she told UPI. "I felt I should tell it like it was. People can criticize all they like. No one has called me a liar." True, they hadn't outright called her a liar, but reviewers dismissed her work as "cheap trash-bin non-literature" in an outcry so intense that Gallagher reportedly changed her phone number and left town for a week.

As for her reason for writing, Gallagher said, "The real living people are rapidly being lost in growing mythology," so that "historians and future generations will be hard pressed to distinguish fact from fancy, reality from myth." It is, Gallagher thinks, a problem remedied if "those of us who are really close to the scene record our honest recollections and experiences." She does it for history, she says. "Knowing Jackie's sense of history," Gallagher muses to the UPI, "she may be grateful."

In truth, Gallagher's account isn't all that scandalous, but given the lack of any news that isn't third- or fourth-hand, given this environment of frenzied interest and the absence of facts, the testimony of former employees—people who actually knew her, who made her dresses and cooked her food—assumes a gravitas. It's frowned upon, accompanied by a whole chorus of *How dare you write such disgusting things about that saintly woman!* But it's also read with relish. And the information revealed is added to the surprisingly small stack of Things About Jackie We Can with Certainty Know.

•

Jackie knew the book was coming and the columnist Maxine Cheshire reports that she did nothing about it. But she is, apparently, neither as grateful as Gallagher imagines nor as passive as Cheshire believes. In retrospect, from the archives, we can piece together the behind-the-scenes machinations.

After the serialization's first installment, a lawyer friend writes *Ladies' Home Journal*, pointing to "inaccuracies" and requesting that they run some sort of "note" before the next installment of the series. (Copies of this correspondence are in her personal files at the JFK Library; it was written, no doubt, at Jackie's direction.) The lawyer especially takes issue with Gallagher's claims to the historical importance of her account. Alas, in a letter dated July 10, the magazine's editor replies that the issue has already gone to press so there's nothing to be done. "There are many kinds of contemporary history," he points out, noting, "This book represents a gossip and personal kind of portrait which some persons are bound to resent."

Three days after this reply, the reporter Vera Glaser runs a curious column reporting that she has gained access to Jackie's "private papers," which reveal the book by Jackie's "tattletale secretary" is "a deliberate hatchet job." Given access to "secret source material . . . fascinating candid papers" that included "the former First Lady's verbatim inside-the-White-House correspondence [ . . . memos] written to express herself with no thought of forming a public image," Glaser glimpses another side of Jackie.

Glaser quotes liberally from these memos, but she does not name their source, which is, in all likelihood, Mary Van Rensselaer Thayer. Since 1965, with Jackie's occasionally begrudging cooperation, Thayer had been working on a follow-up to her 1961 authorized biography of the First Lady. The memos Glaser references are materials to which Thayer had been given access.

Given the level of micromanagement in Jackie's office, this leak must have received her approval at some point. Its beauty being that in the duel against Gallagher, it leaves her appearing totally uninvolved. But she is, again, holding her hand to the avalanche.

On its release in September, the book sells 75,000 copies. It's in its third printing by month's end.

*My Life with Jacqueline Kennedy* is the story of a powerful aristocrat with many foibles and the working-class woman who acts as her administrative lackey, a job with low pay and perks galore. Many critics interpret the book as Gallagher's retribution for not getting a timely raise. More likely, it's lingering hurt over the fact that, after seven years together, Gallagher felt ill-treated in the aftermath of the assassination and then rather too casually dismissed when her employer moved to New York. "She wasn't like a boss in business—we were like sisters," writes Gallagher. "The sisterly resemblance is not strong," one reporter cuttingly observes.

This claim to sisterhood perhaps explains why, although everyone rushes to read her book, Gallagher herself excites so much scorn. Like Mrs. Gallagher, for years now, American women have had a life with Jackie and some have felt sisterly toward her. Yet, for all the ways Gallagher is like these other women, there is a fundamental difference: she knew Jackie in real life. She ironed Jackie's stockings, paid Jackie's bills, went to Jackie's house. A pair of deceased Kennedy pets are buried in the Gallaghers' backyard. While people around the country can buy JFK rocking chairs from the Sears catalog for $39.95, they can't buy that kind of intimacy with Jackie. Gallagher had it and she now appears to be exploiting it. And so, because she dared lift the veil of privacy and, worse, had the audacity to write negatively about the experience, it is almost patriotic to hate her. That hatred is often explicitly cast in classist terms.

Allusions to the French Revolution abound, as though the hordes of former Kennedy employees have begun a Reign of Terror. Were that the case, we're assured Gallagher "would have done wonderfully creative things with the guillotine." Never mind that the press often depicts Jackie as a modern-day Marie Antoinette; now, they are appalled by Gallagher's audacity to do so. From her initial meeting with Gallagher, Gingras describes the employee-employer dynamic as "queen vs. peasant." Columnist Mary McGrory's review of the book declares it "a communications breakdown perhaps unequalled since Marie Antoinette talked to a milkmaid at Versailles."

"It really isn't a nasty book," Gallagher protests, to no avail. The press repeatedly plays up the book's "scandalous" details in their reviews and coverage. Almost as one, they spring to the defense of a woman whose remarriage they celebrated, not even a year before, by declaring her first husband must be rolling in his grave.

When Gallagher goes on *The Today Show* for an interview, Barbara Walters appears visibly uncomfortable in her presence. Walters quotes from the book—"Jackie Kennedy was like a sister to me and neither time nor distance can erase the memories of the years we shared together"—then chastises her guest that "not everyone will agree that this is how sisters should write about each other."

•

But no one is sure how to write about Jackie. Marylin Bender, who reviews the Gallagher book for the *New York Times*, is researching a profile that the *Times* ultimately kills due to the editorial staff's squeamishness over the "the presumptuousness of passing judgment on a living figure." Bender interviews Annette Kar Baxter, then an associate professor of history at Barnard and a pioneer in the emerging field of women's studies. "Jacqueline Kennedy is a difficult figure for America to confront," Baxter tells the *Times*. "Because she represents the ultimate in tragedy and the ultimate in hedonism."

That same hedonism is on display in Gallagher's memoir. While readers revel in the details, that reveling neither eradicates their repulsion over such excess nor their disapproval of such things as Jackie's so-called "champagne tastes" being revealed. It's hypocritical, but puritanical America has a hard time with hedonism— at once denying, desiring, and ridiculing luxury. It's a difficulty Jackie's story highlights, especially in the years to come.

For, in retrospect, these years to come—the so-called Onassis years, her Greek years—appear her most hedonistic. She's supposed to represent America at its best, but now she's a figure of European luxury, wealth, and intemperance, exciting both envy and interest across the country. What Gallagher's book says is that this isn't a new development: she was like that all along. And so maybe Camelot wasn't such a magical era. Maybe America's queen had always been a bitch.

Still, like the voters of Massachusetts to Ted Kennedy, they rally around her. Never mind that last year they disowned her for marrying a toad. Because one so wants to believe in something, and it's easier, preferable, to imagine Gallagher doesn't know what she's talking about. To direct all vitriol—both recent and lingering—at the former First Lady's former secretary, the twelfth child of Italian immigrants. Merely a member of The Jackie Show's supporting cast, Mary Gallagher provides a convenient foil so that the Jackie fascination can persist, unabated, while the disgust siphons off onto someone else. As Truman Capote once said, there was always, "underneath all that adulation . . . a tremendous resentment and envy."

•

She looks different these days, when she returns to New York. The bouffant is gone, replaced with a casual, "heretofore unveiled vibrancy." A new Jackie who—according to the *Boston Globe*—"shunned hostessing black-tie affairs for folksy goings-on . . . bypassed cosmeticians to concentrate on looking vital and healthy"; a barely recognizable woman embracing the fashions of her new home base, decked out in "puffy harem pants, silk shirts and vests dangling with fake Turkish coins."

"The feeling among top New York designers now is that Jackie-O is above fashion," the *Globe* reports. "She is in the Best-Dressed Hall of Fame and has enjoyed all the prestige, publicity and adoration that a dazzling fashion image can bring. Now she has other worlds to conquer." Reportedly, she orders pantsuits, coats, and dresses in the colors of the Greek flag from the couturier Valentino, who observes: "However Jackie goes, so goes fashion." Fashion—in clothes, in culture—is, to be sure, taking surprising turns.

OBSCENITY. NO ONE'S ENTIRELY CERTAIN OF THE DEFINITION. The prevailing attitude continues to be Supreme Court Justice Potter Stewart's 1964-era threshold for identifying obscene materials: "I know it when I see it."

But the standard of acceptable talk and writing in America has changed enormously in the last few years and, increasingly, Americans casually encounter books, magazines, and movies characterized by a sexual bluntness they'd been previously spared in the mainstream. "We're in a historical crisis in American society," an English professor at Columbia informs the *New York Times*, "a crisis of extremely rapid social change and a crisis of which the Vietnam war is a symptom rather than a cause. It's clear that the old, solid middle-class values that people at least give lip service to are no longer adequate . . . large numbers of people have a need to see or read about sex."

Because many others want no part of that, obscenity is both the hip, new thing to rally for and the hip, new thing to rally against: the latest in a long line of perils come to corrode America. "Is this society moving toward a 'new freedom,'" the *San Bernardino County Sun* asks, "or is it beginning a wild descent into the darkness where there is complete abandonment of standards?"

It seems total nudity now counts as a form of free speech. This isn't, many think, what the Constitution's framers had in mind.

The scourge of "bottomless dancing" seizes California. A flurry of arrests ensue. Police haul two women into a Sacramento court. Suzanne Haines and Sheila Brendenson—both twenty-two, both billed as "bottomless go-go dancers"—are arrested on charges of lewdness when they perform naked at the Pink Pussy Kat beer bar. The trial lasts five weeks. As part of the defense's contention that such dancing is in keeping with "contemporary community standards," jurors partake in a screening of the Swedish skin flick *I Am Curious (Yellow)* as well as a field trip to the Pink Pussy Kat, where they watch one of the women perform the dance for which they'd both been arrested.

On October 1, after eleven hours of deliberation, a predominantly male jury rules for acquittal. Obscenity for the win.

Or is it? The local sheriff raises his fists to the heavens and vows, "If they are there tonight and they're dancing bottomless they're going to get arrested." On the advice of her lawyer, Miss Haines does not dance that evening; Miss Brendenson retires.

• 

In New York, on an unseasonably warm afternoon four days later, Jackie and Ari arrive in separate cars to catch a movie at the Cinema Rendezvous Theater on West 57th Street. Halfway through the movie, Jackie leaves Ari in the theater and goes alone to the lounge. In the lobby, she encounters three photographers. She asks the manager to order them out. They leave. Then she leaves too.

Walking out of the cinema, she allegedly goes six feet out of her way to attack photographer Mel Finkelstein with what he will later describe as a "judo trick." Finkelstein lands on the sidewalk but recovers in time to take a shot of her walking away.

The following morning, Nancy Tuckerman talks to the press—an event, at this point, terribly rare and, therefore, an indicator of the gravity of the brouhaha. "I congratulated her this morning," Tuckerman tells reporters, "but she said she hadn't done it."

The doorman at the Cinema Rendezvous backs Jackie. So does Peter Tufo, an assistant to New York's mayor and an eyewitness, who tells the *New York Times*, "I know a judo toss when I see one. She didn't use any judo." Finkelstein himself later tells the *paparazzo* Ron Galella that he'd tripped, but by that point the story had taken on a life of its own.

• 

In London, the *Times* reports Mrs. Onassis had been in a "scuffle," and quotes Finkelstein saying, "She was very professional about it." The following week, trying to suss out the truth, *Life* magazine stages a reenactment. In it, a woman wearing a turtleneck, plaid skirt, and penny loafers walks innocently down the street—the sign for 57th St. Wines & Liquors, visible in the background, attesting to the setting's authenticity—whilst a man wearing a suit and bogged down with photography equipment assaults her.

The costuming is provocative. As the *Times* and nearly every news outlet noted, "Mrs. Onassis [was] wearing a short leather skirt, dark stockings, a ribbed sweater and a multi-colored headscarf"—an outfit, in its chic aggressiveness, nearly as provocative as the film she'd gone to see, though not quite.

She and Ari were at a screening of *I Am Curious (Yellow)*, "the controversial Swedish film dealing with sexual fantasies," hailed as "a landmark likely to shatter many of our last remaining movie conventions." The previous spring, the film was hauled before the U.S. Court of Appeals, which—to the consternation of many—refrained from labeling it obscene, thus making *I Am Curious (Yellow)* the first commercial film screened in America that legally and explicitly depicted sexual intercourse. Produced at a cost of $150,000, it had already netted $5 million by October 1969, despite (or perhaps due to) the fact that, under the new rating guidelines established in November 1968, it was listed as X.

"Naturally, Jackie Onassis was conspicuous outside 'I Am Curious (Yellow)'," jokes one commentator. "She was the only one who wasn't carrying some sort of picket sign."

In their coverage, the press always mention she was leaving the cinema and had been there to see the "sexually explicit Swedish film." All of which makes it seem as though, if she floored the photographer, it was because she didn't want America knowing she'd been watching porn.

She was, undoubtedly, there and had gone to see *that* movie. A connoisseur of sexual gossip, she'd long been titillated by the private lives of others so it's not all that surprising that she *was* curious. She is, at this time, trying to be "with it": wearing leather skirts and boots and gold chains, hanging out with bohemians and dabbling in the counterculture. It makes sense that she wants to see what the fuss is about over this film.

That she leaves the movie to go to the lounge approximately twenty minutes in is often overlooked. If she went to the movie, it's likely because she wanted to and likewise, if she left, it's likely because she changed her mind. Maybe she had her limits and, discovering she was a woman who could only sit through twenty minutes of *I Am Curious (Yellow)*, she left. Or maybe she just had to pee.

It's hard to know what went on inside the theater. Clearer is what went on outside, which actually tells us less about her movie-going and more about her increasingly fraught relationship with the press.

THE *PAPARAZZO* RON GALELLA, THEN PUSHING FORTY, IS A BURLY go-getter. The idea of *paparazzi* and the word *paparazzo* have been around since the release of the film *La Dolce Vita* in 1960, but it began as a European phenomenon. Galella's angle is unique in that he thinks of it as an actual craft: "candid portraiture" or, as his business card bills it, "Photography with the PAPARAZZI approach."

Manhattan is his studio. "By shooting on location, I got celebrities being themselves in their environment," he says. "I catch them as the Real McCoy, I catch them as they are, genuine emotion." Andy Warhol is reportedly a fan, but many of the famous people Galella photographs are not.

Galella has been shooting Jackie for a few years now and, on September 24, he swings by 1040 Fifth to see if he can get a few shots to sell. An autograph collector outside the building informs Galella she is in Central Park with her son. Galella finds the pair riding bicycles and takes several shots before she notices him, at which point she, according to Galella, gestures to the three Secret Service agents present and demands, "Break that man's camera!"

The agents chase Galella, who manages to lock his equipment in his own car before they force him into theirs and drive him to the police station, where Secret Service agent James Kalafatis files harassment charges against him. In court the following day, Galella pleads innocent and, without having to post bond, gets released.

Photographer Mel Finkelstein isn't a *paparazzo*. He's on staff at the New York *Daily News*. But at this point, coming so close on the heels of the spat with Galella (an incident that received far less press coverage than the business outside the sex movie would), she sees anyone with a camera as a threat.

There'd been photographers around for years. She never liked them, never fully accepted they were going to be a part of her life from then on. Of her time as First Lady, legendary White House reporter Helen Thomas recalled, "She waged a three-year war of independence with the press. Looking back, I would say it ended in a draw. We won a few, she won a few." It was a war she waged more fiercely after leaving Washington, D.C. Freed from her official role, she was even less willing to tolerate the hoopla—the photographers, in particular, who grew more insistent, more belligerent, with each passing month.

Dining with friends at Maxim's that spring, she reportedly said of the *paparazzi*, "They seem to be everywhere. . . . I would not be surprised to have a flash bulb go off in my face when I'm in the shower."

Everyone says she's fallen from her pedestal and she's no longer a Kennedy, but still it feels like they're closing in. She's the most famous woman in America, a country she hasn't really left, and Americans—even if they don't always like her—are still unrelentingly obsessed.

On Tuesday, October 14, she and Ari take the kids to see the New York Mets beat the Baltimore Orioles in Game 3 of the 1969 World Series. The *Boston Globe*'s Harold Kaese reports he couldn't see the field for all the sportswriters piled up in front of him, gawking at Jackie Onassis. He records their conversation:

> "Which one is she? What's she wearing?"
> "She's wearing a white dress and black hair."
> "I think I see her. Is she carrying a flashlight?"
> "No. That's one of her diamonds."
> "Which one's her husband? I only see a big guy."
> "They say he's small. Maybe he's under a seat."
> "It's his pocket book that's big."
> "If you go down, he'll give you an autographed diamond."

"I think I see him. He looks like a Greek."

"He ought to. He is a Greek."

The wife of a Mets pitcher observes, "She's a mess. It looks like she never combs her hair." The mother-in-law of one of the players quickly shushes the woman, saying, "Well, if you had her troubles, you might look like that."

"Here I am, Jackie," a male fan shouts to the former First Lady, sitting with her family in the stands behind home plate. "Try a judo on me."

It's a cacophony that accompanies her everywhere she goes. But as the photographer she supposedly felled outside the sex movie said, "That girl can handle herself!"

HER FAME IS SUCH THAT EVEN ARI'S CHILDREN BECOME supporting players in her drama. "I have been told that Alexander Onassis, 21, son of Aristotle Onassis, is the richest young man in Europe, that he will soon marry a woman twice his age. What's the scoop?" a reader from Milwaukee asked the gossips. They answer: "He is extremely fond of Baroness Fiona Thyssen. . . . Fiona and Alexander have been seen frequently on the ski slopes of Gstaad."

He's a dashing young man—not conventionally attractive and not much taller than his father, but he exudes nonchalant confidence and is, Kiki Moutsatsos remembers, "the person Mr. Onassis loved most in the entire world." Charismatic and sexy, he's a hard worker, a characteristic that charms his father, who confides to Kiki that he's kept his company, Olympic Airways, as long as he has because working there gives such pleasure to his son.

Alexander is sensitive, gentle, and kind, which perhaps makes it even more startling how much he hates his stepmother. Not her, he's careful to clarify, but the world she comes from and represents: cossetted Newport and the pretentious American privilege of which he feels she is a product. "It's not that I have anything against her personally," he tells a friend. "But she's not our type. She goes with orchids and champagne. We mix with garlic and saltwater." She's too delicate, he thinks, too refined and rarified to blend into the world in which she's now moving.

Bad enough she's a misfit, but she also destroys any lingering hopes for both Alexander and his sister that their parents might reconcile. These hopes endured during their father's years-long dalliance with Maria Callas precisely because he had not married her. Now their parents' reconciliation seems impossible, and his son blames Jackie. To Kiki, who would become his secretary, too, Alexander swears he'll never sleep in the same house as "that American woman"; he holds true to his word, decamping to the Athens Hilton when she first arrives and setting up permanent residence there.

Distance doesn't ease the tension. "Alexander despised Jackie," maintained Costa Gratsos, a friend and employee of Ari's. Gratsos tells a story of a night out at Maxim's, where Ari, his wife, and son were watching a showgirl flirt with an older man. As Gratsos remembers, Alexander said to his stepmother, "Jackie, surely you don't think there's anything wrong in a girl marrying for money, do you?" Pointedly, Onassis remained silent. He did not rebuke his son.

An obvious slur against his stepmother, it's also a parry against his father—debasing Ari to just another old man manipulated for his money. A big element of Alexander's anger toward her seems to have been displaced rage against his dad. Alexander is annoyed that Ari keeps trying to orchestrate his future as heir to the family business and that his father keeps trying to break up his relationship with Fiona Thyssen-Campbell—who is divorced, has two children, and is only three years younger than Jackie. Alexander is twenty-one, but surprisingly mature, and he thinks he knows how he wants to live. That his father keeps interfering is infuriating and he retaliates accordingly. If the American woman gets caught in the crossfire, so be it.

Ari's aware of what she's up against and tries to smooth the way, confronting his children about the marriage, telling them how much he wants them to like his new wife, and appealing to their emotions by emphasizing how much she reminds him of his own dead mother. When Alexander and Christina won't listen, he leaves in frustration and Ari's sister Artemis steps in. She speaks to Alexander and Christina all night, telling them how much Jackie loves her own children and how she will love them if they give her the opportunity. But they don't listen to their aunt. Later, Artemis tells Kiki Moutsatsos, "They said that if I truly loved them, I would not love this woman."

•

While Alexander dislikes his stepmother from the first, Christina's relationship with her appears more uneven and not always so bitter. On several occasions early on, they're photographed going to church together. In 1972, Christina tells a reporter, "Maria [Callas] never liked me very much" and claims, "Jackie is my stepmother and great friend." But it was not easy to be Christina's friend.

"That girl was not at all right," observed an acquaintance. "Ari was not a good father at all but she was doubly unfortunate because the tradition is that the father's the one who takes care of the business, takes care of the money, that provides and it's the mother that brings up the children, and in a way her mother was quite incapable of bringing up her children."

Christina's mother, Tina, was barely out of her teens when her daughter was born; there were rumors that Ari abused his wife in an effort to terminate the pregnancy. Whether or not this happened, Christina believed she was unwanted and developed severe depression, suicidal impulses, and weight fluctuation as a result. When her father remarried, Christina was eighteen, with thick dark hair, and "wonderfully soulful eyes, Judy Garland eyes," a friend remembered. But she lacked the delicacy of her beautiful, blonde mother and also her brother's confidence.

After dining with Christina in April 1973, James Mellon will write in his diary: "She can be touchingly honest and unassuming, but is also capable of telling repeated lies and embroidering on them." He concludes: "I like her a great deal, but she is definitely a problem case and is sure to be someone's impossible spouse."

Kiki, who often saw Christina in the office, believed, "She did not have one completely happy moment in her entire life."

Into this melodrama, Jackie arrived. Chic, sophisticated, famous the world over for her poise, style, and slim figure. By some accounts, she tried to help Christina with a makeover, arranged for electrolysis, took her shopping, scheduled appointments with a diet doctor. For a while Christina enjoyed the attention; and then she rebelled, angrily announcing that she would not allow herself to be remodeled into a boring American fashion plate.

But her attitude is inconsistent, and her feelings toward Jackie seem also to have depended upon her closeness to her brother. In 1972, she publicly praises Jackie, telling a reporter that she "always tries to please him [Ari] in everything. Whenever they are together, she seems to fall more in love with him." She characterizes her stepmother as her "good and close friend." Just a year later, she surprises a friend by launching into "a sudden bitter tirade" against Jackie and Caroline, declaring them "creepy and standoffish," and saying, "They let you know very fast that they don't want to have anything to do with you." It's a declaration suggesting she, at one time, wanted something to do with them but felt she'd been rebuffed.

Jackie grew up in a blended family, so she knew how such things could work. Despite the tumultuous atmosphere of her stepfather's Newport and Washington homes, the Bouvier (née Lee) and Auchincloss families' merging seemed mostly a success. Yusha Auchincloss—Hughdie's son from a previous marriage—remembered that Jackie introduced him as her brother when he went with her to meet Black Jack Bouvier. "She did have a tremendous sense of family," recalled a cousin. "After Tante Janet married Uncle Hughdie [in 1942] and they were all together—his children from other marriages, her children—Jackie never once spoke of step-this or half-that. To Jackie they were all her brothers

and sisters. There was a great mothering quality about her." With
Alexander, that quality seems to have been thwarted because, as he
said himself, he did not need a mother. With Christina, it appears
she tried, for a while at least.

"She wanted to be totally relieved of annoyances in life," a friend
remembered of her during this time. "Any kind of little irritations
and anything, she didn't want"—conflict, especially. Though she
flagrantly rebels, often passive-aggressively, on strategic occasions,
she deplores direct confrontation. This avoidance is unrealistic, but
it may explain why, once it becomes clear there is going to be no
relationship with Alexander and that any relationship she may have
with Christina will be exceptionally fraught, she doesn't try harder
to make it work, despite it being a disappointment to Ari that she
doesn't have a better relationship with his kids.

During this time, an artist friend observes, she is "a person hiding from in-depth experience in life . . . on the surface of life trying to remain there." Undoubtedly, she sees what's going on with
Christina but there's no way she can help without it consuming her,
without it dragging her back into the abyss of depression and loss.
So she pulls away and stays on the surface, where it's easier, where
she can pretend she's escaped and she is free.

BUT THE PAST PULLS HER BACK. AS THE DECADE ENDS, ONE
last blow.

After years of brutal incapacitation from the stroke he suffered
in December 1961, her former father-in-law, Joe Kennedy, is near
death in late November 1969. At some point, she jots her thoughts
on a piece of yellow lined paper:

Now Mr. Kennedy is sick and Jack is gone.
    Mr. Kennedy had seen Jack nearly die so many times.
He used to say that Jack was touched by destiny. But those
were happy summer evenings at the Cape [ . . . ] when we

were all eating Mathilda's fish chowder—and you thought that meant only happy things—to be touched by destiny.

Dear Grandpa—you brought all the joy of my life—more than one should dare to hope to have—and because of that—all the pain. I will remember you—and I will love you until I die.


She adores Joe. When she first entered the Kennedy orbit, he stuck up for her. When his kids kept pestering her to play touch football, he'd send them away and insist she sip tea with him on the front porch, just the pair of them, chatting about their travels around Europe, books they loved, gossip they'd heard.

"I loved Mr. Kennedy," she later tells Arthur Schlesinger. "He had a charm. He was so warm if he like[d] you and he always like[d] me. . . . And he amused me and he was wonderful to me." But she was realistic about the old man too; she knew "he was suffocating to live with" and she didn't shy away from telling him that. "He was so strong. . . . Jack used to say that Mother would be the happiest widow . . . you can't live in a house with anyone that strong and not—well, I mean, he made Teddy stutter. He practically made Mrs. Kennedy stutter."

In Jackie's hands, though, he seems to have been putty. Mary Gallagher remembered "the great fondness Jackie held for him," and how "They could sit and happily scheme together and be as playful as two little children." Jackie had once said of him, "Next to my husband and my own father, I love Joe Kennedy more than anybody in the world." She said she'd never known anyone else who, "when you saw them, you were so glad to see them."

On November 18, 1969, Joseph Patrick Kennedy dies.

He's buried on November 20: Bobby's forty-fourth birthday.

At the burial, Jackie clutches Cardinal Richard Cushing's hand.

According to the papers, she "repeatedly started to leave only to return to the grave."

## SATURDAY, NOV. 22, 1969 ★

EARLY DECEMBER. SHE READS A MAGAZINE ARTICLE ABOUT how her friend Kitty Carlisle Hart is chairing a bed-tour committee at a veterans hospital in Queens. She calls Hart and volunteers to spend an afternoon visiting the servicemen.

"I had no idea that these very young men, teenagers, were just thirty-six hours away from the battlefield," remembers Hart. "Row after row, panicked or stunned, in bandages . . . some of them were dying as we spoke to them. And Jackie just went from bed to bed, and she talked with them [ . . . ] No hanging back. I just followed in her wake, because she was doing it all herself. She just knew what to say, and what to do. No fear, hesitation, or anxiety. She cared a great deal about these poor souls."

•

She's a "private operator": overwhelmed by large-scale problems, she chooses individuals or projects where she can have a real impact, preferably working behind the scenes. She doesn't see herself as a philanthropist, and her involvements are usually spontaneous, evolving through existing friendships and her own interests in the arts and culture. This is how she became involved with the husband-and-wife design team Leslie and D. D. Tillett and their company Design Works.

The Tillets were superstars of the textile world, and she'd been a fan of theirs for years. They'd done work with the State Department, invested in communities in South Korea, and consulted with nascent businesses in China, Lesotho, and Peru, advising local entrepreneurs how to develop their native handicrafts into commercially profitable businesses. They said that if Jackie would connect them with a design team, they'd do the same in the U.S. She connected them to Brooklyn's Bedford-Stuyvesant community, where in the mid-1960s Bobby Kennedy had been involved in establishing two joint citizen corporations that would work to revitalize the area. Design Works was born.

In December 1969, Jackie quietly finances the leasing of a space so the company will have an outlet for selling its merchandise in Manhattan.

# 1970

ELLIOTT GOULD *Reveals Why He's More Of A Man Without Barbra!*

# screen stories ®

## THE *ONLY* MAGAZINE FEATURING FULL-LENGTH MOVIES!

DEC. 50c

**7** YEARS AFTER DALLAS JACKIE CRIES:

*"Don't Make Me
A Widow Again!"*

# WHAT SHE DOESN'T KNOW IS THAT THIS TIME SHE'S THE TARGET!

*INSIDE!*

"Song of Norway" —
Even better than "Sound of Music"

D.C. GOSSIP COLUMNIST BETTY BEALE RINGS IN 1970 WITH a report that "Paris-types" have written friends in town saying that, the week before Christmas, Onassis escorted Callas to a dinner party. The guests there had, in Beale's words, "come away with the impression that the Jackie-Aristotle union is not so united." But when the Onassises spend Christmas together at Lee's country home outside London, they seem as united as ever, so it's hard to know what to believe.

It's a blip followed by quiet followed by a maelstrom that boils down to two words: Dear Ros.

•

On February 10, Maxine Cheshire reports in the *Washington Post* that a cache of "highly personal letters" from Jackie has been removed from her friend Roswell Gilpatric's locked safe and they are now to be sold at auction. Gilpatric is totally unaware of this until Cheshire herself, curious how the letters came to market, calls for comment. Only then does Gilpatric realize his letters have gone missing, at which point he exclaims, like the dupe in a penny-dreadful: "It's extraordinary . . . incredible! They have obviously been purloined by someone with larceny in their heart."

It's a story of improbable characters. Immediately after speaking with Gilpatric, Charles Hamilton, proprietor of the autograph gallery, rings up the *Times of London* to report that, during this call, Gilpatric's "voice was shaking and he said he was concerned that the sale, if it went through, would ruin his friendship with Mrs. Onassis."

Former Deputy Director of Defense Gilpatric is a lawyer, and by then in his mid-sixties. There were rumors of a romance when he accompanied Jackie to Mexico during the heyday of the David Ormsby-Gore speculation, but it was widely believed at the time that she was engaged to Ormsby-Gore and, anyway, he was married then. "He's very cultured and charming," a Kennedy family friend observes of Gilpatric now, "and a real lady killer with those dancing blue eyes and blond hair."

A reporter for the *Washington Post*, Cheshire always gets good gossip on the Kennedys. She reports on these stolen letters every day for a week and the deeper she digs, the sketchier it gets.

Enter the man who consigned the letters on the thief's behalf. Theodore B. Donson, age thirty-two: he swears he was "duped, deceived," contacted by "a mysterious third party" later assumed to be a night stenographer, no longer in Gilpatric's firm's employ. Donson has no idea how to contact the stenographer, and seems to believe he's been set up as a fall guy. He seems aware of the implausibility of his story. When Charles Hamilton, the autograph hocker, suggests Donson explain himself further to the press, he declines: "No one would believe it. It sounds like an Alfred Hitchcock story." Soon enough, it begins to sound like a novel by Jacqueline Susann.

Coincidentally, Madelin Gilpatric—Ros Gilpatric's third wife, from whom he has been estranged since 1968—files for separation on the day of Cheshire's first column about the letters. When a reporter for the *Chicago Daily News* dials her up, Madelin Gilpatric answers the telephone, and she is surprisingly loquacious.

"They were very, very close," Madelin informs the reporter. "I have my own feelings about that, but I won't go into them. Just say it was a particularly warm, close, long-lasting relationship." She continues: "I'm really most sorry for Mr. Gilpatric. I'm sure it was quite a shock to see this spread around."

Madelin isn't the only one worried about the effect all this is having on "Dear Ros." Jackie worries as well. Enough that someone—whom the papers only identify as a "spokesman" but whose speech pattern is similar to that of Nancy Tuckerman—announces Jackie is "very upset" over the theft and concerned about the distress it must be causing her "very good friend." When asked whether

Jackie caused the Gilpatric's separation, the spokesman denounces such claims as "so untrue and sort of unfair" because Gilpatric is a friend of both the Onassises and had been a friend of Jack Kennedy's. They're all just friends; nothing sordid here.

The content of the statement is more telling than the fact that a statement is made, because—after the business with the judo flip at the sex movie—Nancy Tuckerman and various people at Ari's Olympic Enterprises increasingly refute tabloid rumors on Jackie's behalf. Based on this denial, it seems she's worried about three things: the theft, how much the theft has upset Gilpatric, and the rumors suggesting she's involved in the breakup of his marriage. Understandably, she doesn't want to be perceived as a home-wrecker, which would have implications for Gilpatric's marriage as well as her own.

At the heart of this melodrama lay the four letters themselves— the earliest dated April 1963 and the most recent from November 1968—which amounted to a total of 578 words. The letter of June 13, 1963, constitutes the bulk of the word count at 419, and Maxine Cheshire heralds it as the "one which will interest historians the most" due to its brief references to members of the Kennedy administration. But the November 1968 note is the most titillating.

In October 1968, upon hearing news of her impending marriage, Gilpatric told reporters, "I hope that she has a happiness that certainly is entitled to her. I wish her that." Her November 13 letter, written during a period the press describes as her "honeymoon" (though she'd been married nearly a month and was already back in New York), was a response to his public support. In its entirety, it read: "Dearest Ros—I would have told you before I left—but then everything happened so much more quickly than I'd planned. I saw somewhere what you had said and I was very touched—dear Ros—I hope you know all you were and are and will ever be to me—With my love, Jackie."

"The Jackie-watchers," the *New York Times* reports, "as usual hung on every syllable." In the wave of press coverage around Mary

Gallagher's book the previous summer, Vera Glaser's column on Jackie's White House memos was rather lost, and so, given the lack of her private writing available then, the "Dear Ros" letters are shocking: so familiar, so intimate and loose, so different from how one imagined she would write. And, ultimately, that's what it comes down to. That's why these letters are such a big deal: the gap between what's expected and what actually seems to be is so very, very vast.

Much was made of the intimacy—that a married woman was writing a married man in this way—but it's a tone sustained across her correspondence. "Dear Dear Ken" begins a typical letter to the economist John Kenneth Galbraith, which concludes: "I had to tell you ONE MORE Time – ♪ ♪♪ You're Sensational, That's All ♪ xo Jackie." In another undated letter written from 1040 Fifth, she writes Galbraith, "And thank you for your long and touching letter—You have always been the deepest friend—how lucky I am—I hope I will see you more—and I hope you always know how much I really love you." It's the tone of her letters to women as well. "I can't find any adequate way to ever say thank you for all you always are—full of love and delights and making happy things happen for me," she wrote Galbraith's wife, Kitty. But because so few examples of her writing are available at the time and because the Gilpatric letters lack any context beyond their media cacophony, they hold the illusion of being meaning-ful: an aberration rather than the normal tone she uses in letters all her life.

The Gilpatric letters also hint that there remains—in spite of all the words already written about her, all the ink spilled and "facts" known—a secret Jackie, yet unseen: casual, flirty, friendly, polar opposite of the ruthlessly well-composed woman seen in pictures. If the William Manchester serialization ordeal and Mary Gallagher's book exposed elements of the *real* Jackie, the "Dear Ros" letters edge even closer. They also deepen the longing for more.

The Jackie-watchers are beguiled by the possibilities. And Jackie-watchers don't always look as one might imagine. A week after the "Dear Ros" story first breaks, the *Chicago Tribune*'s longtime White House Press Corps member retires. To commemorate his leaving, President Nixon poses for photographs with the newsman. As they pose, the president of the United States asks him, "How come the *Tribune* didn't have those Gilpatric letters? They were really something, weren't they?"

They are, indeed, something, though there isn't any consensus on what they are, what they signify, or what their fallout will be. Friends are afraid they're such a big deal, such a violation, that they'll drive her further from America. "After this mess," one tells reporters, "Jackie will probably move to Greece for good."

•

But then, nothing happens. The Os are in New York. Celebrating Valentine's Day, they wind down the evening in a nightclub, where they drink a "love-potion" from a champagne glass with two straws.

A few days later, Earl Wilson—the "Earl of Broadway" gossip—catches up with Ari, who shrugs off all that Dear Ros stuff with a dismissive laugh, and Wilson comes away from this chat thinking, "Quite obviously, Jackie and Ari understand each other, and do not give up their old friends."

"Jackie and Onassis have the happiest marriage I have ever seen," the decorator who's helping her with the house on Skorpios enthuses to a reporter in Peru. "He's the most charming man I have ever met. They have a mutual admiration for each other. Both are witty. They have lots of laughter and a real appreciation for each other. And Jackie has her freedom." That is, as ever, the most important thing.

ALL ALONG THERE HAVE BEEN WHISPERS ABOUT ARI AND Maria. But behind the headlines, life appears uneventful for Jackie and Ari. Later, Ari will talk of divorce, but that won't begin in earnest for a few more years and, when it does, Maria Callas never appears to be a factor—it will always be about punishing his wife. For now, it seems he just wants to have his cake and eat it too.

He continues to meet Maria from time to time. "She never lost touch with Onassis," her friend Stelios Galatopoulos claims. "At first her feelings were divided, oscillating between proud reluctance to have anything to do with him and longing to be with him," but then "their old relationship began to develop into genuine friendship."

"After his marriage we never quarreled," Callas later tells a biographer. "We discussed things constructively. He stopped being argumentative. There was no longer the need to prove anything either to ourselves or to one another." An employee who saw him with both women on Skorpios felt he "was never as warm, as relaxed, as passionate" with his wife as he was with Maria. With Maria, "he was so alive, so contented."

He relies upon Maria for stability and advice, while with his wife, when the conversation turns toward business, he says it will bore her and suggests she leave the room. He protects Jackie from those matters, treats her like a princess—though the fact that she later accompanies him on several business trips suggests she is more willing to play a role in this part of his life than he usually permits. Coming from a culture where a wife's greatest achievement is to be an asset in her husband's career, she wouldn't have been averse to this. But because of their relationship's length and their ongoing joint business ventures, Maria already knows his whole world.

His sister Artemis knows what's up. She gossips about it with Kiki, and the pair of them conclude Jackie knows too. How could she not? At a dinner party, someone mentions Maria and Artemis notices that her sister-in-law gets quiet. When she bids Jackie farewell that evening, she reminds her that Ari loves her totally. Artemis later tells Kiki, "She is not a stupid woman. She has to know. But she is smart enough to know also that she is the woman my brother married and the woman he wants to spend the rest of his life with."

Her husband relies upon this other woman, and it seems she tolerates what goes on in private. This is, after all, nothing new. Hadn't Jack Kennedy been a pathological philanderer? Aren't all the men she's close to unfaithful to their wives? She deserves better, but maybe she doesn't expect it. Years later, when her former sister-in-law Joan Kennedy is thinking of leaving Ted, Jackie will tell her:

> Look, it's a trade-off. There are positives and negatives in every situation in life. You endure the bad things, but you enjoy the good. And what incredible opportunities. . . . If the trade-off is too painful, then you just have to remove yourself, or you have to get out of it. But if you truly love someone, well . . .

In this instance, the trade-off seems to have been worth it and so, again, she puts up with her husband's behavior and lives her life. In the wake of the "Dear Ros" letters, however, the rumors about his relationship with Maria resume with renewed vigor.

"Is Jackie's Marriage Over?" the columnist Sheilah Graham asks in mid-March, noting Ari "seems to be spending more of his time these evenings with Maria Callas." Rumor has it that when Lee Radziwill declines a film role, she does so with the declaration, "I can't leave my sister at a time like this."

The story dies down in the papers for most of April and May. But Ari is believed to be with Maria in some way or another, though he is also with his wife that spring. The Os split their time between Skorpios, Athens, and Paris; then Jackie flies to Boston for a meeting of the John F. Kennedy Library Foundation, to Newport for a meeting of the Newport Restoration Foundation, and then on to New York.

THIS STORY OF THE LOVE TRIANGLE WILL EXPLODE IN LATE May; it unfolds amid a series of other troubling events, seemingly disconnected. And all these stories neighbor one another in the newspapers, a circumstance that lends the fracture of Jackie's marriage a typographical equivalence to the fracturing of her homeland.

These are scary, tiring times. No one knows what will happen next, and every time it looks hopeful, like things are beginning to come back together, it all goes to pieces again. America is coming apart.

First, near-tragedy as something goes horribly wrong with Apollo 13. For six uncertain days, the world waits to see if America can bring its astronauts home. And then, as *Life* puts it, "hurtling along with no visible means of support, clinging to a course by the force of momentum, sustained most fragilely by their own makeshift devices and finally, joyously, arcing with jaunty arrogance toward the chanciest of goals," they splash into the Pacific on April 17. A huge sigh of relief.

Three days later, after visiting the Apollo 13 crew in Hawaii, President Nixon gives a televised address from San Clemente, California, and announces plans for the withdrawal of 150,000 American troops from Vietnam. The war is ending. At last, all with be well. And yet . . .

A week and a half later, during a televised address from the White House, the president tells Americans: that very evening in Cambodia, "American and South Vietnamese units will attack the headquarters for the entire Communist military operation in South Vietnam. . . . This is not an invasion of Cambodia," he declares, but that's how it looks to many. The response from certain corners of the war-weary country is vehement.

Over the weekend, the head of the Senate Foreign Relations Committee is besieged with telegrams from folks opposing the move into Cambodia 10 to 1. There are protests at college campuses, demonstrations at Ohio's Kent State University, the University of Maryland, and Stanford. Some suggest that American colleges be shut down for the remainder of the year to halt the protests.

In Philadelphia, during Sunday services at a home for disabled children, a twenty-two-year-old organist makes an announcement:

"In light of President Nixon's invasion of Cambodia, we'll sing a hymn of peace today." When the Episcopalian minister conducting the service commands him to play "Onward Christian Soldiers Marching as to War," the organist walks out.

It is a weekend of heightened emotions.

Come Monday morning, among the political class in D.C. there's a recognition that the "Cambodian adventure" is not an event occurring in isolation. But according to the *New York Times's* correspondent, there is also "a bitter and ugly spirit" regarding this "sudden lurch into Cambodia": "The Capitol is angry . . . it is puzzled and troubled. It cannot understand or explain the events of the last 10 days . . . within a week, everything was changed."

That afternoon: a report circulates that four university students have been killed by the National Guard at Kent State.

A reporter on the scene describes it:

> The troops formed in regimental order on the football field with their backs to a fence. Demonstrators surrounded them on three sides. A student leader . . . led a group of demonstrators towards the encircled troops. The students tossed rocks about the size of baseballs. Suddenly a volley of shots broke out. By the sound and intensity, one immediately thought they were blanks. It was inconceivable the troops could fire such a barrage at the demonstrators. . . . One victim lay in a pool of blood on a concrete walkway. His skull had been split open by a bullet, his eyes were crossed and blood was pouring from his mouth and nose. Students screamed for ambulances. . . . Enraged students yelled "Kill the pigs, kill the pigs." A professor wept. The crowd dispersed.

"This should remind us all once again," the president tells his fellow Americans, "that when dissent turns into violence it invites tragedy." One editorialist, and many listening, interpret the remarks as victim-blaming.

On Friday night, at a late press conference, the president clarifies. "I want to know what the facts are," he says. "I have asked for the facts. When I get them, I will have something to say about it." Then he goes on to reiterate that "when you do have a situation of a crowd throwing rocks and the National Guard is called in . . . there is always the chance that it will escalate into the kind of a tragedy that happened at Kent State."

·

Later that night, Richard Nixon cannot sleep. He asks his Cuban-born valet, Manolo Sanchez, to accompany him to the Lincoln Memorial. With three Secret Service agents, the pair arrives at the Memorial at 5:00 a.m., where they encounter a group of young people camped out for a demonstration the following day. The president talks with them for half an hour, discussing—"in earthy language"—his Cambodia policy, his world travels, America's racial problems, and the environment. After telling the students to have a good time and not to "go away bitter," the president and his valet go to the Capitol, where Nixon gives Sanchez an overview of American history; followed by a visit to the Mayflower Hotel, where the president has corned beef hash with an egg for breakfast. The president, arriving back at the White House at 7:30 a.m., declares this jaunt "one of the most interesting experiences of my life."

To everyone else, it looks damned weird and only adds to the general sense that no one is in charge and the country is coming off the rails. On May 10, in a letter to the editor of an Ohio newspaper, an American writes: "Many of us are confused and even more are frightened by what is happening in the country. . . . I am scared, not so much for my physical safety, but for America, and even more so for mankind because I feel something is drastically wrong."

·

Many agree. A new Jackie book is published. It's a pseudo-academic study of the movie magazines, entitled *"Jackie!" The*

*Exploitation of a First Lady.* In it, author Irving Shulman suggests that the Jackie phenomenon is partly to blame for the current state of "American normlessness" and the ruination of American journalistic standards. And it is American women, Shulman contends, who are at fault.

To blame are the "unthinking" people, "a class of poorly educated fan magazine readers—mostly women—who wanted to drag her down off her heroine's pedestal." The movie magazines, Shulman contends, cater to "childish minds in older bodies" by conveying "uterine tidbits" and a "clitoral interpretation of life" exclusively to "the average American woman who might better serve society if she could be altered to lay eggs like a bird, and then be compelled to sit on them until they hatched." And from there, the mainstream press, sensing profits, followed suit.

In his haste to cast blame, Shulman dismisses the movie magazines and broader interest in Jackie as a feminine affliction that, in appealing to the "febrile imagination" of "America's mod mother," has somehow seeped into the mainstream press and infected the national life. "To charge fan magazines as the principal agent of American normlessness oversimplifies the problem," he writes, before suggesting that they are nonetheless "a dangerous virulence," which has "corrupted every branch of popular media" and contributed to the nation's perceived moral decline.

Ironically, in his 1966 and 1967 interviews with movie magazine readers, Shulman noted that many believed "the best features of American life were incorporated in Jacqueline Kennedy." They also felt that reading about the lives of famous people made them feel better about their own. "Jacqueline Kennedy is real; 'Jackie' is a myth," but "The myth is far more popular than the reality," Shulman concludes, never wondering what useful purposes the myths might serve. "One can only wonder what possible use still another publication of this sort can have," a reviewer sighs, noting it's bound to be a bestseller regardless.

Headlines at the newsstand that May of 1970 cry: "Jackie and Ari to Divorce?" (*Modern Screen*), "Intimate! Behind Jackie's Letters of Love" (*TV Radio Mirror*), "Gilpatric Isn't the Only Married Man She Dated!" (*Screen Stories*), "Whispers That Shocked the Jet Set—Ari Puts a Stop to Jackie's Shopping Spree! Why They Spent Their Holidays Apart!" (*Movie Mirror*), "Onassis: It's All Over Between Jackie and Me . . ." (*Motion Picture*).

W HEN  SHE  WAS  RETURNING  TO  THE  U.S.  IN  LATE  A PRIL, Jackie told reporters she would be splitting her summer between America and Europe, likely returning to the continent in mid-July. According to other reports, she said she'd stay on until the end of June.

It's impossible to determine why her plans changed, but it's probable that the events to come made that change in plans appear more meaningful than it was.

On May 4, Eugenie Niarchos—the sister of Ari's ex-wife, Tina— died under suspicious circumstances in Greece. Maybe Ari had planned to come to Jackie in New York and now couldn't. Maybe he needed her in Paris. Maybe she really did want to surprise him there. Maybe there are other factors of which we know nothing.

What we know is that, at some point, she decided to fly to France, a circumstance that would have excited very little attention had Ari and Maria not gone to dinner at Maxim's the night before and been photographed leaving the restaurant together.

The story goes viral.

The Italian tabloid *Oggi* provides a comprehensive report that captures the gist of the story as it was told at the time: Ari remains at Maxim's with a group of people until 4:00 a.m., and—despite his having "always carefully managed to avoid photographers" when he "revisited his ex-flame"—this time, upon leaving, he is photographed smiling ("not a forced smile") alongside Maria. "As always," after that, he remains for a few hours at Maria's home on Avenue Mandel then returns to his own home on Avenue Foch.

According to *Oggi*, across the Atlantic, his wife is "warned by a friend" while her husband is still at Maxim's and so she flies out of New York on the next plane to Paris and arrives at 7:00 a.m. on Saturday, May 23.

"She was tired and rather untidy," according to the tabloid. "Her face was drawn, her hair uncombed," and she has no luggage. "Her appearance had all the appearance of something improvised."

She arrives at Avenue Foch from Orly Airport at 7:30 a.m.; "Aristotle, unaware, still asleep."

"At this point begins the vaudeville," *Oggi* trills, with Ari and Jackie quarrelling all day before they don formal wear for "a dinner of reparation" and appear at Maxim's, where they are seated at the same table that Ari and Maria sat at the night before.

•

The reports of Ari being photographed with Maria, and Jackie's arrival in Paris the following morning, coalesce into evidence supporting the rumors of marital discord that have been circulating in the European tabloids for months—all of which is now reported in the United States, often on the front page. Press accounts universally present her arrival in Paris as a response to Ari's dinner the night before, despite the near practical impossibility of her receiving a warning prior to her eight-hour flight out of New York.

May 25, the Os leave Paris and fly to Greece. In Europe and the U.S., this is interpreted as a last-ditch effort to save their marriage. And it isn't just the tabloids: it's the *Los Angeles Times*, the *New York Times*, *San Francisco Chronicle*, *Newsday*, the *Boston Globe*. Everyone is reporting on this.

The UPI quotes the London *Daily Telegraph* quote from a French friend who says, "There seems definitely something not altogether right about their marriage at the moment." Meanwhile, the Onassis camp claims all is well, it is nothing, and the Onassises simply came to enjoy the Greek weather. But they are aware that the world is watching. And, significantly, she does not hide.

On Tuesday afternoon, she goes shopping with her sister-in-law. Then, she and Artemis go to a bistro for a snack. As they leave the bistro, reporters call out to her, asking, *Are you angry that your husband has returned to his mistress after he promised not to see her again?*

"Oh my God," she says, "what will they think of next?"

It's a dismissal that does nothing to stop the story's momentum. The rumor mill rumbles on, augmented now by a curiously specific report that she's going to file for divorce on June 10. Nancy Tuckerman issues "a vehement denial," saying she has talked to Jackie: Jackie is in the best of spirits . . . Jackie loves Greece . . . Jackie has no plans to leave. Left unsaid but just as obvious: this is a story Jackie does not like and one she wants to kill.

The Os are still in Greece, planning to host some astronauts, their families, and a small group of friends for a cruise to Rhodes, Mykonos, and Corfu. That's the story out of Skorpios. It's almost believable until, back in Paris, reports swirl that Maria tried to kill herself on the day her rival was drinking ouzo and laughing off reports of marital rift.

Officials at the hospital where Maria's reportedly been taken quickly refute this, announcing that she isn't there. Publicly, Maria maintains she took too many lozenges for her laryngitis. Privately, she *was* hospitalized for a barbiturate overdose, and this overdose—like others before and after—seems to have been entirely accidental, an effort to quell insomnia. Callas laughs it off to a friend, saying: "The press cooked up a dramatic story about my having attempted suicide. What nonsense all that was!"

The announcement that Jackie and Ari's plan to host the astronauts is indefinitely postponed solidifies the connection between the "suicide" and the ongoing Jackie-Ari drama, and it does nothing to convince anyone of the solidity of their union.

But much like the "Dear Ros" letters, photos of Ari and Maria are not actually that incriminating. The pictures were not widely published in the U.S. and so it is their existence that titillates, and also the real-time development of the story after that initial dinner, rather than the images themselves.

When Aristotle Onassis has dinner with Maria Callas at Maxim's in May 1970, it hits the papers in less than a week: a serialized telling of Jackie's husband stepping out and her trying to patch it up. It's like an item out of the movie magazines except there it is every day in the morning paper, Jackie's personal crisis amid all America's other troubles.

It's a crisis with special resonance in light of contemporary fears of a divorce epidemic. With mounting divorce rates, new no-fault divorce laws, and, in particular, the growing trend of middle-age divorce, divorce suddenly seemed to be everywhere. Dubbed the "Twenty-Year Fracture," one psychiatrist explains that, in such cases, divorce often resulted not from the couple's sexual incompatibility or a worsening of the marriage, but from "a bettering of their own idea of individual freedom" and a longing for independence—two themes, coincidentally or not, always prominent to Jackie's story.

And hers is a story as compelling as ever, now, as the president says America's pulling out of Vietnam only to slip into Cambodia in the dead of night. Many Americans in a war-weary America in which the American family appears to be falling apart wonder: *Where are we are going? What are we doing? What will happen to us?* The sun sets and rises, and there's Jackie—an American abroad, in uncertain circumstances—her marriage in peril, jeopardized by a late-night dinner. Hers appears a comforting, controllable uncertainty, bound by the newspaper columns and word limits, neutralized by the knowledge that Jackie is a survivor and Jackie will be okay. Jackie is, ultimately, always okay.

And so the unfolding love triangle provides a welcome distraction. Something you read in the morning paper and wonder about during the day. Far less worrying than whether the National Guard is going to shoot your kid at college or what the president will do next.

She is still the most famous woman in America and her husband seemingly prefers the company of someone else. There have been whispers ever since she remarried, but here it is for real, out in the open at a restaurant in France. Denials all over the place but it's getting harder and harder to deny.

"WHAT WILL THEY THINK OF NEXT?" SHE ASKS THE PHOTOG-raphers, and then she goes about her summer. Which doesn't mean it doesn't hurt, only that she refuses to acknowledge it in public, or even to the people who know her and see her every day. Kiki notices that she doesn't "appear to sit alone in Greece . . . and fume over her husband's infidelity"; it is simply as if it did not happen. The curtain in her mind drops and she spends the better part of the summer putzing around Skorpios, often away from the cameras, reading and studying Greek culture.

She spends time with her Greek friends, particularly Niki Goulandris—a woman working in philanthropy, politics, and paint-ing. Goulandris is in the middle of a project on peonies, and Jackie accompanies her on expeditions searching for new species to paint. The pair also spend hours wandering around ruins and museums together.

She loves reading about something and then going to see it for herself. She's drawn to the idea of lost civilizations, whole histories remembered only through the fragments left behind. "[O]ne won-ders," she writes, at "all the secrets we will never know."

•

The children arrive in mid-June. Caroline is twelve now; John, nine. They're a close, tight-knit family: the three of them, as one friend later put it, "locked onto each other in a way that families almost never do." They are her "vengeance on the world," she says, though she worries: "Probably I will be too intense and they will grow up to be awful." She wants them protected but not cocooned, and she insists they have every opportunity to experience life like other children. When she feels they're surrounded by too many Secret Service agents, she writes the agency that they must not always feel they are under protection—which, she worries, will act as a constant reminder of the violence in their lives, the ongoing risk. She does not want them growing up afraid.

She hopes to open their world, to make sure they fully develop as people in their own right, not stunted by the shadows of their parents. Yet, inevitably, the memory of Jack Kennedy remains. Caroline and John reportedly often asked questions about their father, but they also knew how hard it was for their mother. When he was reading a picture book about his father, upon turning to a page showing the motorcade in Dallas, John exclaimed, "Close your eyes, Mummy!" and ripped the page from the book. Caroline later admits that, growing up, she felt it was her responsibility to protect her mother.

Jackie is less of an absentee mother than most women of her social background, but she is also not with her children all the time, particularly in the early years of this second marriage. She's always had help—first Maud Shaw, the children's nanny through 1965, and then a string of others until she hires Marta Sgubin in July 1969. And she is often in and out of New York during the school year, rendezvousing with her children on the weekends.

Marta goes everywhere with the kids—New York during the week, Newport on some weekends, and, on others, they meet up with the *Christina* in the Caribbean. And then, in the summer, they fly to Greece. A "fantastic, different life," Marta recalls, one "I hadn't even known existed."

A "gutsy mother," Peter Beard called Jackie, suggesting she allowed her children to take chances. She also makes a point of putting them in situations that challenge them. She's concerned they'll become spoiled, and so she frequently sends them off on what she calls "character-building experiences." John, especially, was "always being sent off to have his character built," his sister later observes.

Years later, Caroline will recount how her mother sent the pair of them on a day trip to an island and instructed them to climb a volcano, telling them she would meet them at the bottom: "And so we went all the way to the top just like we always did whatever we were told, and then on the way down we heard these engines roaring, and . . . when we got down to the bottom of the mountain, they said, 'Here, your mother left $20 and she said that she'll see you in a couple days.' And we were like, 'WHAT?!'"

When she came to collect them, they gave her the silent treatment.

·

Caroline is reserved; nearly as tall as her mother by then, with her mother's thick, wavy hair, sandy blonde and worn long. She also shares her mother's dislike of the press. In most photographs she appears sullen—the typical stance of a teenager who isn't quite comfortable in her own skin and is keenly aware of the camera's lens.

She has her father's mien. "Caroline looks at you like Jack used to look," Rose writes in her diary, "feels out the situation in her own mind and reserves an opinion and then goes on to listen, to act, but always with certain reservations." A Kennedy cousin says of Caroline and her mother, "They're like one soul."

Jackie has a great deal of confidence in her daughter. "Caroline is Caroline," she says. "She will do fine no matter what." Her son is a different story.

He's a cutup: boisterous, charming, with a mop of unruly brown hair worn controversially long, and a devastating Mick Jagger impersonation. Often unfocused and less academic than his sister, he struggles against authority and routines—later, biographers will suggest that he may have been diagnosed with dyslexia and ADHD—and all the expectations already settled upon him. But he's a good kid, a lively one, maybe a bit lost but brimming with such energy and joie de vivre you'd not know it.

John's ability to cope with the future seems less certain than Caroline's. He was so young when his father died. Jackie had concerns about his lack of a father, his ability to find his way. She deliberately surrounds him with men who knew his father, men who can teach him to be a man, men specifically versed in Kennedy masculinity—in part due to a fear she expresses to multiple people that he will wind up "a fruit," some casual homophobia on Jackie's part.

Even Ari's children are fond of Caroline and John. When the children visit Skorpios, Alexander and Christina break their rule and dine with the family.

•

Telephoto lenses had been around since the nineteenth century, but they'd combined with the new *paparazzi* phenomenon to shocking result. Elizabeth Taylor was an early victim: the *paparazzo* Marcello Geppetti caught the married actress kissing her married costar, Richard Burton, on a yacht during the filming of *Cleopatra* in June 1962. Since then, the *paparazzi* continued training their long-range lenses upon the private lives of the famous.

In contrast, the photographers Jackie dealt with over the years were usually up in her face, which is why she hated them so much.

There were occasional incursions from telephoto lenses: long-range shots of her and the children taken through the White House fence and, later, pictures of her leaning out the window of 1040 Fifth watching a St. Patrick's Day Parade with Caroline and John. But she'd been largely spared the intrusions of being photographed unaware in private—a circumstance that was about to change.

•

In its June 26 issue, *Life* runs a three-page spread of photos "taken with a telescopic lens on the beach at Skorpios, the private Onassis island in the Ionian, the wine-dark Onassian sea." The photos also appear in U.S. newspapers publicizing that issue of *Life*.

In the photos, she's oblivious to the cameras, strolling across the sand in a bikini and bathing cap, carrying flippers. She and Ari frolic in the ocean. Ari cuts his foot on a piece of glass. Jackie, brow furrowed, doctors it. He goes inside. She applies sunscreen.

Banal activities, but they present a story quite at odds with dramatic tales of their marital breakdown. The images portray a pair who, according to *Life*, appear "as happy as any twosome on the sand at Atlantic City."

The pictures are controversial. "Sirs: Disgusting!" reads one letter to the editor. "It staggers the mind to think that you would deal with a photographer who has nothing better to do than lie in wait all day off the coast of Skorpios hoping to take telescopic pictures of the Onassises."

The following month, another set of images emerges in *Paris Match*. "It's Jackie O as you've never seen her before," trilled *Women's Wear Daily* of these images, which showed Mrs. Onassis practicing yoga—"derriere en l'air." But these pictures aren't widely printed in America until the tamer images of her yoga practice pop up in the movie magazines as "Jackie's Love Exercises" later that summer. Her derriere retains its sanctity, for now.

SHE'S MOVING ON, LIVING HER LIFE, BUT WHAT TO DO WITH THE past? The papers focus on her love life and her life with Ari, while including the reminder that she is "John Kennedy's widow"—a circumstance with implications they don't dwell on, despite continually evoking it.

In public, she appears to be breezily enjoying a carefree life of travel and privilege, unconcerned about the rumors of Ari and Maria. But in private she's plagued by memories of the murder and frequently references her first husband's death. On a particularly bleak day aboard the *Christina*, she tells Artemis, "I know I should be happy now, but all I can think about today is my first husband and what happened to him in Texas. Sometimes I think I will never be able to be truly happy again. I try but I cannot forget the pain . . . I am just waiting for it to return."

She experiences physical discomfort, neck pains she attributes to the events in Dallas. "She told me she had a pain in her neck that doctors all over the world had tried to cure," reveals an Austrian masseuse who treats her. Initially, the pain—which surfaced a few days after the assassination—was believed to be a form of delayed whiplash, but it persisted. "She had the pain in her neck, sometimes she was crying," recalled Kiki Moutsatsos. "She could hardly pass this event."

There's no medical diagnosis, then, nothing to explain what she's enduring, but the symptoms of post-traumatic stress disorder are there: her persistent reexperiencing of the event, avoidance of people and places associated with it, emotional numbness, hyper-vigilance, exaggerated startled response. Based on the testimony of the people around her, it's clear this was an ordeal woven into her everyday life—triggered by the ringing phone, fireworks, car backfire, a slamming door. It's impossible to predict; anything can do it and suddenly she's in that nightmare of the bloody back seat.

The designer Emanuel Ungaro only meets her a few times, but from those encounters he's struck by the "undercurrent of fear," and mentions how, when he sees her in 1969, it's "almost as if she were trembling all the time." At an airport, James Mellon watches a man approach for an autograph and, when she recoils, he's stunned to realize she actually fears for her life. For all the talk of her marrying for security, protection, and bodyguards, she often goes out unaccompanied when the children are not around. She covets normalcy and she doesn't want her whole existence governed by these fears. And so, as Mellon told me, "She would just go through an airport like anybody . . ." though, he was quick to add, "anybody could have shot her."

She's "truly a deeply shattered person," says a Greek friend, noting that beneath all the charisma and wit there is "somebody who had been absolutely shocked." Her face is "entirely labored by these tiny crack-marks everywhere," observes another, who attributes it to the shock of Jack Kennedy's death, recalling that, physically, "She was like a piece of glass that had been shattered and put together. Like crackle glaze on porcelain." The photographer Cecil Beaton sees it, too, writing in his diary, "Her white skin has shadows and creases as if underneath the surface something had broken out of place."

While he encouraged her to talk about her feelings when they met in 1963 and promised her sanctuary in 1968, Ari struggles with the depth of her continuing grief and also with the intrusions of her Kennedy life. A friend notices that she rarely talks about Jack Kennedy: "She normally says very little about him because Ari is jealous of the memories she has of this good-looking, idealistic, and charming young man."

She's adamant about starting over, but perhaps now that notion begins to look a little naïve. She struggles with expectations: the fact that, though everything seems ideal on the surface, she cannot forget the past. She's gotten what she wanted, after all; she is free. They're still very much together. Despite the rumors, the marriage still seems to be working in its own way. Walking along the beach, slipping into the ocean, they appear as happy as anyone else during these strange, tiring times.

Still, any sense of safety Ari can give her seems illusory at best. He is a famous businessman, she the most famous woman in the world, a pair with twin targets on their back.

ON JULY 22, SIXTY PASSENGERS BOARD AN OLYMPIC AIRWAYS flight from Beirut to Athens and then on to Rome. Come the Athens stop, a group of men—identified in contemporary reports only as "Arabs"—hijack the flight on the ground and hold the passengers hostage for seven hours while negotiating with the Greek government for the release of two Jordanian men, who are then on trial for terrorist acts.

On Friday, July 24, after the hijackers release the hostages, Onassis holds a press conference where he reveals that he offered himself to them. "I went down to the plane," Onassis recounts, "and a man came off to see me. The conversation was conducted with me looking at the barrel of his tommygun."

The *Daily Herald* in Provo, Utah, runs the story "Onassis Bargains for Lives" on page four. The *Dixon Evening Telegraph* in Illinois has "Stock Gone Down, Says Onassis" on page seven. The *Kingsport Times* in Tennessee has "Maybe Onassis Should Have Offered Jackie" on page one.

The story is wired cross-country, then packaged by the various newspaper editors—different titles, different tones, and, from that, different readings. Onassis is a hero. Onassis is a joker. Onassis is a joke.

Though, as Onassis explicitly said, "It was no joke."

She hates guns. "Objects of death," she calls them. A rifle killed Jack, a revolver killed Bobby. And now here's Ari, willingly staring down a gun at close range.

•

There's another story circulating that day. A tiny report that runs on page eight of the *Holland Evening Sentinel* in Michigan, but which is picked up in surprisingly few U.S. papers. "Man Held on Charge" is the title. It reports that, the day before, British police arrested a man for threatening to kidnap and kill Aristotle Onassis and his wife.

•

On July 28, she celebrates her forty-first birthday with her children, husband, sister, and assorted other relatives. According to UPI, "The day was not marked by any of the noisy celebrations which often go with Greek Birthdays." The AP reports the complete opposite, recounting how she received "[a] helicopter full of gifts" and that the *Christina* was "bedecked with flags and festooned with colorful lights."

"[H]ousehold sources" inform the press that Ari gave his wife "the best yacht in the world, to be completed by the same date next year" at a Japanese shipyard. Reading this, Eunice Kennedy

Shriver tells her mother, who speaks directly to Jackie to find out if it's true. Jackie says it isn't. Rose notes in her diary: "These stories go around all the time."

Perhaps more reliable—though there's no evidence supporting this story, either—is the report that he gave her another gift of gold earrings commemorating space flight. This pair, by the same Greek jeweler who'd designed the Apollo 11 earrings, are even trippier: "The earrings hang on strands of gold wire which fit around the entire ear. A large spiral effect is created and 'man's movement in space' is duplicated by the earrings as the wearer moves her head."

"I couldn't think of anything more matching for a person like Mrs. Onassis," the jeweler tells the AP. "She's a real space woman."

•

In early August, she and Lee take their kids to Hyannis, where the Kennedy compound isn't as peaceful as they probably had hoped. That summer, Rose had been bedeviled by tourist boats going by every half hour, all day and into the evening, narrating the Kennedys' lives over their loudspeakers: *And right over there, that's the Kennedy compound, three houses on six acres of property, white frame clapboard structures—and Bobby's house—he lived there until he was shot down by Sirhan Sirhan—and the president's house—where he lived until he was shot in cold blood by Lee Harvey Oswald—and Jackie, as I know you all know! She married a certain man by the name of O-nassis—and the main house? It has a four-car garage!*

At her house and the other houses in the compound and up the shore, Rose records, "It is very much as though the radio is going all the time."

Ari joins them for the weekend, and the Os pop up later in New York, sparking the headline "Jackie Onassis wears tablecloth" when she catches a chill while lunching and a waiter wraps table linens around her shoulders to create a blanket effect.

On August 11, Ari is back in London, where, speaking to a reporter of the *Evening Standard*, he addresses the rumors of an impending split, declaring:

> We are both ideally happy and anybody who says that is not the case doesn't know what they're talking about. All this is complete mythology. It is unbelievable. It is absurd. Unbelievable mythology. What I want everyone to know is that there is no rift in my marriage to Mrs. Onassis. People invent these malicious stories because they have nothing else to do, because it amuses them. It has been obvious that there is nothing behind the stories but still they persist.

He says that he's heading to Greece that weekend to meet his wife, already on her way there.

Which brings us to August 15: Maria Callas's name day—a day, in the Greek tradition, similar to a birthday but corresponding to the day of a saint's death. August 15, 1970, is a Saturday and Ari is in Greece, on Tragonisi—an island owned by a friend and competitor of his. While he's there, a photographer with a telephoto lens gets a shot of him kissing Maria Callas.

On August 25, the story breaks in the U.S., with a report that color photographs have appeared in the Italian celebrity tabloid *Gente*. The spread is entitled "Callas Has Won."

Several holes remain in this story: the photographs of Ari kissing Maria were not included in the contemporary British and American reports and they're not available online now, so it's hard to say for certain what they actually showed. American summaries of *Gente*'s report mention that the pair went swimming and had a beach picnic with their companion, and they characterize the kiss as one of "greeting" so it's highly possible—especially in light of the hysterical reception of the incredibly tame shots outside of Maxim's a few months before—that the photos themselves are not all that incriminating.

Much like the incident at Maxim's, the drama of this episode seems to revolve entirely around Jackie's perceived reaction to it. "Mrs. Jacqueline Onassis," according to the UPI's translation of *Gente*, "when notices of her husband's amusements reached her in America, returned abruptly to Athens."

Given what Ari himself already said about her preexisting plans to return to Greece, that her return is precipitated by the photos seems inaccurate. But this is forgotten in the press, where everything is now about Jackie trying to win back her husband's love.

*Time* magazine reports: "Responding like a dalmatian to the fire bell, Jackie flew to Greece, to Onassis, to the yacht Christina, and to squelch the rumors."

The same day "a photograph said to show her shipowner husband kissing soprano Maria Callas, a former yachting companion," is published in *Gente*, Mr. and Mrs. Onassis arrive in Capri, a picturesque island in the Gulf of Naples. It's a preplanned vacation with her husband involving a rendezvous with Lee and Stas, who are in Amalfi at the time. Also, Jackie had heard a friend living in Capri was ill and was eager to visit his wife. However, according to media accounts, the locals interpret this visit as being "specifically intended to allay rumors the Marriage O. is foundering."

SHE'S INCREDIBLY VISIBLE IN CAPRI: AT THE MARKET, A shop, a café with her sister and niece, ordering ice cream from a vendor, shopping with Lee, strolling barefoot with the couturier Valentino. She's even photographed buying a copy of *Gente*. Ron Galella, who gets this shot, senses she's "annoyed" that he has.

Galella is shooting her every move. In most of the photos she smiles enigmatically and looks serene. However, there's one where she sits in a café. If she had wanted her picture taken, she is, by this point, over it. If she hadn't wanted to be shot at all, she nonetheless humored him and now she's had enough. She beckons the waiter to her table; she talks to him as she looks toward Galella.

In Galella's picture, she points directly into his lens and she is visibly annoyed.

But pictures don't tell the whole story; they freeze it at strategic points. Looking at Galella's pictures from Capri, it appears she went for a walk and, because some of his shots are so close they capture the texture of her skin, one would think Galella's shooting with a zoom lens. But he wasn't the only *paparazzo* in Capri that afternoon, and it's in those pictures that it becomes clear how physically close Galella was—so close that, in some shots, you'd mistake him for a bodyguard.

In the evening, she goes for a walk with Ari. Another photographer records this. His photos are of Jackie ordering an ice cream cone and eating it, her and Ari walking down the street, sitting in a café with Stas and his kids, Anthony and Tina.

In these café pictures, as the family sits at their table, Stas smokes a cigarette and Jackie and Ari listen to the kids. They're sitting outside. In one shot, a horde of people inside the restaurant press against the window, staring out at them like children looking into a cage at a zoo. It appears the group is dining privately and the chaos is kept indoors. But a shot from another angle reveals that, in reality, they're crammed close to a number of other tables and those people are watching them as well.

The photographers, the crowd, flashbulbs popping, and the buzz of all those people pressed against the glass—and yet the group appears peaceful, involved in themselves and ignoring the attention directed toward them. Maybe she wants to be seen, but there's a defiance here too—in going out when she knows the whole world's watching, in refusing to stay holed up on the boat. Instead, she continues to do all the things anybody does when they go on vacation. She sees the sights. She sits in a café in plain view, chats with her nephew as though she hasn't a care.

•

She's getting a lot of attention in Capri but her friend Count Bismarck's ill health and Ron Galella's pursuit don't make it into the papers, which are more concerned with her marriage and how she looks. They think she appears notably different, more bohemian: hair parted in the middle and slicked back in a chignon; her casual, printed gypsy skirt slit to mid-thigh.

Looking at all these photos out of Capri, *Women's Wear Daily* proclaims, "There's a new Jackie O. . . . The only thing that remains the same are those famous shades."

Yet another new Jackie, like the new Nixon. It's getting hard to keep up.

THERE ARE WHISPERS SHE'LL ACCOMPANY ONASSIS ON A trip to open a new social club at the Belfast shipyard of Harland & Wolff—a Protestant shipyard in which Ari's a major shareholder and which is building two tankers for his fleet.

The Os arrive in Belfast, where 150 Harland & Wolff employees and their wives are treated to a buffet lunch. They are, says one attendee, "really nice and chatty."

It's a good trip, with a few unfortunate incidents. As the UPI report has it: "Jacqueline Onassis came to Northern Ireland for the first time Saturday in a three-hour visit enlivened by a bomb scare and by an evangelist who assured her there was room for her in heaven."

The social club being christened is very near an area of Belfast where sectarian violence has been flaring all year. Just the night before, a bomb went off, killing a local man in what police identified as an offshoot of "the ongoing Roman Catholic-Protestant conflict."

So everyone is already on edge when, only minutes after an evangelist ran across the street shouting at Jackie that there was room in heaven for her, police receive a telephoned threat. Pedestrians and traffic are diverted, but the deadline passes without incident. The buffet goes on.

A cynically lighthearted tone characterizes the reports and minimizes the genuine threat of violence. In West Virginia, the

*Beckley Post-Herald and Register*'s page two report, entitled "Jackie Has Lively Visit to Ireland," is headline-adjacent to stories about bombings in Canada and L.A. Bombs are enjoying a certain vogue and, coming after the hostage situation and the kidnap threat, and especially given that Jackie is the most visible Catholic woman in the world—and this is a Protestant shipyard in Belfast, September 1970—the danger is real.

*It was no joke.* That's what her husband told the press after he stared down the barrel of the hijacker's gun. But both of them were, by this point, kind of a joke, whether he liked it or not.

•

A popular joke at the time: "Some mornings Jackie's husband wakes up and says, 'Today I feel as wise as Aristotle' and other mornings he says, 'Today I am as rich as Onassis.'"

CONCURRENT WITH THESE PLOTS AND THREATS, A SERIES OF STO-ries on the money the Os spent in their first year of marriage slowly rolls out in papers around America. The figure consistently posited is $20 million (with inflation, approximately equivalent to $145 million in 2022) and the articles are excerpted from a book to be called *The $20,000,000 Honeymoon,* in which author Fred Sparks takes all the rumors circulating since 1960 (Jackie as clothes horse! Jackie as spendthrift!), rumors that were cousins of the stories dis-tilled into Mary Gallagher's book the previous summer as Jackie's "champagne tastes!"—and he supersizes them.

From fall of 1970 into the summer of 1971, Sparks's stories appear in papers across the land. An ad for the book runs in the *New York Times* with *Library Journal*'s assurance that "The facts are sensa-tional but never vulgar." *The $20,000,000 Honeymoon* is serialized in the Hearst papers, which means it cascades across that empire into spring and summer 1971. After running all twelve parts, the papers have nearly printed the entire book.

•

The Os spend a lot of money. Maintaining multiple homes, a ship, and an island, their baseline budget is extravagant by anyone's measure, especially given the economic climate of the time. According to *Life*, unemployment has risen from 3.5 percent to 4.8 percent in just one year, and inflation, a problem that "touches everyone," has "been surging like a red tide."

And then there's Jackie, eating at fancy restaurants and ordering Valentino in bulk.

But these stories find readers in enormous numbers—even for a syndicated piece, they have an extraordinarily broad reach in the Hearst newspapers. They're stories readers can escape into, imagining Jackie's closets, Jackie's clothes, Jackie's vacations, how incredibly pampered and loved Jackie must feel.

Sparks's story is a dramatic retelling of the greatest hits of the prior two years: the marriage, the spending, the sex movie, and Maria. And the Os are made to seem, for all their reckless spending, like an ordinary couple. So, if Ari drank, it was only because "Ari is no different from the thousands of American commuters who, on arriving home in their suburbs on the 5:26, rocket directly to the booze closet seeking a liquid nerve pacifier." If Ari drinks, it's because he's just like you and me and "The need to 'unwind' is universal." And his wife, like so many other wives, "has had to force herself to coexist with her husband's dry martinis," even though "Like anyone who cherishes superior cooking, Jackie believes that a man who has marinated his taste buds in tobacco and alcohol for 30 minutes couldn't tell the difference between *foie gras* with truffles and a pizza."

Sparks's stories, with their titillating gossip and their snappy prose, run for months on end: an intoxicant, a comfort, carrying the message that Jackie is, in the end, *just like us*.

Americans don't even have to buy the book. It's easily accessible in the magazines on the newsstand and at the beauty parlor, and it's in the local paper too—not even buried in the back in the women's pages, but in the front section. These recaps of the first year of Jackie's marriage, Jackie's $20 million honeymoon, are treated as news.

Next to all the other news—the war, hijackings, kidnappings, campus protests, police brutality, the bombs in the streets—there's Jackie: queen of distractions. A whole world away from all that awful stuff, she's protected by the millions of the man she married. Jackie is safe.

"Jackie has impact," one writer suggests. Because people are tired, anxious. Like those family members flocking to Skorpios, they want to escape. Readers expect entertainment and that is what they get from her. They don't need any more reminders that the world is unpleasant and unsafe.

The novelist Anita Loos gushes to *Women's Wear Daily*: "God bless Jackie—the only thing that can make us forget the bomb." She makes you forget that you're waiting, always anticipating, thrown forward into the anxiety, again and again—like Jackie, telling the story from hell, again and again—always anxious, because this is the present and, in the present, we never know what will happen next.

"Get a load of the movie magazines," columnist Jack O'Brian tells his readers. "Non-actress Jackie Kennedy Onassis still reigns supreme." Constancy at the newsstand, though change is in the air.


THERE'S THIS MIDI-CRAZE, BUT IT'S MAYBE TOTALLY manufactured.

The mini hem length is out, so *they* say, and everyone's going midi. It came about, according to one designer, because "fashion was in a rut. . . . Women were shortening their old dresses instead of buying new ones" and the industry needed to give women a reason to buy new clothes. Enter the midi (23"–25" in length) and, more dramatically, "the Longuette" (25.5"–33"). Intended for, according to the vice president of Marshall Field's department stores, "that strange woman . . . who wants to be the first out of the hen coop with the latest oddity. She'll go to any length to be *au courant* and we make a lot of money because of her."

It's a marketing juggernaut to which many women are deeply resistant, a recalcitrance summed up in an October 1970 *Wall Street Journal* headline: "Women Call It Sleazy, Dowdy, Depressing; but Designers Say It Will Catch On Yet." A reporter notes, "It is, in some quarters, considered a capitalist conspiracy [as] the longer skirt length requires higher prices at a time when inflation is on the rise."

The midi is a tough sell. "The straight ones with the slit up the front make you look just like a French whore," one twenty-two-year-old tells *Life*. "I feel I'm in an old bad Russian movie," says another. Obviously an intolerable circumstance in America, where one's clothes should make one feel free, not French, or—worse—Russian.

In its cover story on the phenomenon, *Life* quotes newscaster Barbara Walters as loving midis. Quickly, in a letter to the editor, Walters complains that *Life* has misrepresented her position. She notes that, as a TV broadcaster, she remains "behind a desk 98% of the time and my skirt length is a complete mystery to the audience." Also, she writes, "it is only very recently and very timidly that I have tried wearing a skirt below the knees."

•

*Women's Wear Daily* has been pushing the midi trend hard for months and, from the beginning, Jackie has been a part of the marketing campaign. In the autumn of 1970, readers are told she "came out of Paris with no less than six Longuettes from Philippe Venet, two from Givenchy and two from Ungaro boutique." They're also told that, when she ran into a friend on the streets of an unseasonably sizzling New York, she apologized for her minidress, saying—like the star of a clothing commercial—"Don't look at me now. I'm so embarrassed to be wearing such a short dress, but it's so hot. I can't wait to wear my new long dresses."

As supporting evidence that the mini is dead, *Women's Wear Daily* runs a cover photograph with a big X printed over her knees, informing readers they may never again see so much leg from the former First Lady because she's going Longuette and, according to Valentino—the lord of Longuette himself—"She looked perfect in whatever Longuettes she tried on."

According to John Fairchild—legendarily tyrannical editor of *Women's Wear Daily*—she is still "the world's leading fashion heroine." In large part because, in the mid-1960s, she single-handedly dignified the mini, "because the masses concluded that if a woman of her stature wore a mini, they would not be corrupted if they did likewise." Now, her hems have dropped and those short skirts are embarrassing; clothing manufacturers are prodding other women to follow her example.

As a predictor of trends, however, Fairchild seems to have lost his way. At a Harvard Business School forum on the midi phenomenon, he asserts that women of the future will wear midis and go topless, so his crystal ball is cloudy at best.

JACKIE HAS OTHER THINGS ON HER MIND. ON NOVEMBER 2, after a long fight against cancer, Cardinal Cushing of Boston dies. "I loved him and will miss him terribly for the rest of my life," she says in a statement released after she learned of the death of the man who had officiated at her wedding to Jack Kennedy, at the gravesides of her two infants, and at Jack's funeral. "The world has lost one of the greatest men who ever lived. His life was built on love; to heal rather than to divide."

Upon her remarriage, Cushing had been a vocal advocate on her behalf. "This idea of saying she's excommunicated, she's a public sinner, what a lot of nonsense," he told the press. "Only God knows who is a sinner and who is not." She had broken a law of the Church, he said, but she had not broken with God. "I assure you," he told another reporter, "she is a valiant woman of modern times." This stance prompted such an uproar he opted to retire early.

When she visited him shortly after, accompanied by Ari and the kids, the cardinal reportedly took her aside and said, "Now, Jackie, when everyone from the pope on down was belting your head off, I stood up for you, so I've a right to ask you: Are you happy?" She said yes.

"Apart from my family, from all the ties of blood and marriage—the person that I truly love in all this world is you, Your Eminence," she wrote the prelate in March 1969, reflecting on the debt she owed him: "So many people we loved are gone. I was so hostile to God after he took Jack. You, more than anyone, brought me back to Him. Now, because of your example, I have the deepest faith that cannot ever be shaken again. So I owe my life—and the lives I will try to give my children—to you."

•

At the lying-in-state and before the funeral, she's expected but doesn't show. The air buzzes with a general hum of "Where's Jackie?" At the bakery across the street from the cathedral, middle-aged women keep asking the man working the counter whether Jackie's coming—as though he will, naturally, be the first to know.

She comes down from New York for the funeral. In the photographs, she looks beautiful and serene. Wearing a black quilted suit, just above the knee—not a midi, probably Chanel—and a black mantilla covering her thick, light brown, windswept hair.

A little over a year later, as these images of her at the cardinal's funeral are projected on a screen in a courtroom, she'll cite this occasion as one in a list of instances when Ron Galella got close to her and members of her family and frightened her. Her voice falters as she says of Cardinal Cushing, "I loved him."

## SUNDAY, NOVEMBER 22, 1970

Back in New York, she and John go cycling in Central Park. There's La Cote Basque with Lee, ice cream with the kids, shopping at Bonwits and Maximilian and Cartier, buying housewares at Saks. A performance of *Hair*, where she sports a truly atrocious wig.

Christmas comes again. She's probably in New York.

On the editorial page, in a year-end roundup of a local Illinois paper: "Santa Claus and his elves are getting almost as much privacy as has been granted, for several weeks, to Jackie Onassis." But there's plenty of noise and "news" to fill the void.

Princess Margaret's psychic looks deep into Jackie's womb and predicts the New Year will hold pregnancy and a miscarriage, while the astrological competition foresees an accident for Ari. It seems the rumor of Jackie's birthday yacht is finally put to rest when Jackie's own mother, Janet Auchincloss, tells D.C. columnist Betty Beale that the story is absurd.

# 1971

Drug Scandal Rocks Jerry Lewis' Family SEE PG. 50

# MOTION PICTURE

50¢ JANUARY

## WHY JACKIE CAN NEVER GET ENOUGH

A dollar-by-dollar look at Mrs. Onassis as wife, lover, consumer

RAQUEL WELCH SAYS: **"I'M ASHAMED OF MY BODY"**

DEAN MARTIN SOBS: "I want my Jeanne back"

SUNDAY, JANUARY 3. THERE SHE IS. SWEATER PULLED UP over her nose, sunglasses over her eyes, head covered in a giant fur hat—walking with Caroline through the snow in Central Park. The photo is by Galella.

•

In late January, Pat Nixon invites her to the unveiling of the official White House portraits. In response, Nancy Tuckerman is dispatched to the First Lady's office hand-carrying a letter.

"I really do not have the courage to go through an official ceremony, and bring the children back to the only home they both knew with their father under such traumatic conditions," Jackie writes. "With the press and everything, things I try to avoid in their little lives, I know the experience would be hard on them and not leave them with the memories of the White House I would like them to have." She proposes a compromise, suggesting she bring Caroline and John for a private viewing, with no advance notice given to the press. Upon reading the letter, Pat Nixon tells Tuckerman to set a date.

•

On February 3, she visits for the first time since John Kennedy's death. The Johnsons had tried to get her to return, but she refused. The house held memories and, she said, even the sight of the building was too much. "Even driving around Washington I'd try to drive a way where I wouldn't see the White House."

"I don't think I ever would have gone back if I could have helped it," she says later, "but when our portraits were presented I sort of had to."

She tours the State Rooms with Caroline and John, accompanied by Pat Nixon and her daughters, Julie and Trisha. Julie finds her "subdued." The president joins them and they all have dinner. Julie notes that when Nixon joined the group, Jackie's "mood changed again and she became, as he recorded later in his [personal] diary, 'very bright and talkative.'"

She's an incisive and shrewd judge of character and it appears she's rather beguiled by Richard Nixon. She's known him casually for twenty years, through John Kennedy—a man Nixon, despite his jealousy and their rivalry, considered a friend. Possibly she senses the president's insecurities, just below the surface.

"He is not a broadly confident man and probably never will be," observed a sympathetic editorialist. Lacking the cool confidence of Jack Kennedy, Nixon is full of nerves, every news conference a "real agony" and "ordeal" of "exquisite uncertainty." An "egg-walker, treading delicately upon thin shells," he tries to appear to be making "confident plunge[s]," but his "quest for the right phrase" only leads him "into entangling thickets" betraying the fact "He has no natural fund of small talk."

The "great pain of his life is that he chose fields of endeavor—politics and high public office—where displays of confidence are supposed to be worn like a uniform," a circumstance with which she, a fundamentally shy and introverted woman who is nonetheless ambitious, can sympathize. They've chosen paths that go against the inclinations of their temperaments, a commonality that bonds them beyond their connection to John Kennedy. They feel like outsiders in the America they both symbolize and to which they both belong. After this dinner, she tells her mother she thinks he's "a fascinating character with a lot of complexity" and "an extremely brilliant mind."

They get on well. At one point, he says she tells him: "I always lived in a dream world."

This is a man who eagerly read the reports on the "Dear Ros" letters, so he's a Jackie-watcher himself and he knows this dream-world line is a tantalizing note on which to close this scene in his memoirs. Here's Jack Kennedy's widow at his dinner table—he'd gotten her here when even Johnson, that persuasive son of a bitch, could not—and she's opening up to him. He wants the whole world to know that and only that. He tells us little else and doesn't contextualize this statement beyond the fact that he didn't want to distress her or make the conversation sad.

He wants to please her. And she is pleased. "Can you imagine the gift you gave me," she writes him the following day, "to return to the White House privately with my little ones while they are still young enough to rediscover their childhood. . . . Thank you with all my heart. A day I always dreaded turned out to be one of the most precious ones I have spent with my children."

She reportedly tells her mother that she's "impressed" with Pat Nixon, who she finds very "warm and gentle and understanding." She also telephones Rose Kennedy, who writes that "she was elated that everything had been so private and so quiet."

When the portraits are unveiled in the East Room a few days later, a "misty-eyed" Pat Nixon tells reporters that Jackie "loved being back. . . . She really did. I invited her to come back. I think she will."

She won't.

•

Her portrait remains, to mixed reviews. According to Mrs. Nixon, the president feels that, because "Mrs. Kennedy" approved them, "they must be pretty fine." Others are less confident in Jackie's taste.

Bonnie Angelo wrote in *Time*: "Those aren't her hands. She has broad, unglamorous, working woman hands and bit her nails."

"She looks like a witch," says someone else.

According to Helen Thomas of UPI: "That's her look when she would see the Washington press women."

A more hopeful viewer: "I think they'll probably grow on us."

She'd sat for the portrait by Aaron Shikler off and on from winter of 1968 to February 1970, and two starkly different versions emerged. After seeing the transformation following her remarriage,

Shikler rejected the first as too girlish. In it, she's wearing a white blouse with ruffled collar and black skirt, standing before the fireplace at 1040 Fifth and staring directly at the viewer. She looks like an Edith Wharton heroine. Shikler, "the Gilbert Stuart of the jet set," felt it failed to capture her reserve and strength. "Anyone could paint her prettiness," he says. "I wanted to paint the haunted look in her eyes." He began again.

"She has an impassioned quality," the artist reflected. "She has this great inner passion but it's so strongly controlled. I tried to show in the hands that tension stiffly under control but ready to coil out."

The final portrait is lighter in terms of mood and color. In it, she stands, again, in front of the fireplace at 1040 Fifth, wearing a dress by the Irish designer Sybil Connolly.

Everyone notices the hands first, which appear to strain against the fabric of the dress. But when the eye wanders up, her gaze is arresting and directed away from the viewer. Neither sad nor girlish, but extremely attentive, hawkish even, as though she were watching her children and poised to swoop in should they encounter any difficulty.

At first glance, the portrait is sunny, awash in a golden late afternoon light, which spills across the canvas, splashing such brightness over the scene that it almost distracts from the anxiety written on the subject's face. Only when one looks closely does the anxiety surface: the tension in the hands, the uneasiness in the eyes, the defensiveness. She does not look at you directly. She evades your glance.

"You come to it with mixed emotions," a woman at the opening tells *Women's Wear Daily*. Mixed emotions: because JFK died and she did not die with him, and so she continued to live, remarried, and went on. In the wake of her first husband's death, she became a repository of both collective and individual emotions, some repressed, most defying articulation. And now here she is in actual art.

This is, ostensibly, how she wants to be seen: posed, pulled together, a bright, shining light. But there are complaints that she looks contrived, unreal. The ghostly vision in the portrait is, after all, a woman everyone just saw running around Capri. Much like the letters, her presentation of herself here doesn't align. The truth seems to lie somewhere between the pieces, which give the impression something has been revealed only to then fall far short of what is expected and wanted—pointing to a Jackie one cannot, will not, ever know.

According to Shikler, her only stipulation with her husband's portrait was that he not "look the way everybody else makes him look, with the bags under his eyes and that penetrating gaze." She was, she said, "tired of that image." In his portrait, John F. Kennedy is looking down, deep in thought, arms crossed.

The portraits are seldom seen as a pair, though it is as a pair that they assume a provocative dimension. Depending upon which side of his portrait hers is placed, she is either looking toward him or away. He is looking down, deep in thought. She is anxious, tense. He was painted as he was, in 1963. She appears as she is, in 1971.

•

She drafts a letter to Ted and Rose Kennedy regarding Jack's portrait: "I find it enormously moving. ~~You can look at it for hours.~~ ~~It makes you remember~~ I think it has a quality of spirit that one would like future generations to find in the White House portrait of Jack . . . I supposed there is ~~always something wrong~~ never complete satisfaction with a painting of someone known and loved. No one can ever paint all we saw in him—especially if he is not there to sit for it. . . . Anyway, I love it and just pray you will."

Of her own, she writes: "I like the dream-like mood of the picture. The person in it could be from any time and place. It has a ghost quality."

"I would have liked it even more lost in shadows," she tells a friend, "less specific, more impressionistic." It reveals too much.

•

The following week, rumors swirl in Europe that she is dying from cancer. From New York, Nancy Tuckerman issues a denial: "It's not true at all." Jackie "couldn't be more well. . . . I think it's cruel for any newspaper to print such a thing."

SHE STAYS PRETTY QUIET DURING THAT SPRING AND EARLY summer—popping up in Antigua, Nassau, London, New York, saying little.

"There are indications that public interest in Jacqueline Bouvier Kennedy has waned," one columnist announces, a claim immediately undercut by his declaration that the "popular magazines are still featuring 'Jackie' in sometimes semi-libelous contexts on their covers" and that a new "big book" is about to be released.

Enter Mary Van Rensselaer Thayer's "painstakingly written" follow-up to her authorized 1960 biography, *Jacqueline Bouvier Kennedy*. The "first and only authentic narrative" of those "three glittering, strenuous years."

"Bearing the stamp of approval of the former first lady," *Jacqueline Kennedy: The White House Years* lands in bookstores with a pronounced thud.

•

Thayer bills her account as "a true picture which should be of interest to historians as well as living Americans." She seems to have seriously misjudged the longings of living Americans. They're still sending inquiries to gossip columnists and writing Mary Gallagher, begging for a sequel, so the interest in Jackie persists. But "Jackie's Aide Tarnishes Halo" is a much better story than "Jackie Likes Book," and the book's authorization automatically lessens its value. It's dismissed as irrelevant. A reviewer censures it as "neither unique nor historically significant . . . an unrealistic portrait blemished with the tinted paint of the past."

Perhaps there would have been more interest were everyone aware of Jackie's own ambivalence about Thayer's "authorized" project. In the summer of 1968, a few weeks after Bobby's death, when a publisher wrote to inquire whether Thayer was working with her consent, Jackie's response was vehement: "I do know that she is doing a book, however, since I do not have the slightest desire to have any more books written about me, I cannot really say that it has my approval. The only thing I could give approval of is total silence!"

"I hope he doesn't show this letter to Molly," Nancy Tuckerman gently prodded her in response to this draft, "as she is so enthusiastic and thinks you are pleased with the idea."

She seems to have reconsidered sending it, for there is a giant X across the page.

But, come 1971, they're still tussling. When Thayer requests a memo of support, Jackie writes Tuckerman that she envisions a different book altogether, a definitive history of the White House restoration, but she imagines Thayer is "too old to start all over again." She's torn between wanting the material on the restoration to be available and not wanting to reveal any more information about her life. She is also afraid she'll be exploited, as she was by William Manchester and, she feels, by Thayer in 1961.

When Thayer requests photographs, Jackie writes Tuckerman: "I think she should see the book of the W.H.—the before + after pics I took. . . . But don't let her keep it—as she'll reproduce the photos as she did last time + use them + sell them." Eventually, however, she relents: "I suppose if the poor woman is doing a book + the only thing I'll tell her about is the restoration—I might as well give her a few pics—otherwise no one will ever see them but Caroline + John."

She gives in but remains ambivalent. Her lawyer draws up a two-page endorsement that she finds too gushing. Ultimately, Thayer's book is armed with a terse pair of sentences declaring Jackie thinks she's done a "fine" job and that it was good of her to do it because Jackie couldn't do it herself.

She's distrustful of history in general. More specifically, she is skeptical of how history depicts the people involved—and she is, in fact, already a historical figure. Total silence is an option, but because there is already so much misinformation out there, she can't resist trying to correct it. Cooperating with Thayer is the compromise she begrudgingly makes to get the information about the White House restoration into the historical record. She would prefer Thayer write the story of the White House restoration, but what she gets is *Jacqueline Kennedy: The White House Years.*

•

Thayer's book is the first sustained examination of her work as First Lady. It's a flattering portrait, but it also illuminates the contributions of a woman substantially more involved in her husband's presidency than the public and the press realized during the Kennedy administration or in the years since.

Betty Beale covered the Kennedy White House, and even she is startled by Thayer's account. To Beale, the book reveals that "Even when the public thought she might be shirking her duties as a hostess because she wasn't present," Jackie was completely involved and programming every single detail. Another columnist notices Jackie "comes into her own," and the book "does an impressive job in documenting the really monumental results" she achieved during her short tenure: "Jacqueline Kennedy clearly was running the show." While her endeavors were still pinned to the restoration and entertaining, rather than her engagement in diplomacy through letters to foreign leaders or her foreign tours, it was a start.

"We come to it with mixed emotions," a woman said of Jackie's White House portrait, and the same holds true here: Americans could read about how much her hot pants cost and speculate about where she's wearing them, who she's wearing them for, and whether she's pulling them off. They could feel they know so many small, totally inconsequential details about her—nearly every item of clothing she's ever bought—and yet really know so little about who she is. And still a tremendous resistance persists, almost a willful refusal, to seeing her on her own terms.

Betty Beale knows both Jackies, but even she concedes that the portrait in the Thayer book illuminates not only the vast gulf between who she is believed to be and how she wants to be seen, but also, possibly, how she might be. Beale cites a lengthy memo regarding details of Joe Kennedy's visit to the White House, wherein the First Lady gave the chief usher instructions for her father-in-law's care and feeding after his stroke. Reading this memo, Beale reflects, "It is hard to find in this thoughtful daughter-in-law the spoiled rich girl who supposedly spends a cool fortune annually on her own wardrobe."

It's a confusing divide. Is she thoughtful or selfish? Kind or careless? A figure of historical significance or a silly, spoiled girl?

·

Sometime in spring or summer of 1971, she volunteers as a teacher's aide at the McMahon Memorial Temporary Shelter. Once a week, for several months, she goes up to East Harlem to work with the children of drug-addicted parents.

A six-year-old from a different class whispers to an adult: "Didn't she used to be married to President Kennedy?" But the three– and four-year-olds she works with are too young to know that the white lady playing building blocks on the floor is the most famous woman in the world.

She does this privately. Nancy Tuckerman and the public are equally in the dark. They will not hear that she had done this until the following winter, when Maxine Cheshire gets a confirmation from one of the nuns running the shelter. A confirmation given reluctantly, because the nun knows it ensures she probably will not return.

·

That spring, in imitation of a *Life* survey conducted the previous January, the humanities students at Southeast Polk High School in

Pleasant Hill, Iowa, poll students on heroes and non-heroes. Jackie appears on a list of "top ten vote-getters" in the hero category, along with President Nixon, President Kennedy, President Lincoln, Vice President Spiro Agnew, John Wayne, and Jesus Christ.

This isn't as flattering an accolade as it may seem at first glance, as she also appears on the list of "top ten in non-heroes," accompanied by Nixon, Agnew, Cassius Clay, Charles Manson, Joe Namath, and Hitler.

She is the only woman the students identify.



VILLE FRANCE-SUR-MER. CAPRI. SICILY. ARI IS WITH HER, reportedly buying "several thousand dollars' worth" of jewels. The Os sip aperitifs in a floating café and wander the city. In published photographs, she is billed as "The widow of assassinated President John F. Kennedy" and shown strolling with Caroline. Everyone looks happy. Everything seems fine.

In Portofino, she wears "a revealingly tight red sweater" and the Italians wonder if "Jackie Onassis showed up without a bra." The photo goes out across the wires with an obscenity warning that suggests "EDITORS: PLEASE NOTE NATURE OF MRS. ONASSIS'S COSTUME."

It is, a French tabloid reports, "a sweater which left little of the twin charms of her bust to the imagination."

Within the month, questions surface in a syndicated gossip column: "Is Mrs. Onassis one of those bra burners?" *Definitely not!* comes the reply from Robin Adams Sloan (the secret pen name of *Cosmopolitan* articles editor Roberta Ashley). The response buys into the popular belief that all the "bra burners" are anti-men and asserts "The [women's] movement doesn't interest her [Jackie] a bit" because "She liked being a feminine woman—in the company of exciting, stimulating men." No, Jackie isn't "a Women's Lib type," the gossip says; just stylish—"apt to behave as other sophisticated resorters do and shuck her undies."

# Cast your ballot today!

## HAS JACKIE FINALLY GONE TOO FAR?

☐ YES! She's old enough to know better!

☐ NO! The photographers should be shot!

☐ WHO CARES? I'm tired of the whole thing!

Mail your ballot to: THE JACKIE LOOK
TV Radio Mirror
205 East 42nd St.
New York, New York
10017

October 1971, *TV Radio Mirror*

She is, at this point, widely believed to be a figure of European hedonism and lax morals. In an article on the demise of the jet set, Marylin Bender, a reporter for the *New York Times*, asks, "What does Jackie stand for today?" Her conclusion: "Nothing, poor thing. Beyond her role as superconsumer, she stands for nothing. She is the ultimate woman-as-object, since she is woman-to-be-bought."

What is really being said here is that what she stands for isn't "good" and is unworthy of all the adulation she receives for it— whatever "it" is. "It" isn't *nothing*. And, even if "it" isn't explicitly clear or consistent, there are intimations of how Jackie's story trickles down into the lives of the women who read about her; how they use stories of her life to navigate issues in their own.

In the April edition of the feminist news journal *Off Our Backs*, bobbie goldstone asked: "Is she or isn't she? Is Jackie oppressed?" She recalls how Jackie was "a rebel and an outlaw at school," quoting the school headmaster's declaration that Jackie's was the "most inspiring mind we've ever had," and cites her ambition "not to be a housewife." Then she observes that, like so many other women, "even Jackie got the old programming" that a woman's role was to be well behaved and work in the home:

> She got it from her mother who wondered out loud to Jackie's friends why was she always so naughty. She got it from the Chapin School dean who told her that wild horses weren't good for anybody, you had to break them in. She got it from her newspaper boss, who told her he didn't want to hire another little girl (Jackie) who would leave and get married. She got it from J.F.K. who "kiddingly" told a wedding night party that he was marrying Jackie to get her out of newspaper reporting because she might be dangerous to his career.

Hers was an experience mirrored in the lives of many American women and one of which they were, increasingly, becoming aware.

That, as a leader of the National Organization of Women wrote, women "are indoctrinated to view themselves as sex objects; as helpless, dumb and witless, as having unmistakable roles: to be pleasing to men; to bear and care for children; and to consume, consume, consume . . . buy, buy, buy: buy to get a husband, buy to make you more desirable; buy to make your floors shine; buy to care for your children; buy to 'fulfill' yourself." Jackie's story was emblematic of this experience and, as goldstone wrote, "I don't want to sound soap-operaish, but from rebel to obsessive consumer is pretty depressing."

Later, when they're looking back, they'll remember her for hav-ing modeled nearly every role a woman can have in life, but that's less visible in this moment. It's hard to see how a life is being used as it's being lived, though the evidence is there, and it suggests she's not just modeling American consumption.

In celebration of her upcoming forty-second birthday, the syn-dicated medical columnist Dr. Eugene Scheimann finally succumbs to the pleas from his mailbag and acknowledges that "Over the past ten years, the one woman I've gotten the most letters about is Jacqueline Onassis," and that "Women in particular seem to want to pattern their behavior after hers." Most of the letters he receives, he notes, are inquiries into whether Jackie should have a baby—a question about Jackie that is actually, Scheimann believes, women wondering "whether they can and should become pregnant at a later age than is usually accepted in our society for having babies."

This is just one example. There are many. What they are doing here is using Jackie to ask about choice.

JULY 28. HER FORTY-SECOND BIRTHDAY. AS THEY DO EVERY year, her children raid her closets and stage a theatrical. That year, it's *The Imaginary Invalid* by Molière. Lee remembers it as "unforgettable." Though it's maybe not a birthday Jackie will later look back upon with undiluted pleasure as, just a few days before, her stepdaughter eloped to Vegas with a man of whom Ari didn't approve.

Christina had met Joseph Bolker in California that summer. Forty-eight, American, Jewish, a man who would be nobody in her father's eyes. She confided to him, told him her father was giving her a hard time. "He used his children, his family, he used everybody," Bolker later said, after he'd been subdued by the full freight of the Onassis legal machine.

Christina refused to be exploited by her father. "Loving is a quest, not a business deal," she told a friend, asserting her right to make her own choice. She chose Bolker and snuck off to Vegas with him two days before her stepmother's birthday. "Wedding News Hurts Jackie's Birthday," the headlines read. A notion reinforced by the fact that there were no announcements of what Ari bought for his wife, no reports of a party.

A spokesperson refuses to accept questions regarding the wedding but, by all accounts, the father of the bride's fury knows no bounds. His friend and employee Costa Gratsos is reportedly his first phone call, and there is so much screaming Gratsos assumes "a major deal had collapsed." Which, to Ari's mind, it probably has.

He's been trying for a while now to marry twenty-year-old Christina off to Peter Goulandris, heir of a wealthy Greek shipping family (a mutually beneficial merger). Reportedly, an engagement had been in the offing four or five times, but Christina kept backing out. Ari believed he would prevail, because didn't he always?

But he didn't understand his daughter. He was oblivious to Christina's desperation for his attention, eager to be loved by her father as her brother was or, at the least, to be for her father something more than a pawn in a business venture. As Kiki Moutsatsos observed, "Mr. Onassis could never have a conversation with his daughter without telling her what to do."

Ari's fury seems endless. Coming from a man who is often apoplectic, this is unparalleled. "Ari went ape," attested his aide Johnny Meyer. "I'd seen him fly off the handle plenty of times but never like that. He was rampant, he was mad enough to chew nails."

Kiki Moutsatsos recalled, "I could not imagine any human being withstanding that unbroken wrath."

His anger, though precipitated by Christina's elopement, likely ran deeper. He'd taken a number of hits in business recently; his fortunes were not what they once were, and his failure to control his daughter—the way it was meant to be in these Greek shipping families, where sons were the future of the family business and daughters were bartering chips—seemed representative of power lost on a larger scale. He was drained by boredom when he didn't have a fight on his hands, and this was a fight if ever there was one. As his business took a downturn, increasingly his family would supply the drama that sustained him.

Immediately, he cuts her off financially.

His aides call it "the Christina problem." It is also, to some degree, a "Tina problem," as it's reportedly Christina's mother who, hearing her daughter is living with Bolker, suggests she either return to Europe or marry him. Christina secretly receives money from Tina, a move of uncharacteristic generosity given that, in the words of her brother Alexander's girlfriend, "To get Tina to break into a five-pound note was a goddam miracle."

But Tina's motivations aren't disinterested. There's already a "buzz-buzz" in the papers that Tina had plans to marry her late sister's husband—Ari's old rival Stavros Niarchos. Conveniently, Tina crowed of Ari to a French friend, "Joe Bolker has replaced Stavros as the man he loves to hate."

There's little Jackie can say or do to help the matter, but she stays by her husband's side from mid-July through nearly the entirety of August. Both stay out of view, no comments. In America, they're gearing up for the gala opening of the Kennedy Center for the Performing Arts and she's expected to attend. People wonder what she'll wear, who she'll sit by, how she'll look. But that summer, she mostly avoids the looming collision with her Kennedy life, and stays in Skorpios, soaking up the sun, skirting the family drama.

•

The family drama, however, is unavoidable. Lee is recovering from a hysterectomy and staying on Skorpios with her children. Peter Beard, a friend brought over in the capacity of an informal babysitter to entertain the kids, is also there. Beard is a photographer and an artist. Jackie invites him to Skorpios because he's good company, because John and Caroline adore him, because he's good looking, and because her sister is depressed. He and Lee are drawn to one another like magnets.

Lee's marriage to Stas has been troubled for years. He was older and he loved her deeply. But, as she later told a reporter, "I was a foreigner married to another foreigner, living in a foreign country. That's fairly difficult in a way. We both missed our own countries a lot." For a 1967 profile entitled "Girls Who Have Everything Are Not Supposed to Do Anything," she told *Life*, "One reason we get on so well is that we're both essentially loners. . . . It can be so exhausting to be polite, you know."

But she wanted more, and like her sister, she wanted to escape. "The world I grew up in—of family business and bridge playing and special schools—that was something I wanted out of," she said. "It couldn't have been more pleasant, you understand, and yet it had no meaning for me." And so she went to Europe and then she came home to America and tried theater and TV. "My deep regret," Lee tells Andy Warhol, "is that I wasn't brought up or educated to have a métier. . . . The only thing that gives you any real sense of fulfillment is to accomplish something, no matter how small or insignificant it might be considered."

But nothing seems to stick; she is always just Jackie's sister. Always one of those "whispering sisters," and the lesser one at that. Now, here's this sexy American artist—five years her junior, just back from safari, and he's into her. She is enamored.

When they separate at summer's end and Peter returns to Kenya, Lee pursues him with countless impassioned letters. Jackie thinks Peter is good company and she's grateful to have him around the kids, telling them about photography and adventure and life, but she doesn't approve of the affair, and she makes that clear. She adores Stas and she hates that Lee is being so cavalier.

•

In the middle of all this domestic drama, Stas's brother dies, leaving him an absolute wreck. In a letter to Rose Kennedy, Jackie writes of Stas's grief and Lee's ill health; she says that she feels her presence is needed with them. And so she skips the opening of the John F. Kennedy Center for the Performing Arts and goes to Warsaw instead.

When she arrives, the communist government plays it cool, wanting to avoid close associations with the aristocracy of the dispossessed princes, the former First Lady of a democratic country, and a Catholic funeral. But Polish TV news covers her arrival and an article in the Warsaw morning paper reports details of her visit.

There is considerable public interest in her, at home in America but also abroad. In Poland, that interest comes to a head in a small town on the outskirts of Warsaw upon which thousands now descend.

The news reports leave no detail behind: her dress is black; the bench she sits on is yellow; the service lasts forty minutes. Though loads of Polish aristocracy attend, the *L.A. Times* observes, "It plainly was Mrs. Onassis . . . who was attracting the crowds." At the requiem Mass, the officiating priest spends fifteen minutes clearing the crowd from the steps so the mourners can get through. At the cemetery, as the pallbearers carry the coffin in, the crowd trails in their wake, pushing to see her and asking, "Where is Jackie?"

It's a family funeral and 4,000 people have turned up to watch.

It's too much. Ten minutes before the service concludes, she leaves. The crowd follows, shifting in her direction, crushing against her. And, feeling them closing in, she runs.

Out of the cemetery. Into an adjacent potato field. Panicked.

And still they follow. Hundreds of them in pursuit.

Seeing the spectacle from the road above, the operator of a passing streetcar stops to help her. Police beat back the curious

Jackie-watchers trying to board with her and she is taken, without further incident, to her limo parked up the road.

.

The experience was harrowing. Her kids were with her, so she either consciously left them with Lee and Stas, or was so spooked by the response of the crowd that she entirely forgot them. All those people, all that noise. Her effort to take control by leaving leads to nothing but awareness of how little control she has and how unprotected she is.

A few days later, Nancy Tuckerman reports to the press that she was "extremely frightened." It was a "dreadful experience. . . . People were literally trying to rip off her clothes."

Tuckerman tells reporters that Jackie had told her "she had never been so frightened in her life." A phrase that jars, given all she's experienced.

.

The gala opening of the Kennedy Center for the Performing Arts is one week away. Already, she's wary of attending. She skipped the Center's preview in late May. Early speculation is this had to do with the fact that, in President Nixon's absence, the Secret Service wouldn't be able to guarantee her full protection, though—despite the brouhaha in Poland—inadequate security seems an unlikely excuse.

These things are always difficult—returning to Washington, remembering Jack in public—and sometimes, when it's too difficult, she refuses. That's probably what happened here. Between Stas's grief, Lee's depression, the scene at the funeral, and the crowds anticipated in Washington, D.C., there were many reasons for her absence; but there was also the brutality of these public remembrances. They don't seem to be getting any easier, and she tries to avoid them whenever she can. And so she stays in Greece and lets the Kennedys go out in their finery and play royalty in the city they once ruled.

On the day of the opening, she and Ari are spotted fishing off Skorpios. "Despite what many hoped, the Onassis marriage is working out groovy," Fred Sparks reports. "Jackie has all the money she needs—zillions!—and, more important, she has her freedom, a freedom she didn't have as the wife of the most important statesman on earth."

·

"Photographers still stalk Jackie Onassis here. But in Greece, doesn't she have more privacy because of Ari?" asks a reader from Tampa. No, no, came the answer, "the paparazzi buzz around Skorpios like a plague of locust," with one of them catching "full frontal nude snaps of the 42-year-old former First Lady of America."

The negatives circulate among the tabloids, along with an offer from an Athens attorney "on behalf of an unnamed party"—Ari?— of $25,000 for their return. Freedom, indeed.

·

She allows *House Beautiful* magazine into 1040 Fifth to take color photographs of her dining room and library, two rooms featuring the Design Works fabrics. They appear in the September issue.

Americans have read about her nearly every day for the past ten years, but they know very little about her home beyond its address. And now here she is flinging open the doors.

They are invited to know: She keeps a strand of Greek amber worry beads on her coffee table. . . . There's a fabric called "Fish Head Plaid" in her dining room and "Large Feathers" in her library . . . it's surprisingly homey, surprisingly normal. . . . As Maxine Cheshire reports, "She hasn't been living like Marie Antoinette."

They're also told that "Mrs. Onassis first said 'yes' and then 'no' and then 'yes' again," and that it took "more than a year of coaxing" for her to agree to these photographs that reveal how she uses these designs in "her private 'at home' world." This reluctance makes the images feel even more precious, because Jackie herself was uncertain she wanted to reveal so much; she wasn't sure she wanted to let us in.

IN OCTOBER, CHRISTINA LEAVES BOLKER AND RETURNS TO
Europe. But Ari's victory is diminished by Tina's marriage to
Stavros Niarchos.

Tina's sister Eugenie had been married to Niarchos before her
death under suspicious circumstances in May 1970 and now, just a
year later—as Ari says, "the grave had hardly closed on her sister"—
here Tina was marrying him. Ari, according to Costa Gratsos,
"behaved like an injured lover."

The press reports describe Ari as ill-tempered. "Leave me alone,"
he says brusquely to the newsman waiting outside his Athens office.

"He is trying to marry Tina to tease me," Ari tells a friend who
tells the papers. "The S.O.B.s are gathering in Paris to hurt me."

That the news is accompanied by claims that "Niarchos is now
thought to be even richer than Onassis" also grates.

Two marriages he disapproves of. Two women who have defied
him.

•

Thanks to Christian Kafarakis—a former *Christina* steward who
was briefly in Ari's employ before he married Jackie—the gossip is
that the Onassises have a 170-clause marriage contract stipulating
separate bedrooms and detailing Onassis's "greatest generosity,"
which keeps his wife "sheltered from want."

The *New York Times* reports the marriage contract rumor on
November 1. Reading the article and presumably remembering
her previous conversations with Jackie's financial advisor, André
Meyer, Dorothy Schiff imagines "Meyer made outrageous demands
on Ari in an effort to bust up the projected marriage." Schiff, who
also knows Jackie, surmises Ari was angry and Jackie "told him to
forget the whole negotiation and flew over to marry him without
any agreement."

The specifics of Schiff's version aren't verifiable, but the spirit
seems accurate: several accounts report that, after the marriage,
Meyer was distraught that he hadn't been able to negotiate a deal for
Jackie, a circumstance supporting the idea that she could have done

better for herself and didn't. It's provocative that a woman whose need for financial security was typically identified as her great flaw didn't do more to secure her financial independence at the outset of this marriage, and also an indication of how much she trusted Ari.

The next day, Nancy Tuckerman publicly denounces the rumors as "ridiculous . . . really quite unfair and unkind" and "fabricated"—a denial that also runs in the *New York Times.*

In private, Ari is more forceful. Talking to his aide Johnny Meyer, he reportedly scoffs, "Anyone who believes that garbage can go fuck themselves."

•

But this story of the boat steward captures the public imagination. How many Americans have even seen a marriage contract, much less one with 170 clauses? A columnist in Maryland reports: "Area women are buzzing about that marriage contract Jacqueline Onassis has with her husband." One woman informs the columnist: "The next time I marry, I'm sure going to get a contract like that one."

This likely mythical document is always referred to as a "contract" (rather than a prenup) and, therefore, framed as a business deal. And much is made of its specification that the couple occupy separate bedrooms at all times and the financial arrangements ($10,000 a month for clothes, $7,500 a month for cosmetics and hairdressing, $625,000 per year for Jackie's "comfort, pleasure and children"). But, beyond all the money, there are other surprising provisos, like how "Jackie has absolute license" to travel, and a stipulation that the Os are to be together over summer holidays and principal Roman Catholic feasts.

Combined, these details support the themes that characterize their marriage as the press portrayed it: money over sex, apart more often than together; the very things that make their marriage appear unconventional. But they also lay out the practicalities of how such an unconventional marriage might work. No one knows what is going on with Ari and Maria, but Ari and Jackie are still together,

and they look happy enough. Reading these stories, you might imagine perhaps a marriage contract has something to do with that.

The story of the marriage contract is entertaining precisely
because it is so unbelievable. A reporter at the *Boston Globe* discusses the reports with his wife. "I read every word of it and I'm
sure every other wife and mother who saw it did the same," she
says, even though she admits that it's so overblown that she doesn't
think it's true.

•

Sometime in mid-November, around Caroline and John's birthdays, she drafts a statement. It is her "greatest wish," she writes,

> that there may be an end to the wealth of misinformation
> which continues to appear in print. All the speculation and
> inaccuracies concerning our family life and way of living are
> totally unrealistic and out of proportion. While I do not
> care for my sake, I do care for the sake of my children. This
> is what I think about most (now that they are older?) of all
> on their birthdays /—that somehow all this erroneous folk-
> lore (xx all these myths?) will cease to be written. It's what
> matters most of all to me.

At the bottom of the page, she scrawls a note to Nancy
Tuckerman: "by 'way of living' I really mean money. Does it sound
that way to you?"

The memo is filed for later use. It seems never to have been
released.

•

The marriage contract story, which appears to substantiate
Sparks's claims that Jackie is rolling in dough, is still circulating
when two people the press universally refers to as "Mrs. Jacqueline
Kennedy Onassis' aunt and cousin" are revealed to be living in an

"indescribably filthy . . . crumbling, 28-room mansion" that presents a "health hazard to occupants."

Mrs. and Miss Edith Bouvier Beale: seventy-six and fifty-four, respectively. The Bouviers were a wild and rowdy bunch but, in a family of strong characters, this pair are the most colorful by far, a trait that always drew the young Jackie Bouvier to them. A Bouvier cousin remembered how "Little Edie" had been a fashion plate, "one of the first girls to wear skintight latex bathing suits" at the Maidstone Club in Southampton, while her mother, always called "Big Edie," was "a wacky Auntie Mame who had no use for conventions and a hearty disrespect for respectability." At family gatherings, Jackie always made a beeline for Big Edie, whom she later called "a genteelly subversive influence."

In 1924, Big Edie's husband, Phelan, purchased a mansion called Grey Gardens. Twenty years later, when he divorced his wife via telegram, Phelan Beale provided her a pittance for upkeep. Little Edie returned to live in Grey Gardens with her mother in the '60s, and by 1971, their circumstances had deteriorated to an appalling degree. No running water, failing toilets, fleas, and twenty-five violations of the sanitation code. The situation and the stench were so appalling that when the investigation team from the Department of Health and Sanitation came out, three members vomited.

The head of the health department's housing and sanitation division declares of the Beales, "These are unfortunate people."

Unfortunate, maybe, but also amazing copy. It's like something out of Faulkner. Little Edie shouting down to the reporters from the second story window. Big Edie always calling, "*EeeDIE!* Where is my champagne cocktail?" Both of them closed up in what the *L.A. Times* calls that "haggard-looking, three-story mansion," but which Little Edie sees as "oozing with romance, ghosts and other things."

It's the "other things" that concern the neighbors, who wonder where the Beales' famous relative is during all of this, how she could let it get so bad. Jackie's aunt and cousin living in squalor! And Jackie, with all that money, out on her island, doing nothing.

The Beales hope she won't hear about it. "She is fond of us and we are fond of her," Little Edie tells the reporters. "I told mother tonight that I'm going to write a letter and tell her all about it." But, truth is, she can't help but hear about it as it's all over the papers. "Jackie's Kin Found Living Amid Filth" . . . "Mrs. Onassis' Cousin Says Raid Hurt Sale" . . . "Kin Hopes Jackie Doesn't Find Out."

In reality, it has little to do with her. Big Edie has two adult sons—the women are hardly alone in the world and taking care of them is the Beale boys' responsibility, so Jackie says nothing. Asked if the Beales' famous relative knows what is going on, Nancy Tuckerman replies, "Mrs. Onassis is very fond of all her family. This is a personal thing."

## MONDAY EVENING, NOVEMBER 22, 1971
*"Where the Spirit of the Lord Is, There Is Liberty."—II Cor. 3-17*

SHE TRIES TO ENJOY HERSELF. EARL WILSON REPORTS SEE-ing the Os out at Casino Russe, tangoing and requesting Russian songs from the balalaika player. She wears "chic pants" and "gently and good-naturedly" guides her husband away from the blonde with whom he is dancing. The conclusion: "Jackie as Mrs. Onassis is separating herself from the Kennedy tradition and image."

•

The following week, Design Works makes a splashy debut at the Metropolitan Museum of Art. "It's a moment of glory for Bedford-Stuyvesant," says Design Works' head, C. Mark Bethel. Not only because it catapults the fabrics into a broader and wealthier level of consumers, but because it provides a template for how work can revitalize a community's economy.

Ethel Kennedy, Bobby's widow, arrives. Two minutes later, Jackie enters, whereupon "Everyone in the room—1,050 persons, a security guard—senses the excitement of her presence," and surges toward her as her companions form a protective circle around her, linking hands.

Jackie is loquacious, telling reporters she used the fabrics in eight of the bedrooms on Skorpios and three of the rooms at 1040 Fifth, and now she's heard they're doing rugs and she wants to see those. "I want to see everything," she says. "I love the fabrics." Scheduled to stay for only fifteen minutes, she remains for ninety. She watches the performance of the George Faison Universal Dance Experience and, as she leaves, she tells reporters, "I wish I could stay longer. I feel like dancing, too."

*Women's Wear Daily*: "When Jackie O believes in a crusade she really turns on."

FRED SPARKS, THE BEALES, AND THE MARRIAGE CONTRACT story aren't the only unwanted attention she's been getting. In the autumn of 1970, Ron Galella sued her, claiming that in sic'ing her agents on him and telling them to "break his camera" in September 1969, she interfered with his livelihood. She countersued, claiming he made her life hell. He sued for $1.3 million; she sued for $1.5. Working their way through the legal system, the suits are about to be presented in a New York court together, before a judge with no jury.

On December 3, in an initial affidavit, she swears Galella makes her "an absolute prisoner" in her apartment because of "the intimidation and harassment" that would come from "any venture onto the sidewalks." She asks the court to prevent Galella from making her life "miserable."

"Does she look to you like a woman who is being tortured?" Ron Galella asks of her appearance in his photographs. But the still image obscures and, in this case, glamorizes the reality.

"It was like a lens making love to a lens, the minute the camera was there," the editor of *Women's Wear Daily* suggested. "Her whole demeanor turned on when she saw a camera." But what John Fairchild casts here in sexual terms can also be interpreted as a hypervigilance, not just around cameras but the flashbulbs and the pushing crowds that accompany them.

These are not still scenes: she doesn't just walk into a room, encounter a photographer, smile, and have her photo taken. A reporter from the *Saturday Evening Post* records how, upon her entry at an art event, everyone exclaimed, "There she is!" and "the words seemed to hit Jacqueline Kennedy like the wail of an air raid siren." It's a tense, often overwhelming moment and her response is visceral, not sexy. She freezes and the shutter snaps and the photo renders serene a woman who is, in reality, distressed.

A journalist once complained to Bobby Kennedy, "Jackie wants it both ways," and argued that if she truly wanted to be left alone she just wouldn't go out in public. If she really "does not want to be bothered by publicity," Merriman Smith wrote in 1966, "there is one sure way of avoiding it—play in seclusion." But she doesn't see total seclusion as an option, and so she tries to command the attention on her own terms. One columnist notes of her situation with Galella that "Her problem at such times is twofold: to discourage Galella and yet to look as good as possible in the pictures he is taking." Because, ultimately, he will get the picture: better to have it be a good one than an unflattering shot.

Elizabeth Taylor and Richard Burton's bodyguard had recently roughed up Galella, so Jackie isn't alone in her dislike of his tactics, but she is by far his most profitable subject. The photographer estimates earnings of $15,000 a year on his Jackie photographs alone (equivalent to nearly $104,000 in 2022), such a substantial figure that *Life* jokes, "Mrs. Onassis might well list him as a dependent." He's aware of his debt and acknowledges it, saying, "I know that I'd be almost nothing without her."

And, in his own way, he tries to be respectful, usually donning a suit when he photographs her and destroying unflattering photographs. He has no wish to embarrass her, he says: "I want to make her look good, but spontaneous, natural, the way she really is." But she doesn't like his tactics, or that when he shoots, he calls her "Jackie baby."

Like Fred Sparks and Mary Gallagher and everyone poring over the 578 words of the "Dear Ros" letters, Galella is trying to get to the Real Jackie. *Life* calls it a "three-year telephoto love affair" and, if it isn't necessarily love, it is certainly addiction of a sort—to the thrill of their encounters, the game of it, the chase. Speaking to *Esquire*, he suggests it's a game she plays well: "[She's] always trying to outwit me." Galella needs something new and different in each shot if it's going to sell and sell high, but she often repeats outfits and wears lots of black—both of which curtail his profits. She is "fascinated" by his tactics, he thinks. "And why not?" he asks. "We have a lot in common. I'm persistent. I get what I want. So does she. She wants to dominate, to do things when she wants."

"Oh," he says, "she's foxy, all right."

•

Always, the press and so many of those watching believe she is playing a game. Up and down the newsstand there's general agreement that, in the words of *Life*, she "hates publicity and yet loves her celebrity." Gossip Sheilah Graham notes, "Her behavior is often spectacular . . . and the press has a sixth sense and is always there when it happens." A columnist asserts, "Mrs. Onassis doesn't like being jostled by fans, but likes the wave of recognition she creates. . . . The lady enjoys being a celebrity."

The movie magazines are a bit gentler in their critique. "It's conceivable that she's genuinely annoyed at the harassment of the lensmen," *TV Radio Mirror* allows, "but would be even more disappointed if she were ignored." *Screen Stories* places much of the blame on the media, admitting that the Jackie stories are "not exactly red hot material for scandals," but "Jackie is news. Jackie's name sells papers, Jackie's face sells magazines."

Of course, these publications contribute to the frenzy. "Jackie. Jackie. Jackie," Galella notes.

> Everything depends on Jackie. Jackie is international, the biggest star all over the world. She doesn't have to do anything but step out of her door to make news. . . . There are at least fifty fan magazines and they'll all buy pictures of Jackie. *The National Enquirer* will buy any new pictures of Jackie at any time. [They] never get tired of her.

She says she wants absolutely nothing to do with the movie magazines, but her relationship with them isn't straightforward, as she also reads them.

Her White House Secret Service agent Clint Hill recalled that "She loved to read the tabloids—especially if there were articles or photos of her in them." One of her maids reportedly told Galella there was a closet in 1040 Fifth that Jackie kept stacked full of magazines and newspaper clippings, and Galella himself caught her buying issues of magazines featuring her on their covers. These claims are supported by the inclusion of movie magazines in the JFK Library files and a pile of approximately 250 Kennedy-related magazines in the 1995 Sotheby's auction of her estate, including issues of *Modern Screen*. After *Photoplay*'s editor testified on her behalf at the Galella trial, Jackie's lawyer asked for a subscription on his client's behalf, saying, "She thoroughly enjoys reading those stories about her," as one newspaper reported.

Part of that enjoyment may have been in seeing which of her acquaintances were tipping off the press. In Nancy Tuckerman's archives at the JFK Library, there's a copy of the one-off movie magazine *The New Jackie*, from summer 1970. A corner is folded down on a page that includes this observation:

> "Jackie gives me the feeling that she's the dependent type, a leaner, a woman who takes her opinions from men

whose opinions are worth having." One old acquaintance (male) who ran into her after a long time away admitted, "I forgot how beguiling she can be—that feathery voice comes down to a whisper so you're leaning in her face to hear, her attention is absolutely concentrated on you. Jacqueline absolutely exudes femininity. She makes you feel you're Mr. Big."

In the margins next to this section sits an X in blue ink. We are left to wonder at its meaning.

Whether she reads them for entertainment or to sleuth out leakers among her acquaintance, she isn't the only Kennedy wife reading these magazines. Joan Kennedy avoids them like the plague, but Ethel reads them religiously and reportedly saves clippings in a scrapbook. "Every week she had me cutting articles out of *Photoplay, Modern Screen, Movieland*, and all the rest of them," remembers one of her assistants. A columnist for the *Boston Globe* notes that when Ethel comes into the salon, she demands complete privacy and carries a pile of movie magazines with Jackie and Ari on the cover. When a reader asks a gossip whether the people in fan magazines read about themselves, the response is that Ethel Kennedy does and, according to one fan magazine editor, Ethel told him she "reads the movie magazines all the time and will even stop and fluff up her hair for photographers, saying, 'I want to make myself beautiful for Screen Stars.'"

The curious reality is that all the Kennedy women are reading stories about themselves—in the papers, the movie magazines, gossip columns, and books. Rose reads Gail Cameron's biography of herself and is bedeviled by the inaccuracies. JFK's sister Eunice sees a rumor in print about the yacht Ari is reportedly buying Jackie for her forty-first birthday and asks her mother if it's true. The news that her former daughter-in-law was chased by the mob in Warsaw also comes to Rose via newspaper report.

They read stories about themselves and wonder to one another whether they are true. Then maybe they ask Jackie or Ethel or whomever the story is about for confirmation. "I talked with Jackie last night as I had heard a rumor she was not well," Rose writes in her diary, "and she said she was feeling fine." Even as the Galella trial is going on, Rose notes, "Jackie phoned and we were discussing some of the ridiculous stories printed about her in the fan magazines."

•

She is often believed to be complicit. Her friend Franklin Roosevelt, Jr. tells Dorothy Schiff that Nancy Tuckerman tips off the press whenever Jackie goes out. But he also says Jackie hired a big public relations firm after the assassination, a claim for which there is no evidence. Schiff discusses something similar with Jackie during a lunch meeting and records: "She mentioned something she has said before, that she is a very private person. She said that all those women who are in the columns all the time have press agents," the implication being she finds this distasteful.

There is, however, evidence of contact with select members of the press: the editors of women's magazines (particularly *McCall's*), certain reporters, and publishers. Sometimes this involves Nancy Tuckerman or her press secretary Pamela Turnure taking a lunch or placing a phone call, providing background. Often, it occurs under the auspices of correcting misinformation.

She's disturbed by the disconnect between who she is and what she reads about herself. "I picked up the newspaper today," she tells a friend, "and read this story about this absolutely horrible woman—and it was me."

"I don't know of any public figure whose public image was at greater variance with private reality," one of her friends later recalled, and Jackie's interventions with the press seem to have been about bridging this gap. Most often this is done through denials and authorized public statements, to which she increasingly resorts during this period. This fits the pattern of trying to dispel stories rather than promote them, but it's a flawed approach that is, in part, responsible for further fueling the stories she hopes to kill.

For, once one detail has been denied, everything subsequent requires a denial. She couldn't deny the story of the judo flip outside the sex movie then say nothing about the "Dear Ros" letters or the boat steward's claims. It's all or nothing and silence would, from then on, be interpreted as confirmation. And so the denials keep coming, which often means rumors from Europe are given new life through denials in New York. So the stories keep coming too.

•

There are so many things she cannot control. Her sister says just the ringing of the phone excites fears of bad news. But she thinks she can control the constant violation of her privacy and keep Galella from getting up in her face and bothering her children and calling her "Jackie baby." It's important enough to her that she submits to being part of the total circus a trial will inevitably become. It will make a point and perhaps keep Galella at a greater distance, although she must realize it is, ultimately, futile. The people want pictures. Galella knows this, intimately.

"As 1971 draws to a close," a columnist notes, "women everywhere, whether in or out of women's organizations have been jolted out of diaper-changing oblivion and into the realities of war, pollution, politics, morality, and other of life's bruises . . . lib has made today's woman aware and conscious that she is living in a world of change." And yet, Galella says, "ugliness isn't what all the women in the drugstores and the supermarkets with their copies of *Modern Screen* and *Cosmo*" want. Americans are, he thinks, "tired of war and ugliness and poverty and conflict." They want "glamour, beauty, wealth and success stories about famous people . . . Jackie at the tennis court on a lovely fall afternoon in Central Park." They want "to see her as being even more beautiful than she really is," which is what he gives them.

So much is so depressing—war in Vietnam rolling on endlessly, unemployment up, the U.S. dollar down—that it helps: these pictures of Jackie on a bike, Jackie in a café, Jackie shopping at Bonwits, Jackie with her slender figure and her millions wearing old jeans, hair blowing in the wind. Galella's pictures make her accessible, and they keep her on the newsstand and in people's minds and lives. Glamour, beauty, wealth, and success, Galella says. But also connection.

Americans know so much about her. Maybe not facts, but stories. They know her shoe size and her address and where she shops, but they also know how much remains private still. And it feels like with just one more story, one more picture, one more magazine profile, they might figure it all out: who she is, why she matters, why they care.

# 1972

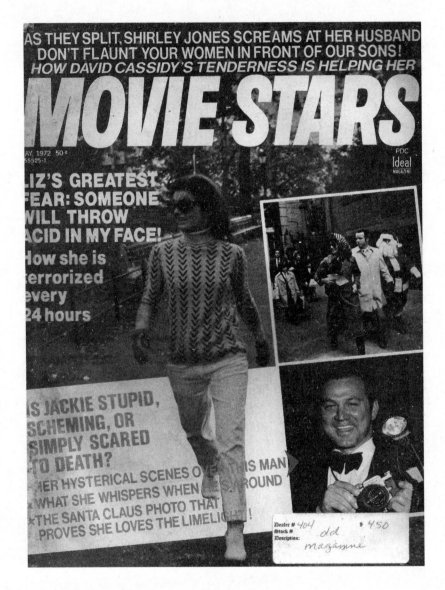

AS THEY SPLIT, SHIRLEY JONES SCREAMS AT HER HUSBAND
DON'T FLAUNT YOUR WOMEN IN FRONT OF OUR SONS!
*HOW DAVID CASSIDY'S TENDERNESS IS HELPING HER*

# MOVIE STARS

AY, 1972 50¢
55525-1

PDC
Ideal
MAGAZINE

LIZ'S GREATEST
FEAR: SOMEONE
WILL THROW
ACID IN MY FACE!
How she is
terrorized
every
24 hours

IS JACKIE STUPID,
SCHEMING, OR
SIMPLY SCARED
TO DEATH?
★ HER HYSTERICAL SCENES OVER THIS MAN
★ WHAT SHE WHISPERS WHEN HE'S AROUND
★ THE SANTA CLAUS PHOTO THAT
  PROVES SHE LOVES THE LIMELIGHT!

THE BRITISH PAPERS REPORT A MASSIVE FIGHT IN THE VIP lounge at Heathrow. An airport official tells the *Daily Telegraph* about a "heated exchange of words"; according to a Pan Am employee, it was "a flaming row." The rumors are loud enough that Ari refutes them, telling newsmen in London, "someone made the whole thing up." "I am afraid this story comes from some of my lesser friends," he contends, friends "who seem to be trying either to bury me or divorce me. It is complete nonsense. I am joining Jackie in New York next week. I would say that we are a happily married couple."

•

On February 17, the Galella circus resumes, and she takes the witness stand. The courtroom is jammed with spectators. They come for the whole day or just on their lunch breaks, eating sandwiches out of brown bags while they absorb details of Jackie's limousines, vacations, and shopping trips. "There is Mrs. Aristotle Onassis, in person, and one can stare for hours," a journalist writes of this scene. "There she is on the witness stand, facing a crowd come to see her, saying she doesn't think the public is interested in her."

Given the context, her claims appear ludicrous. People *are* interested, which is Galella's counterargument. His lawyers claim she doesn't have the same privacy rights as anyone else and that photographs of her are uniquely desirable due to the sense that her lifestyle "represents the American dream." Her lawyers contend this is about a "Peeping Tom," and base their case on newly developed theories that oppressive surveillance is a privacy violation, even when carried out in public. It's an area of law that is unclear at the time, and, according to one analyst, "the lack of clarity is further compounded by the fact that Mrs. Onassis is a former First Lady, the wife now of one of the world's richest men and a perennial entry on the lists of both the 'best-dressed' and 'most-admired' women."

The crux of her case lay in her lawyers' distinction between public figures and private people. Her contention seems to have been this: The attention she received stemmed from her position as the wife of President John F. Kennedy and, while he chose to be a public figure, her marriage to him did not automatically make her one. And so, because she neither sought the status of being a public figure nor earned it, she felt she should not be treated the same as an actress or a politician or someone whose career depended upon their visibility. It's a definition seemingly undermined by her occasional public appearance at events like the Design Works exhibition. But in such cases, there was nearly always a link back to the Kennedys, and so her participation in public life was still, as she saw it, strictly limited to promoting the legacy of her husband and his brother.

From her perspective, this definition makes sense. The old adage that a woman's name should appear in print only when she was born, when she married, and when she died would have been heard often during her youth (I heard it often enough during mine, fifty years later). And while that may not necessarily have been the life for her—she wanted adventure and discovery and something different—she also couldn't have foreseen how much attention she would receive because of her life with Jack Kennedy.

It was unprecedented: the story of no other American woman had ever been followed so closely.

As the public sphere continued expanding through the 1960s and into the 1970s, her attitude increasingly contradicted the prevailing trends in America. More and more, people exposed their private lives, letting the cameras in and revealing all, but she wouldn't. Given the generation and class she grew up in and her continued insistence on protecting her privacy, her argument that she was not a public figure makes sense.

It was also completely untenable. Adhering to a strict split between public and private lives was no longer possible in 1972. It wasn't just that her position in American life had changed; American culture had changed too.

•

Ari is reportedly angry she's suing Galella. He thinks it's a waste of time and that they're bound to be photographed anyway so why bother. Plus, the European photographers are way worse. At one point, Ari tells Galella he's "like a baby compared to the *paparazzi* in Europe." And even as the Galella trial is ongoing in New York, back in Greece, the *paparazzo* Nikos Koulouris is taken to court and sentenced to a six-month prison stint for his repeated and aggressive attempts to take photographs of Skorpios. Witnesses on the Onassises' behalf told the Greek court that Koulouris had thrown rocks at John Jr., made Jackie's life "unlivable," and that Ari was thinking of giving up the island as a result. To Ari, Galella seemed more of a bother than a real threat.

Once the suit is moving forward, Galella approaches Ari, who says, "I hear you're suing my wife. Maybe we could settle this for a couple of thousand dollars . . . I don't want publicity." Ari doesn't want publicity, but he also doesn't want to pay. When Galella offers to settle for $100,000, Ari demurs, saying it's "too much."

In early May, it's reported that the United States government has filed suit against Galella, too, barring him from taking photographs of Mrs. Onassis and the kids because his "outrageous behavior" interferes with their Secret Service protection. Jackie is triumphant. But skepticism persists, as does the impossibility of what she wants.

A reporter asks a photographer friend: "Do you think she really desires all the privacy?" The photographer's response: "It's my own impression that what she really wants is a maximum of publicity when she has some reason for it, and a maximum of privacy when she's off-stage, as it were. And that combination is as impossible as being a gregarious hermit, or a chaste prostitute."

THE 1972 PRESIDENTIAL CAMPAIGN IS RAMPING UP. ALABAMA'S SEG-regationist governor George C. Wallace has an edge over the other Democratic candidates, George McGovern and Hubert Humphrey, in the Michigan and Maryland primaries taking place on May 16. Wallace makes a campaign appearance at a shopping mall in Maryland the day before. After speaking for thirty minutes, he turns to leave the podium and moves into the crowd of 1,000 people to shake hands, when suddenly, a man yells, "Hey, George!" sticks a gun in Wallace's stomach, and pulls the trigger. The bullet lodges in Wallace's spinal column, paralyzing the governor from the waist down.

If there was a chance Ted Kennedy was going to run in '72, it evaporates now. But they knew all along that this was a risk. In that month's issue of *Good Housekeeping*, an interview with Joan Kennedy conducted prior to the Wallace shooting reveals that her husband receives hundreds of death threats each week. She admitted to living in constant fear that he would be murdered. "I would do anything that Ted would want to do and I certainly wouldn't make it difficult for him if the presidency is what he wants—someday." But, she admits, "I hope it's not this year."

"It is getting to the point," an editorialist observes, "where presidential candidates are going to be harder to find than the guns with which deranged zealots can so easily wipe them out."

•

Public life is dangerous. That notion has been reinforced in her life, time and time again. But if she says she isn't a public figure, then what is she? She's photographed. She communicates with the press and details of her private life make it into the papers on a regular basis. She looks like a public figure, and it's further complicated by the fact that her husband is a businessman who needs publicity.

When she and Ari take a sightseeing/business trip to Iran, it makes the American papers. Onassis is negotiating a deal with the Iranian Oil Company to transport crude oil to international markets. He meets with the Shah and goes to a party with a belly dancer. His wife takes a solo overnight trip to Isfahan and Shiraz. Their public embrace upon her return appears, in some American cities, on page one.

While they're in Tehran, a twenty-two-year-old journalist from a local newspaper approaches one night and asks her for an interview. She declines. But the next night, Maryam Kharazmi approaches again and this time, she consents. Kharazmi remembers:

> I asked her what differences there were in her being Mrs. John F. Kennedy and then Mrs. Aristotle Onassis. "People often forget," she answered, "that I was Jacqueline Lee Bouvier before being Mrs. Kennedy or Mrs. Onassis. Throughout my life, however, I've always tried to remain myself and I'll continue to do this as long as I live. I am today what I was yesterday and with luck what I will be tomorrow."
>
> She reminisced about her days in Washington, explaining that she was working as a journalist-photographer conducting interviews when she met Senator Kennedy. "I don't dislike reporters," she declared. "It's just that I get afraid of them when they come at me in a crowd. I don't like the crowds because I don't like impersonal masses. They remind me of swarms of locusts. But having been a reporter myself, I'm aware of what problems a journalist encounters . . ."
>
> When I asked her if she felt better as private Mrs. Onassis than public Mrs. Kennedy, she smiled and replied, "That's a leading question. I'm a woman above everything else. I love children and I think that seeing one's children grow up is the most delightful thing any woman can think about.
>
> "I have been through a lot and suffered a great deal. But I've had lots of happy moments as well. I've come to the conclusion that we must not expect too much from life. At its best life is not too secure and one must seize every moment as it comes.
>
> "Every moment one lives is different from the other," she went on, "the good, the bad, the hardships, the joys,

the tragedies, loves and happiness are all interwoven into one indescribable whole that is called life. You cannot separate the good from the bad. And perhaps, there is no need to do so."

When Kharazmi asks if the stories about her are accurate, she replies, "The truth of the matter is that I am a very shy person. People take my diffidence for arrogance and my withdrawal from publicity as a sign of my supposedly looking down on the rest of mankind."

"Jackie Onassis Not Really Arrogant, Only Shy" scream the subsequent headlines.

Her statements are revealing in that she so rarely speaks about herself in public, but she also doesn't reveal anything new here: she is the same as she always was; she's been through a lot; life is hard, every moment different; reporters are frightening. It's all anodyne stuff.

Curiously, no one wonders why she consented to an interview now on the heels of her legal fight against Ron Galella's contention that she is indeed a public figure. But her flashes of frustration indicate the public image to which she is responding and perhaps why she is speaking out at this particular time. She's particularly bothered by the questions about her husbands, and her answers betray a desire to be seen on her own terms.

There is something about this interview that's far more open and introspective than any other she gives. It's an especially startling contrast to an interview she gives the D.C. reporter Betty Beale a fortnight later. Speaking with Beale over the telephone, she sounds recalcitrant and bored. She "was reluctant to answer personal questions," Beale notes, informing readers that she is "still a very private person." Reminded that the movie magazines feature her relentlessly, she asks Beale simply, "Who cares about movie magazines?"

Beale swears, "One could almost see via the telephone wires the twinkle in her eyes" as she responds "No, I hope not" to the question of whether she would ever write her memoirs and notes the hint of "almost a giggle" when, responding to the clothes horse rumors, she says she usually wears jeans. But, contrasted to Kharazmi's account of her in Iran, she sounds decidedly dimmed down.

At Ethel Kennedy's request, she's flown to D.C. to attend a graveside memorial Mass for Bobby at Arlington on June 6, and a performance at the John F. Kennedy Center for the Performing Arts the evening before. It's a strange time to be giving an interview, but the key to this sequence of events seems to be that she's staying at her mother's house. It is Janet who convinces her to talk to Beale and, according to Beale, it is Janet who suggests she go see Leonard Bernstein's *Mass* at the Center the night before Bobby's memorial.

Involved in the Center's planning for nearly a decade, Janet was co-chair of the Washington Finance Committee when her daughter was First Lady, and co-chair of the dinner parties held around the preview in May 1971. She'd expected her daughter to attend each event, and as each approached, she informed friends and Center personnel her daughter was going to be there. And then she wasn't. The preview passed, then the gala, and still she hadn't shown. Beale noted after the September gala, "It is doubtful if Jackie Onassis has many fans left here after copping out from the premier," but "the person who suffered the most embarrassment when the former First Lady said she was not coming was her mother."

It isn't a good time to be embarrassing Janet. Hugh Auchincloss's brokerage firm had suffered "severe reverses" during the recent economic downturn, which forced him to put Hammersmith Farm on the market in November 1971. "Hugh D. was born in the house, so you can imagine how hard it is for us," Janet confided to Betty Beale, suggesting they hoped to keep a guesthouse and a cottage on the Newport property and to continue to live there.

Janet is a proud woman, and it is a comedown to live in a small house in the corner of the estate that was once just one part of her vast kingdom. It's a humiliation, as was her daughter's seeming disavowal of her work to promote the building of this Center in her son-in-law's memory. It likely wasn't intended as a jab at Janet; mother and daughter seem to have been close during this period. Rather, it reflects Jackie's continuing fear of public commemorations of President Kennedy, which she has avoided since her remarriage in 1968. But this time, for her mother, she relents.

•

The White House press corps finds her in a "conciliatory mood," a circumstance that, two weeks later, still has them "marveling at the 'new' Jacqueline Kennedy Onassis who smiled, spoke to them and found everything beautiful when she visited the John F. Kennedy Center for the Performing Arts." During the "Mass" itself, "Jackie remained cool, placid, unchanged." After, she goes backstage to thank the performers, and one of the choirboys exclaims, "Poor Ms. Onassis," as the cameras crush in.

•

Tuesday, June 6, 8:00 a.m. The Kennedy family, along with friends, Bobby's dog, and a cabal of press, gathers at Arlington Cemetery for a folk Mass to commemorate the fourth anniversary of his death. It's an emotional morning. From Bobby's grave, the group moves to the nearby hillside where Jack lay and she stands before his grave. She is "strained and tired," according to the papers, her beauty "taut with emotion."

She looks like a bystander rather than the widow, so well does she stay in the background. But there is a moment, in front of Jack's grave, where she loses her composure. The surrounding camera shutters snap and the image they catch is one of a woman wrenched with grief.

She remains just for a moment, amid a crowd of Kennedys and milling onlookers, crosses herself, and then approaches a nearby priest to accept Communion—an act from which, as the wife of a divorcé, she is barred. This creates a minor brouhaha, such that later, the chief celebrant excuses himself to the papers: "It would have been a gross affront not to give it to her." Though it is made clear that the Church's policies haven't changed, and it is wrong of her to have done this.

As *Women's Wear Daily* puts it, "She came for two memorial masses, one in a graveyard, the other on a stage" and "Both involved men she loved." Her nerves are shot. Immediately after the service, she and her daughter return to New York. Soon, the papers say, they will be off to Greece.

JUNE 12, 1972. "HER FACE STILL APPEARS MONTHLY ON ONE movie magazine cover or another," *Women's Wear Daily* notes, and "even though her name has fallen to lower positions in those 'Most Admired Woman' polls, the public still considers Jacqueline Kennedy Onassis a Super Star."

"I think she's one of the most influential women on all levels," says the fashion designer Halston. "She can't help but be. She's the most famous woman ever in history."

•

On Sunday, June 18, the *Washington Post* breaks a strange story: in a series of early morning arrests, five men—one of them director of security for the Committee for the Re-election of the President— have been taken into custody after what authorities describe as "an elaborate plot to bug the offices of the Democratic National Committee," which is located within the Watergate complex, a series of office and residential buildings that sit on the Potomac River near the John F. Kennedy Center for the Performing Arts.

A strange story that no one takes too seriously. On June 19, President Nixon's press secretary calls it "a third-rate burglary attempt."

·

The papers describe Martha Mitchell as a "fluffily feminine, chiffon-laden woman with upswept blond hair and a Southern accent," and a penchant for saying "the unthinkable . . . sometimes outrageously." She is the wife of John Mitchell, President Nixon's former attorney general, and she is one of the rare colorful characters in an administration with few superstars. In October 1970, *Life* put her on its cover, noting, "Whenever she is in the public eye—which is often—Martha Mitchell almost always looks as if she's having a grand time."

Mitchell has a fondness for calling journalists in the dead of night and, because she lives in an apartment in the Watergate complex, she's known as "the warbler of Watergate." In the summer of 1972, her husband is head of the Committee for the Re-election of the President.

On June 26, from a hotel in California where she claims she is being held against her will, Martha Mitchell makes a much-publicized "tearful" telephone call to the UPI's White House reporter Helen Thomas. In this call, she refers to herself as "a political prisoner," alludes to bruises and "dirty tricks," threatens to leave her husband if he doesn't leave the Committee, and tells Thomas, "They don't want me to talk." The exclusive goes out under the headline "Martha May Leave Mitchell," as though what she described were merely a domestic dispute. A week later, Thomas files a follow-up piece backing away from her original report and casting Mitchell as a loudmouth for whom the telephone has been both her "trademark and her undoing."

The following week, *Life* reruns a series of photographs from the year before and reports that, since Thomas's initial article, "John Mitchell, who has always stood by his volatile wife, collected Martha at the suburban New York country club where she had been hiding out and then took her away with him."

Martha Mitchell will be blamed for all of this. In a 1977 interview with the broadcaster David Frost, Nixon contends that John Mitchell was "too smart to ever get involved in a stupid jackass thing," and that "if Martha Mitchell's emotional problems hadn't preoccupied her husband," the crime later known simply as "Watergate" wouldn't have happened.

Martha Mitchell will be gone by then, dead of multiple myeloma in 1976. At her funeral, a floral tribute contains the message: MARTHA WAS RIGHT. In 1986, a decade after her death, a psychologist will introduce the concept of the "Martha Mitchell effect": "A misinterpretation of a person's justified belief as a delusion."

THE COURT DISMISSES THE GALELLA CASE AND GRANTS Jackie a permanent injunction requiring the photographer to maintain a distance of fifty yards from her and seventy-five yards from her kids.

A few weeks later, the Greek government arrests eight Greeks and four West Germans, and accuses them of planning a series of kidnappings, robberies, and bombings intended to overthrow the military regime. One of the suspects informs the police that they had plans to kidnap John F. Kennedy Jr., and to blackmail his mother "for as much money as we wanted."

•

"She is a lady who loves attention—only she wants it her way," writes the gossip Jack O'Brian in late July; but even he admits she endures "vicious little embarrassments which shouldn't happen to a French poodle." For instance, the people who crowd outside the children's schools, exclaiming how stuck up she is because she doesn't smile at them. And then they follow her all the way back to 1040 Fifth, commenting on her clothes and her legs, as though Jackie and her kids aren't real people but animals in a zoo.

O'Brian blames the movie magazines and "The continuing phenomenon of . . . dedicating covers endlessly to the female Kennedy Mystique." For it is this "permanent vulgarity," the "angles pursued in these recklessly uninformed rags" and their "trivially reckless misinformation," the "constant errors" and "fictionalizing of fact," that he thinks give the "gawking sensation seekers," these "sidewalk fools," their sense of entitlement. Because "No corner of the Kennedy-Onassis life is safe from fanmag fiction," consequently, her fans consider that same life "a Free Show."

But, in dumping all the blame on the movie magazines, O'Brian conveniently ignores the fact that news magazines, newspapers, and television news—along with gossip columns like his—are reporting the free show too. Her story saturates America.

CAPRI, SARDINIA, CAPRI AGAIN.

July 28. Her forty-third birthday passes with little fanfare in the press, largely eclipsed by the headline: "Jackie Is Paying Bills." When Big Edie Beale tells reporters Jackie and Lee are taking care of everything, Little Edie corrects her, saying, "Oh, mama, for heaven's sake, it's their husbands who are actually paying."

"Aristotle Onassis paid for the repair of the house," says William vanden Heuvel, an old friend Jackie and Lee hired as an attorney for the Beales. "He was very interested. He frequently chatted with Mrs. Beale on the telephone and found her quite charming."

The Os are photographed at an outdoor table at a café in Capri, casual and relaxed. She wears a simple T-shirt and has a scarf wrapped around her head. John Jr. is with them. His hair has grown long. It has just been announced that five men have been convicted in the plot to kidnap him.

According to the American Dairy Association she is "six pounds overweight" and dieting with "fat free cream cheese" ordered from a French farmhouse, delivered via private plane.

"People are film-star crazy," declares Paul Trent, author of a new text on movie stars. And yet, he admits, "People are more interested in Jackie Onassis than movie stars nowadays."

OCTOBER IN NEW YORK. SHE PLANS TO JOIN HER CHILDHOOD friend Senator Claiborne Pell's reelection campaign in what is billed as a four-and-a-half-hour whistle-stop tour through Rhode Island and described by the papers as "her first public activity in a political campaign" since Dallas. But this is more attention than she bargained for. One week later, Nancy Tuckerman announces she's withdrawing: she thought she was just accompanying Pell as a friend rather than a campaigner, and "she feels that her appearance in this campaign activity could be detrimental in her lawsuit in the Ron Galella case."

"She has tried to maintain herself as a private person," Tuckerman tells the press. "If you go out campaigning it puts a different light on the situation."

Privately, she throws a party for Ari that makes all the papers. Held in the Champagne Room of El Morocco, it's to celebrate their fourth wedding anniversary. Eight round tables, pale pink linens, pale pink and white carnations with pink rosebuds.

"She wore a black top, a long white skirt and a heavy gold belt that looked Moroccan," remembers her friend, the reporter Gloria Emerson. "I thought she had the smallest rib cage of any grown-up woman I have ever known." But to Emerson, who has known her since the 1950s, she seems like her old self. After all that has happened, Emerson thinks, she seems happy.

"The El Morocco crowd," writes Earl Wilson, "said she'd never looked prettier nor given such a chic party, and guessed that the tab for 65 people (avec caviar) would be memorable." As he leaves, Ari jokes to an aide, "Don't you pay this! Make sure Jackie signs the tab."

"My friend is indeed an amazing man," a friend of Ari's marvels to Kiki Moutsatsos on this anniversary occasion. "I believe he can go on forever with both Jackie and Maria in his life. They both know what's going on with the other woman, and seem capable of living with the reality of the situation."

There have been changes, of course. "We could all see that [the marriage] had been stronger and more loving when it had begun than it was now," Kiki admits, but "it was far from over."

Shortly after their anniversary, he gives her a document to sign: "Mutual Waiver and Release." Drawn up by his lawyer, it's dispatched over to 1040 Fifth. She seems not to have understood exactly what it was, but she signs it anyway, assuming he will take care of her.

•

Tuesday, November 7 is Election Day in America. When she votes, photographers descend. She appears friendly though dazed, and gamely poses for them in front of the voting booth. When they follow her into the road, she tells them to be careful. As she briskly walks away, a man with a camera around his neck tips his cap to her. She sees this and turns back to give him a small wave before disappearing down the street.

Her former brother-in-law Sargent Shriver, Eunice Kennedy's husband, is running for vice president on the presidential candidate George McGovern's ticket. According to the Gallup poll, McGovern is in for a major defeat, with Nixon leading by a whopping 26 percent. It is the first presidential election since President Nixon signed the 26th Amendment in 1970, lowering the voting age from twenty-one to eighteen. An amendment for which public support had been building since World War II, often around the cliché that if a man was old enough to fight then he should be old enough to vote. A record 80 million Americans are expected at the polls.

"I'm voting for America," Tricia Nixon declares. "I'm voting for my father." Ari reportedly favors Nixon as well, though his wife contributed to McGovern's campaign and also to the reelection of Rhode Island Democratic senator Claiborne Pell under the designation "Jacqueline Onassis, housewife."

Running on a platform of "Peace, Strength, Stability" and the idea that America needs Nixon "Now more than ever," the president carries forty-nine states—earning 520 electoral votes when only 270 are needed to win. With this, "The greatest landslide in history," Nixon declares. "We are on the eve of what could be the greatest generation of peace—true peace—mankind has ever known."

It's a landslide owing a lot to the McGovern campaign's blunders. But, reelected, the president appears reborn. "Nixon [has] the image of a cold and crass and calculating politician without compassion," a columnist muses, but it is, he believes, an image far removed from the reality, for "The real Nixon is a warm, rather shy, basically decent human being . . . the real Nixon is a patriot who would sacrifice his tremendous political ambition for the sake of his country." A victory for all Americans, Richard Nixon swears.

"His manner reaps respect," *Life* observes, "but it also compels a feeling that he does not have enough faith in the people to be candid with them." The two example cited are "the Watergate bugging case and the related charges of political espionage."

She's in New York and, on November 12, she watches the conservative commentator William F. Buckley interview the former prime minister of the United Kingdom, her old friend Harold Macmillan, who has recently published his memoirs. She watches the broadcast at 1040 Fifth with John and Ari, and afterward writes Macmillan, evoking the line from Yeats's poem "The Second Coming," about how "the center cannot hold."

*Wednesday, Nov. 22, 1972*

FRIDAY. *PLAYMEN,* AN ITALIAN "WEEKLY GIRLIE MAGAZINE," publishes fourteen full-color photographs "purporting to show

Mrs. Aristotle Onassis in the nude," with both "full frontal and rear views." Images collected by ten photographers during a one-year siege of Skorpios.

The title of the *Playmen* article: "Jacqueline, the Former First Lady of America: A Tranquil Nudist on the Beach on the Island of Skorpios."

As the Americans are quick to point out, the photographs capture her changing out of a wetsuit, so she is hardly a nudist. "To blow up the latter pictures—front, side and back views—and refer to them as 'total nudism as practiced by Mrs. Onassis' seem a bit much when it took 10 photographers equipped with aqualungs and underwater cameras innumerable hours to get them," observes Betty Beale, who's appalled by the "outrageous invasion of privacy."

But there's more going on here, for the pictures are the coup de grâce in an Italian turf war that some are calling "The Battle of the Busts": a fight for market dominance between the established Italian men's magazine *Playmen* and the arriviste Italian-language edition of the American magazine *Playboy*.

The magazines operate under different philosophies. *Playmen*'s editor, thirty-nine-year-old Adelina Tattilo, contends that Italian readers want "real women . . . natural women, flaws and all," rather than "those plastic girls of Hefner's Playboy." The publisher of Italian *Playboy* snaps back that *Playmen* isn't even a competitor because it's pornography.

"Those pictures made ME look great," Galella enthuses, noting that, even at his most intrusive, "I never tried anything like THAT."

It is a step too far as well for Hugh Hefner, publisher of *Playboy*. "Anyone but Jackie," says the "hitherto undisputed king of the manure pile."

●

In public, she is blasé. "I have to live my life," she tells Kiki Moutsatsos. "If I think about the photographers all the time, I will not be able to move out of my bed in the morning." When a friend runs into her at a cocktail party and exclaims, "Why, Jackie, how good to see you with your clothes on," she laughs. "I don't treat it as reality," she tells *Newsweek* a few days after publication. "It doesn't touch my real life, which is with my children and my husband. That's the world that's real to me." But, obviously, the incident is real enough that she feels compelled to speak to a national news magazine.

In private, it must be hard not to think about it. The experience has, Ari says, "spoiled Skorpios for her."

•

The gossips get an influx of letters.

A reader from Florida asks, "What was the reaction of Onassis to that disgraceful nude photo of Jackie published all over the world?" Answer: Ari is "enraged" and summoning lawyers. He is, reportedly, "prepared to sue the world."

•

Actually, it appears he does nothing. Kiki Moutsatsos routinely pays photographers for negatives, but there is seemingly no intervention in this instance. Or maybe there was, and it was unsuccessful. Maybe the September 1971 report of a $25,000 offer was right, and the photographers turned it down, realizing they could score $34,000, $51,000, $81,000—reports of the price vary—from a deal with *Playmen*, and Ari thought, *To hell with it*, and let the photos run. Or maybe there was a deal with *Playmen* all along and the negatives were never on the open market. But the reality was that Aristotle Onassis, one of the richest men in the world, couldn't protect his wife on the island he owned.

Later, there will be claims Ari was involved in all this; that he conspired with the photographers and set up the whole thing, so enraged was he by how much of his money she'd spent fighting Galella. It will also be said that Ari himself claimed this, during a conversation in late 1974. But by then, so much has happened: he is ill and angry, his empire is crumbling, his family falling apart, and he has turned against her.

This claim fit the image he wanted to project—Onassis, always in control, the world at his mercy—at a time when neither had ever appeared less true. It is conceivable he made that claim in 1974, but who knows if it was true.

DECEMBER 4, ANOTHER STRANGE STORY. THE *NEW YORK Times*, page one: "Amphetamines Used by a Physician to Lift Moods of Famous Patients."

It's a giant article featuring the work of eleven reporters. Later, he's known almost exclusively by the moniker "Dr. Feelgood" but, in its exposé, the *New York Times* refers to him by his real name: Dr. Max Jacobson.

Max Jacobson: a German-born doctor then famous in New York for "potions" his patients swore by. "Most say his shots give them boundless energy and more productive and pleasurable lives," the *Times* reports. They likely weren't wrong, as the potion—often described as "vitamins"—included a substantial hit of speed, which explains the co-existent complaints of "enslaving addictions" as well as "wrecked lives and destroyed careers."

The *Times* includes the caveat that "It cannot be said with certainty that the Kennedys or, with a few exceptions, any other specific patient received amphetamine," but it was known Jacobson used "unusually large amounts" of the drug and that he had, at one time, treated both Jackie and JFK.

The doctor moved in glitzy circles and counted several of the Kennedys' friends as patients, including Stas Radziwill, Chuck Spaulding, and Mark Shaw—one of the family's favorite photographers, whose 1969 death from "acute and chronic intravenous amphetamine poisoning" precipitated the investigations into the doctor's dealings. Truman Capote, who had given up the shots after a collapse in Europe, told the *Times* that even though they were identified as vitamins, he believed "they were loaded with 'speed.'"

It's an altogether bizarre story, deviating from typical tales of drug users and addicts—wayward teens and hippies who ran away from their parents to move to San Francisco and indulge in lives of free love. All those stories of Liz Taylor and Dick Burton boozing it up, Dean Martin's drinking—everyone in Hollywood addicted to alcohol and pills. It was understood that the kids and the stars had these problems. But not the president of the United States.

Just try to imagine Dick Nixon taking potions from a man the glitterati called "Dr. Feelgood." Inconceivable! That's what the country got for electing a man who looked like a movie star. A show starring a president with a drug addiction: the leader of the free world, dependent on injections of which even Truman Capote was afraid.

The doctor-patient relationship remained unclear, but Jacobson confirmed he knew the Kennedys, and he had treated them both a number of times in 1961. He also confirmed he was in Vienna with them during the Khrushchev summit and that he gave the president injections, though he did not specify their contents. One of JFK's physicians informed the *New York Times* that, cautioning against the continued use of Dr. Max's potions, he'd told President Kennedy: "No president with his finger on the red button has any business taking stuff like that." This stuff that made a famous fashion photographer declare, "I went berserk . . . I went mad. I was committed to Payne Whitney Psychiatric Clinic of New York in a straitjacket."

•

Some patients rally around the doctor. Jackie does not. Through a spokesperson, she admits he treated her. Beyond that, she says nothing.

According to the gossips, "It was Jackie who discovered Dr. Max Jacobson (through mutual friends)" and, like Eve giving Adam the apple, "it was she who urged the President to try him." The evidence, however, suggests the opposite. According to Jacobson himself, Jack Kennedy became his patient in autumn 1960, taking the treatments to manage campaign exhaustion. Kennedy seems to have relied upon Jacobson in times of stress, and so in advance of his trip to Canada, concerned about his wife's post-partum "chronic depression and headaches," he asked Jacobson to treat her too.

When Kennedy's back pain was aggravated at a tree planting ceremony during their state visit a few days later, he summoned the doctor again. Then, a few weeks after that, in early June 1961, Jacobson accompanied the couple to Vienna for the president's meeting with Soviet Premier Nikita Khrushchev. The White House waited until his trips to Paris, Vienna, and London were over to announce the president's back injury to the American public, at which time it was portrayed as a "new" injury, rather than a recurrence of his chronic back pain. Dr. Jacobson's involvement was not mentioned, but in retrospect, it would have been a crucial component in Kennedy's ability to maintain the public appearance of a youthful, healthy man for that entire month.

During that first year in the White House, Jackie and Jack likely both took the shots on occasion, particularly in that spring and summer of 1961, but there are no indications that either became full-on addicted. Which is how it looks, coming out under headlines like "JFK, Jackie Possible Amphetamine Users."


JUST BEFORE CHRISTMAS, LEE AND STAS SPLIT UP. THE marriage has been troubled for years but the split still comes as a shock, because it's been assumed Stas would continue to grin and bear it. But Stas—who Jackie adores and whose side she takes—finally gave up on Lee. A "foreigner married to another foreigner . . . living in a foreign country," Lee had said. It was difficult.

Just a few years before, the *New York Times* had suggested that "Jackie was never Mrs. Front Porch and her natural playground was Europe." This is how she seems to many Americans: moving between countries with deceptive ease, traversing cultures, somehow transcendent. But it isn't easy, this transience between the old life and the new and, four years in, it's starting to wear. "In New York City, she was Jackie Kennedy Onassis, widow of President John F. Kennedy, mother of Caroline and John; in Glyfada and on Skorpios, she was Mrs. Aristotle Onassis," remembers Kiki Moutstatsos. "It was part of her mystique that she was able to lead both lives and perform each role so effectively . . . it could not be easy for her."

Jackie knows Ari well enough to know how to calm him, how to handle his tempers and mood swings. Kiki thinks she's more adept at it than his sisters, who just flee in tears. "Jackie calmly repeated, 'Yes, Ari,' while he ranted, and waited patiently for the fury to subside," Kiki remembers, noting, as a result, that "this anger subsided more quickly when facing Jackie than with any other person in his life."

She knows how to handle him, but does she understand him? His ex-wife, Tina Niarchos, thinks not, and reportedly tells a French friend, "Jackie will never understand Ari. You can't know men like that unless you were born knowing them." Another woman in these jet set circles observed, "If you marry a Greek you really marry another world." And he is very Greek. One friend recalls Ari telling him, "We Greeks live in Europe, but we are not Europeans. We think like Middle Eastern people." He believed this remark explained the tension that lay between the couple, because "A Middle Eastern man doesn't like a conspicuously independent woman who refuses to play 'second fiddle' to him."

She was never going to play second fiddle, though she knew how. And sometimes, when it was convenient—when the men were gathered round and she could flatter one of them with that laser-like attention she might bestow upon whoever was lucky enough to catch her eye—she would do it. But she didn't do the things she didn't want to do. It was stubborn willfulness, at times self-protective, but it was also a form of independence. She'd grown up in such a ruthlessly mannered society where there was one precise way that girls who wanted to catch husbands had to behave. Jackie wanted to get out and she did, by marrying two of the unlikeliest men. Men were still the way out, and she knew how to flatter them, how to make them feel powerful and sublimate herself and her smarts, strategically—for their benefit and to hold their attention, but also to secure herself. Because that was what it sometimes took to be a woman in this world.

But she wouldn't tolerate bullshit and she'd rather leave the room, sulk in the movie theater, or jump off the boat. This independence of hers, combined with Ari's need to control, is ostensibly the fundamental tension in their marriage at this point. Maria Callas is still around, and he is still seeing her—sleeping with her or maybe just friends, nobody knows—but he thinks he can have it both ways, and his wife seems willing enough to let him. So long as he lets her go about her life as she wishes and she has him some of the time and he tells her stories of Greek gods and heroes and they can, occasionally, go out in the evenings in New York and dance.

One of his friends tells gossip columnist Liz Smith that Jackie likes "being owned so long as it doesn't interfere with her. And it doesn't . . . she found great relief in throwing herself into life with someone like Ari, who will take over completely, care for her, protect her." She is, in this, not so different from some of her contemporaries, whose attitudes toward gender roles are changing, but who are also often reluctant to reject traditional roles within their private lives.

While maybe she wants that kind of relief sometimes, increasingly she chafes against it and, when she rebels, her husband has little patience. He isn't used to being told no, in business or at home; that his wife would question his authority is unimaginable. A guest aboard the *Christina* remembered that, when she corrected a factual error he made, Ari shouted, "Don't contradict me in front of others." In response, she left the table and didn't reappear that night.

"She understood him, but he didn't really understand her completely," says one of her American friends, who felt he didn't get her independence. He married a woman who was broken, on the run, wounded from the losses of Jack and Bobby. But she is stronger now, and while he publicly trumpets her need for freedom and his ability to give her that, it is a setup in which her freedom is still dependent upon him. In reality, this is not the case. She goes her own way, which worries Artemis, who tells Kiki that "Jackie is not doing so well to leave Aristo and go to New York for weeks at a time." She wishes Jackie "would be more of a Greek wife."

"I don't think perhaps Jackie realized that this was completely different to anything she had known before," surmised a Polish friend. "I would say it's not easy for an American. Jackie was very European also but she was an American and it must not have been easy for her."

•

In December 1972, the Athens-based designer Yannis Tseklenis is designing clothes with cartoons of Aristotle Onassis's face on them. "Life is so damn miserable," he says, "I figured it was time to give people a laugh." He's met the man a few times and believes, "Onassis represents everybody's impossible dream."

Asked by the reporter for his thoughts on one of the most prominent issues of the day, Yannis balks: "'Women's Lib'! What's that? You never ask a Greek such an absurd question." Greek men are, the reporter from the *Boston Globe* notes, "historically notorious for the innate putdown of women as secondary human beings."

1973

IND

# TV PICTURE LIFE

STERLING

SEPT.
50c

33697

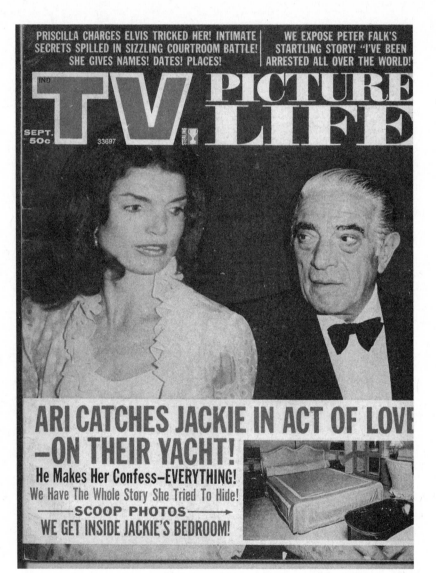

# ARI CATCHES JACKIE IN ACT OF LOVE
# –ON THEIR YACHT!

## He Makes Her Confess—EVERYTHING!

We Have The Whole Story She Tried To Hide!

———— SCOOP PHOTOS ————▶

## WE GET INSIDE JACKIE'S BEDROOM!

IN EARLY JANUARY 1973, A NEW DOCUMENTARY ORIGINATING with Channel 13 in New York begins airing on public broadcast channels throughout the country: *An American Family*. In it, a film crew follows William and Pat Loud and their five children for seven months during 1971, tracking their daily lives to explore modern understandings of the American family and the American Dream.

"Nothing like it has ever been done," anthropologist Margaret Mead writes, suggesting, "it may be as important for our time as were the invention of drama and the novel for earlier generations: a new way of helping people understand themselves." Watching *An American Family*, "one's initial feelings were mixed," observes the UPI's reviewer, but he was nonetheless mesmerized by the fact that "it is real lives that we are watching."

But how many people would allow themselves to be filmed like this? "As compelling as the series is . . . the possibilities for the genre are not likely to be that limitless . . . [it] cannot be so ubiquitous a form as the novel or the drama," the *New York Times* argues, if only because few people would volunteer for such projects. The film's director, Craig Gilbert, takes the opposite view. "More families than you'd believe were willing to do this—almost all of those I talked to," he says. "They're excited by the prospect of someone considering them important enough to spend seven months and more than a million examining their lives." Gilbert took this as a sign that "This country is in much worse shape than any of us are willing to talk about."

But the Louds are not happy. They're indignant over the way they've been portrayed and are particularly disgusted with Channel 13's sensationalized publicity campaign. The versions of them appearing on the television are not, they say, who they are in real life. They have been edited into something else. Watching them on *The Dick Cavett Show* the following month, a TV analyst observes, "It's alright to be criticized for turning in a poor performance if you're playing someone else's part, but to go before cameras playing yourself, and to get poor reviews for playing yourself, that's REALLY Shakespeare's unkindest cut of all."

Later, looking back, historians and media scholars will cite this as the first example of what we now call reality TV.

IT IS REAL LIVES WE ARE WATCHING, REAL PEOPLE.

Jackie is in New York on January 22 when the amphibious plane carrying Alexander Onassis crashes during a trial flight with a new pilot. Ari is with her when the news reaches them that his son is seriously injured. "We were celebrating Peter Beard's birthday, and we found out he had cracked up his plane at Athens Airport and the old man was so absolutely shocked," remembered James Mellon. "He just sat there and looked as though he was already dead."

Immediately, the couple flies to Athens. Another plane, another hospital, another young man fatally injured, more machines to be turned off.

In Athens, the dynamic is fraught. It's a situation involving deeply shocked people with strong allegiances and fierce distrust. Prior to Jackie and Ari's arrival from New York, Christina is reportedly already railing about a "curse," going on about how Jackie has brought death to their family, telling people, "Before long she will kill us all."

Kiki Moutsatsos notices that when Ari, Tina, and her husband, Stavros Niarchos, greet one another at the hospital, they all kiss each other, but none of them kisses Jackie. She is an outsider.

Fiona Thyssen, Alexander's girlfriend, later tells a biographer that Jackie came over and sat beside her, saying she knew Alexander told Fiona everything and that Ari and his son had discussed the possibility of Ari's forthcoming divorce from Jackie. Fiona says Jackie then asked her if she knew what kind of settlement they had in mind. A second source corroborated Thyssen's account, recalling how this incident "showed Jackie's insensitivity, her hard side."

But there is something about this story that doesn't align with anything she did before or after, and there are several ways in which it does not make sense. In such circumstances—with her chronic sorrows rising to the surface, replayed through the horrible news, the plane ride, the hospital—maybe she would have asked this of someone she was close to. But as close as she was to Ari's sister, she never even acknowledged to Artemis her awareness of Ari's continued friendship with Maria, much less the possibility of divorce. In this hospital room full of Greeks, it's odd she'd reveal so much of herself, much less so spectacularly and impolitely. The choice of Fiona, a woman she hardly knew and a woman she knew vehemently disliked her, is equally odd, except for the fact that Fiona may well have been one of the only other non-Greeks there.

Grieving people often do things that do not make sense, but there's a desperation in this scene that strays from her desperation in other moments like it: at Bobby's death, for instance, where she was sent reeling back into her emotions at the time of Jack's death. It's a desperation that begs the question of what Ari—out of his mind with grief—might have said to her on the journey over from New York.

•

The medical effort is futile—Alexander's brain damage is irreversible, but he hangs on. "His brain is dead but his heart is still beating," a hospital administrator announces to the press, taking a slightly more hopeful tack than the Olympic Airways official who, earlier in the day, lamented, "It's all finished. He is dead."

A British neurosurgeon is present, an American specialist en route. When doctors say only divine intervention can save the young man, Greek premier George Papadopoulos orders an air force helicopter to bring the reputedly miraculous icon of the Virgin Mary from the island of Tinos to Alexander's hospital bed. It has not yet arrived when Alexander dies that night. At his deathbed, Kiki Moutsatsos remembers, "Jackie stood beside her husband, her face bare of cosmetics, her lips praying, her skin pale, as if at any moment she might faint."

With Alexander's death, Aristotle Onassis is shattered. Friends tell the papers he's thinking of selling everything and leaving Greece, that he will not be able to continue, so thorough is his devastation over this loss. Family sources inform reporters that he cried all night and twice left the Glyfada house to wander aimlessly around Athens, alone. At a news conference held in his office, his voice cracks with emotion as he tells reporters that Alexander is "dead as a human being. . . . His brain was destroyed . . . his features completely disfigured," and "Nothing could be done for him."

"We all have a certain life span," he tells the assembled press corps with a sigh. "What we don't know is when this span will end." But he takes care to absolve his boy of any blame. A report suggests Alexander was piloting the Piaggio; his father contends that Alexander could not have been the pilot, because had he been, "maybe the accident could have been avoided. . . . I have never seen a more careful, meticulous pilot," Ari remembers, his memory now making an angel of the son of whom he'd been so critical in life.

•

History intrudes. Former president Lyndon Johnson dies the day Alexander's plane crashes. The day Alexander dies, President Richard Nixon announces the signing of a cease-fire in Paris, thus signaling the end of American involvement in Vietnam. The cease-fire will "insure stable peace . . . lasting peace . . . peace with honor," Nixon declares. Hours after he "proclaimed the Vietnam peace which had eluded Johnson so long . . . smiling serenely . . . head held high . . . impressively composed," Nixon joins Lady Bird Johnson for his predecessor's funeral. The president sits, the papers note, in "radiant sunshine." The story directly above: "Onassis Son Allowed to Succumb."

•

Other stories intrude as well. On January 27, after "extensive research during the last year in Paris, New York and London," Fred Sparks is back with an "amusing report on the big spending customers" entitled "Wow! What Well-Heeled Women Spend on Clothes." He identifies Jackie as "the fastest shopper in the West" and the woman with the world's third most expensive shopping habit, behind the queens of Iran and Thailand and just ahead of Elizabeth Taylor.

The world Sparks depicts is one where shopping makes Jackie "as happy as a child in a candy factory," but, as he reveals, she is not alone in her quest for such fulfillment. In 1972, her good friend Bunny Mellon spent $137,000 at Givenchy. The actress Sophia Loren bought four evening dresses, spending $12,500 in a single afternoon. "I'm not kidding," Richard Burton reportedly boasted of his wife: "Elizabeth can spend over $1,000 an hour!" "The dress-mad woman," Sparks says couturier Christian Dior called such clients: the woman "whose whole life revolves around clothes. She can't get enough—not so much to wear, but to own."

But there is more to this than Sparks's glib portrayal suggests. It wasn't just the buying but the ritual of going out. It broke up the day—same with all those long lunches—and gave structure to hours that otherwise might drag on. Asked by a friend why she bought so many things, Baroness Marie-Helene de Rothschild replied, "I don't play bridge or golf. What would I do afternoons if I didn't shop?" It gave one such a feeling of control.

BACK IN GREECE, THE DYNAMIC HAS REVERSED. NOW ARI
is the injured one.

First, he blames the pilot, who is charged with manslaughter.
Then he imagines more sinister forces are at work. "He was convinced that his enemies had plotted the devious act," Costa Gratsos
remembered. When Jackie tries to dissuade him from this belief,
he lashes out at her, telling Gratsos that her behavior here mirrors her inability to accept that John Kennedy was the victim of a
conspiracy. Gratsos, who is no fan of Jackie's, nonetheless corrects
Ari—pointing out, "She never denied the possibility of a conspiracy. She only said that the knowledge of such a conspiracy would
do little good, since it wouldn't restore Kennedy." She didn't want
to aggravate the horrific loss by morbidly probing its circumstances.
Ari has no such compunctions.

He is a changed man. A friend recalls, "The joy went out of life.
It showed in his face, his eyes, the way he walked. It was so sad,
so sad. Looking at him, I found it hard to hold back the tears."
Another friend believed, "Ari started letting go of his life after his
son died. I had that strong feeling . . . he was no longer going to
be satisfied with anything. . . . He began to lose interest. He began
to give up."

People whisper he's having a nervous breakdown. Jackie herself
seems to believe this. Edie Beale recounts that Jackie said Ari "really
lost his mind when his son died in that airplane crash. It wasn't
anything to do with her, it was that tragedy. Jackie said there had
been an argument and [Alexander] just went out in his airplane
recklessly." And after that, "Onassis was no longer interested in
life." To one of Ari's nieces, Jackie writes, "With all my heart I will
try to console your Uncle Ari—I wonder if it is possible to console
anyone for such a loss—but I will try."

She tries in the way that comes most naturally to her in dark
times: travel. She calls up Pierre Salinger and Solange Herter and
begs them to come along on a cruise. To Herter, she says, "I think
the only thing to do is to get him on a boat because he loves that,
and he's drinking too much. Will you join us . . . Go from Dakar

to Guadalupe?" Herter notes the urgency in her voice and agrees instantly, as does Salinger, who brings along his wife.

Herter and Salinger seem to have taken entirely different trips. According to Herter, the seas are rough, the sailing uneasy, and "Ari was drinking himself into a stupor every night . . . bemoaning his fate and cursing the gods." To Salinger, in contrast, Ari is "morose" but he "didn't make a fetish of it, keeping his deepest, darkest thoughts to himself." However, Salinger noted that everyone's nerves were "frayed," and Ari's mood changed if Jackie started to speak about Jack Kennedy; he also wondered about this atmosphere's impact on her kids. Salinger remembered her telling Caroline and John that Ari was grieving and, therefore, he wasn't entirely responsible for his own behavior, which Salinger felt "They'd understand . . . to a point."

Salinger's wife notices that Jackie is "very thoughtful and protective" of her husband. But there isn't much she can do, except whisk him away and surround him with people who entertain him and make him laugh and perhaps, for a little while, help him forget. She's lost children and a husband. Now her husband has lost a child, and it appears she is losing him. Not to another woman, but to grief and loss—sensations she's experienced but which are different for everyone. Like her, he takes to drinking. And like her, he occasionally lashes out—turning against her as, in her own anger and distress after the death of Jack Kennedy, she turned against her secretary, her sister, and anyone who didn't seem to understand the depth of her pain.

He feels she cannot understand him, this American woman. Something his children seemed to have seen. Now he wonders if perhaps they were right all along.

"THERE SEEMS TO BE A LOT OF NEWS—OR RUMORS—ABOUT Jacqueline Onassis, regarding her relationship with her husband," a reader observes to a syndicated astrologer on March 7, asking, "Do you predict that they'll break up?" The astrologer doesn't see a breakup, but reminds readers, "My prediction originally was that she would have three happy years with him and then troubles would begin."

The troubles, it seems, have begun.

•

It's impossible to know when the divorce talk starts in earnest, but in the aftermath of Alexander's death, Ari's attitude toward his wife undergoes a dramatic change. As Edie Beale says Jackie said to her: "He became a perfect horror to live with."

In March they cruise to Haiti; this trip appears to be a tipping point. Later, Ari confides to a friend that, in Haiti, he tried to convince his wife to consent to a quickie divorce so they might secretly remarry. This would effectively disinherit her, but he told the friend he'd told her it would put to rest the idea she'd married him for his money. A wacky plan, obviously duplicitous, and she declined. He also claimed to have offered her "a big payoff" and said she turned that down too. When asked why he was going to so much trouble, he replied: "I don't want lawyers dancing on my grave!"

Clues to Jackie's attitude about such episodes can be found in comments she made to Kiki Moutsatsos. Kiki adored Artemis, but she was also occasionally the victim of verbal attacks Artemis made when drinking. After a particularly nasty series of insults, Jackie took Kiki aside and reminded her, "They can both be difficult people, Aristo and Artemis. But they are not bad people. We must always remember that." She tried to filter out the unpleasant behavior of the people she loved, and to focus on the good.

In April, James Mellon and Lee, who have recently struck up a flirtation, join them for a cruise around the Caribbean. "His mind appears to have lost some of its sharpness," Mellon observes of Ari, noting the pair are on speaking terms though Ari is "drinking heavily." Lee confides to Mellon that she and Jackie stayed up all night with Ari discussing his fortune. "The recent decline in his health and the death of his son have persuaded him to make a new will, but he isn't sure what he ought to do," Mellon writes in his diary. "Jackie is trying to convince him to leave most of his fortune in a trust fund for the benefit of the Greek people, and he is considering this."

Mexico, Puerto Rico, the Virgin Islands, Athens. And Paris.

"We all noticed that Aristo went even more often to Paris after Alexander's death," said Kiki Moutsatsos, acknowledging that he went to see Maria, "his soul mate, the only woman he believed could understand his pain." But any relief found from such visits is short-lived and he is "the same, sad, defeated man" when he returns home.

"He's obsessed with Alexander's death," Maria confides to a friend, citing his fixation on finding his son's "killers." "Aristo has changed," she says. "He really is an old man now."

Jackie is changed too. In her, Kiki senses "a new air of sadness . . . mingled with regret." It's up and down. There are moments when Ari enjoys his time with her, the quiet walks along the beach, the picnics in the sunshine. At other times, he's inconsolable and nothing, nobody, can bring him relief. Kiki sees them walking together and notices Ari looks twenty years older; and even Jackie seems more fragile, both "walking cautiously," as though treading on perilous ground. If he was once her protector, he is no longer.

On Skorpios, he makes nightly visits to Alexander's grave, where he pours two glasses of wine and sits talking to his dead son into the early morning hours. During one lunch with friends, he repeatedly raises his glass to toast his son and announces to the table that he's heard Alexander's voice. "Jackie's eyes met mine," Kiki remembers, "and she shook her head briefly and sadly."

THE TIMES ARE CHANGING. THOUGH, ON AN AVERAGE WEEK-day, 77 percent of adults aged eighteen and over still read a daily newspaper and almost all of them read the paper in its entirety. At a conference of newspaper editors, Gloria Steinem—an American journalist, activist, and feminist who was, in many people's minds then, a major figurehead of women's liberation—tells editors that their reporting is all wrong. "You are using divide and conquer tactics to make women's lib appear not worthwhile," she says. "When women's libbers disagree, it's that fight that is emphasized, not the issues. . . . When I join demonstrations for causes that [are] worth reporting," she complains, "I am only quoted about Jackie Onassis and bra burning."

"Women's Liberation" was "more of a philosophy than a coherent, cohesive political movement," suggested one columnist, noting that it encompassed a

> revolt against dressing to please men; being treated as "sex objects"; being manipulated as consumers in a Madison-Avenue-motivated capitalist society; being treated as "guinea pigs" in the use of the birth control pill; not being free to decide whether to have an abortion or not; and against being treated as "chicks" by their male colleagues . . . the revolt is against the attitude that women are "second class thinkers" unable to play a wholly independent role.

Not surprisingly, given the range of issues involved, Steinem observed, "it's difficult to find people of either sex who understand what women's liberation is really all about."

But it was an idea mainstream enough that when a roving TV reporter asks her a question about women's lib in the February 12, 1971, episode of *The Brady Bunch*, Marcia Brady admits, "If we're all supposed to be created equal, I guess that means girls as well as boys." When asked whether she can do anything boys can do, she answers: "I think I should have the chance to try." Later in the episode, her mother, Carol Brady—hardly a radical—concurs, announcing, "I don't think women's lib is crazy."

Many people thought it was. "Feminists are not all radicals, screaming for a separate slate," a columnist clarified. "We don't expect sympathizers to go out and hit every man with a brick. What we ask is that you re-examine your lives and find where you are stifled—in your careers, in your marriages or both. Then work to change things." The message was often distorted to suggest that women's libbers wanted to be men or to be better than men, to which the president of the Chicago Chapter of the National Organization of Women responded: "You've got to be kidding, no one wants to be like a man who isn't a man. We're talking about something scarier—being women and being equal."

Was Jackie one of these women's libbers? It's cliché but also true to say that it was, for her, a journey. Her views evolved over the years and shifted depending upon the time and her circumstances. In her 1964 oral history with Arthur Schlesinger, she asserted that "women should never be in politics" because "We're just not suited to it," and declared she got all her opinions from her husband. But she also wanted recognition for her achievements. The following year, after a male admirer of John Kennedy's went on endlessly praising the president at a party, she complained, "You'd think I never even existed." This was around the same time that, as a widow, she was reportedly saying "the only way I know is to work through some man."

In 1969, when a *Newsweek* editor mentioned to her that women were fighting for equal pay, she reportedly said, "I don't go for all that. I had no trouble finding a position in journalism as a photographer." Never mind that she got the job because her stepfather called the editor and asked if he was still hiring "little girls." A decade later, it's no longer *I* but *we*, at an event at the Schlesinger Library on the History of Women in America in June 1979, when she quips, "We'll know we have arrived when Harvard men start saying that they graduated from Radcliffe!"

"She read and like[d] *Ms.* magazine, made regular contributions of $1,000 to the Ms. Foundation, supported the Equal Rights

Amendment, and was pro-choice but did so privately, not wanting
to be dragged into the political arena," remembered Steinem, who
wished she'd do more while also recognizing that "wanting her to
use that power from her other lives may be unfairly close to wanting to use her, however worthwhile the cause." Which is not to say
she wasn't used.

•

In late April the publisher of *Photoplay* announces that Jackie is
over; they'll no longer be putting her on their covers. But other
editors stay the path and, after her eviction from *Photoplay*, she
still covers plenty of magazines: *Movie Mirror* ("Caroline Cries:
I Want Uncle Teddy to Be My New Father! Jackie Tells Ari: 'I
Need a Young Man's Love!'"); *Screen Stories* ("Jackie Cries: 'I Can't
Call Him My Little Boy Any More!' John-John Undergoes Sex
Change!"); *TV Picture Life* ("Ari Catches Jackie in Act of Love—
On Their Yacht! He Makes Her Confess—EVERYTHING!");
*Photo Screen* ("Ari Discovers the Love Cult Jackie Belongs To! The
Forbidden Act She Did with a Younger Man! The Sin That Ari Can
Never Forgive!"). And on and on.

Two weeks later, a columnist notes, "The Jackie Factory continues to operate at full tilt." Jack O'Brian writes, "Perhaps you may
not be interested in what Nanny Number 2 or Chef Number 13 has
to say, but enough people are so that any ex-employee who wishes
to hire a ghost writer is assured of a publisher."

•

Joe Kennedy's nurse releases a memoir. "Its seemingly sole selling point" is the fact "that it portrays just about everyone in
the Kennedy compound negatively—except Jack O'Brian Bouvier
Kennedy Onassis."

Ron Galella is readying his own Jackie memoir, which is still a
year off; in the meantime, he talks to the press. "She's a woman of
many moods," he announces. "I don't pretend to understand her,
but I can venture an opinion. She's opposed to the entire press. As

she stated in court, the press annoys and upsets her. So she's using me as a scapegoat to get even with the press."

"Jackie exaggerates tremendously," he says, "when she says I imprison her."

THERE IS SO MUCH CHATTER. EVERYWHERE.

On May 17, the United States Senate begins its Watergate hearings to determine whether the White House was involved in the break-in at the Democratic National Headquarters. The hearings air on all three network channels. "The president did not participate or have any knowledge of activities relating to the cover-up and the president at no time authorized anyone to represent him in offering executive clemency," maintains Nixon's press secretary. But the mood in the White House is grim. One staffer tells *Time*, "It's like the last days in a Berlin bunker in 1945. They're all sitting there waiting for the bombs to drop." Lee Radziwill later remembers of that summer, "Watergate was on the television non-stop and that was consuming." One government official complains, "Nobody's doin' a damn bit of work around here."

According to Alice Roosevelt Longworth, "Everyone is hypnotized by Watergate." President Theodore Roosevelt's indomitable eldest child, always called "Princess Alice," is then eighty-nine. She reports: "One hangs on the boob tube all day long." Which isn't to say it's riveting TV. "Watergate Opening Like Watching Grass Grow," declares a veteran political journalist, who condemns the "colorless and snail's-pace testimony" and "yawn-inspiring recounting[s]."

Offstage, there's a little more action. The day the hearings open, Martha Mitchell resurfaces to hold "an angry, impromptu news conference" in New York, wherein she informs reporters that they can "place all the blame [for Watergate] right on the White House" because "John Mitchell was the honest one in the whole lousy bunch of SOBs." Her husband, she says, told her just the day before that "if anything happens to the president the country will fall apart," but she thinks it will be a "darn better idea" for Nixon to resign than be impeached. Ominously, she tells the press, "I depend on you . . . to protect me and my husband."

•

In New York, Marlon Brando is taping an episode of *The Dick Cavett Show*. "News is business," the actor says,

> and people sell news and, unfortunately, people in my position, people in the public eye are sellable commodities, but they're not any different from Kleenex or Dial soap or anything else. . . . Nobody wants to hear about malnutrition among Indians. Nobody wants to hear that Indians have the highest suicide rate of any group in the United States. That's dull stuff. People come home, they've got enough trouble, and they don't want to listen to that. They want to listen to the fripperies and the foolishness and the fun and the giggles and all that.

As Dick Cavett and Brando walk through Chinatown later that evening, looking for a restaurant, a photographer takes a series of pictures then goads Brando to remove his sunglasses. This is how Marlon Brando's fist winds up in Ron Galella's face—a right hook that shatters five of the photographer's teeth and leaves him with nine stitches and a jaw brace. Galella gets his comeuppance when, the following day, Brando is hospitalized with an acute infection in his right hand. Galella is, readers are reminded, that photographer who imprisoned Jackie Onassis.

•

Jill Ruckelshaus, the White House special assistant on women's rights, is in Philadelphia addressing a conclave of the Interstate Association of the Commissions on the Status of Women. There are currently no women in the U.S. Senate, and she jokes that the women's restroom is being phased out. She's described by one reporter as "a curious blend of the guts and savvy of Steinem, the poise and appeal of Jackie Onassis with the basic personal values of Mrs. Middle America." Ruckelshaus works three days a week and defers to her husband—the acting head of the FBI—but she also boldly admits, "My children are not my entire life." She calls the Equal Rights Amendment "a fight we cannot afford to lose."

Celebrating her twenty-fifth birthday in San Clemente, California, the president's daughter Julie Nixon Eisenhower gives an interview to the AP in support of her father over the Fourth of July weekend. "I think he was really in the dark," she says; "he just had complete faith in everyone around him."

Speaking in Alabama, where he shares the stage with Governor George Wallace, Ted Kennedy lashes out—accusing the president of "trampling upon the creed of democracy" and using "the tactics of the criminal or the power of the law in order to silence those whose ideas of politics are different." A few days later in Atlanta, Senator Barry Goldwater retaliates, telling the delegates at the National Young Republicans Convention, "Sen. Kennedy is the last person in the country to lecture us."

·

You never know what will happen next. On July 16, Nixon's in the hospital with viral pneumonia and a surprise witness is called before the Watergate Committee. Alexander J. Butterfield—"a man who was to many no more than vaguely familiar at best"— reluctantly reveals that Nixon's offices and phones are equipped with recording devices "to record things for posterity, for the Nixon library."

This is shocking and sinister: that the president "bugged" the White House with "listening devices." George McGovern declares it "a violation on privacy." A senator from Oklahoma denounces it as "an outrage, almost beyond belief."

"I read George Orwell's brutal novel '1984' when I was a teen-ager," a columnist writes. "If you haven't read it, I suggest you get a copy from the library and sit down for an evening of unnerving reality."

On July 21, the White House taping system is disconnected. The following day, a columnist observes: "Mr. Nixon [is] in a no-win situation. It is up to him to find an exit. But until he does, one sure bet is that Watergate will continue to go on and on and on."

"NOT ONLY WAS HE FULL OF LIFE, HE WAS A SOURCE OF life," Maria Callas once said of Aristotle Onassis. Now it seems the life is eroded out of him by the death of his son.

Ari lashes out, calling his wife's friends "faggots." She complains of being "stuck on Skorpios all summer long"; complains of her husband, "He is such a loner."

When he's with her, he seems to make being with him as unpleasant as possible. "I can't tell you how many meals I sat through, when Onassis would scream at her," recalled Peter Beard. "He used to make insulting comparisons, right to her face, between Jackie and Callas. He said Jackie was superficial and Callas was a 'real artist.' Jackie just sat around and took it."

Maybe she knows he doesn't truly hate her, just wants her to be there for him in a way she can't be. It seems he wants a Greek wife: always at his beck and call, soothing him when he is troubled, submitting to him. "He used to be the boss of every single thing in his life," James Mellon remembered. "And here was this woman who was used to being the boss of every single thing in her life, plus also she was an American woman with a much more liberated personality than a Greek woman . . . there was chaffing all the time."

People who see her report she is dimmed down. When she accompanies Ari to a friend's home for lunch, he attacks her appearance, shouting, "How can you be seen looking like that?" For a split second she appears hurt then she gently compliments the other women present. After drinking red wine during lunch, Ari stumbles to the beach and, curled up in the fetal position, falls asleep. The gossip columnist Aileen Mehle thinks Jackie looks like she's "been to hell and back." A guest to Skorpios believes she has concluded the only way to "survive with Ari was to maintain her own center of gravity."

It's unclear whether she actually pulls away or if that is just his perception. (Many people, even people who didn't especially like her, suggest it is the latter.) In response, he grows lonelier, angrier, and more determined. He drafts divorce papers again and again.

Callas isn't free, she's seeing someone else, and so he lets things carry on as they are. He'd been burned in the divorce from Tina and knows divorce is a bad option. But, as a friend noted, "the more time he spent alone, and the more things went wrong for him, the more determined he became to get rid of Jackie no matter what it took."

"I wrote several drafts of a divorce petition for him," remembered his lawyer, "and each time I would ask him: 'What is the substance of your complaint? Does she insult you? Does she treat you badly? Does she betray you?' He said, 'No.' 'What then?' 'She doesn't stay with me.'" As the lawyer knew, this wasn't a complaint a successful case could be built on. "I would tell him, 'you knew that her life was in the States. You knew that she had children whose father was a martyred president and they would be raised in the States. And if she goes to court and says, 'Yes, I don't spend as much time with my husband as I would like because I have a duty to my children,' what Greek court would tell her, 'Leave your children and go to your husband'?"

"The trouble with him," Ari's lawyer conceded, "was that he wanted me to get a divorce without saying anything bad about Jackie, and that just could not be done under Greek law, even for a man like Onassis." And so he plots to change the law.

In light of all that's happening that he can't control, his marriage's dissolution becomes an obsession. Reportedly, he hires people to bug his wife's New York apartment for evidence that she's being unfaithful. They can't get past the Secret Service to tap her phones, and the plan comes to nothing.

STRANGE AND TIRING TIMES. THE FIFTH ANNIVERSARY OF Chappaquiddick passes, reminding everyone that Richard Nixon isn't the only man in Washington with a shady past. As the columnist Bruce Biossat notes:

> Had there been no Chappaquiddick, the race [for the 1976 Democratic presidential candidate] would probably be over right now and Ted Kennedy as good as nominated. . . . Yet the sphere of his personal cluster of problems lays partly across the bright orb of his official life. Even as Kennedy demonstrates his skill at using Watergate to unify his party, its reminder of Chappaquiddick undercuts his own prospects.

On August 10, Vice President of the United States Spiro T. Agnew is accused of bribery, extortion, conspiracy, and tax evasions —a litany of wrongdoings he denounces as "damned lies."

Columnists note a "numbing bewilderment" in Washington, because events—which once "seemed to be producing a logical ebb and flow which anyone could grasp"—no longer align and political analysts cannot agree on what is happening. The resulting confusion is "almost smothering."

"Laughter these days in this muggy, scandal-ridden capital is hard to come by," observes an unattributed AP article entitled "Washington Mood Depressed." The article warns, "The sky isn't falling, but on the cocktail circuit and in the green federal work warrens, some insist the government is."

Seventy percent of Americans reportedly accept the possibility of Nixon's complicity in Watergate, but they don't want resignation or impeachment.

The president is counting on this. His strategy, an analyst perceives, is "built upon a belief that his fellow Americans, while not ready to forget, are willing to forgive."

The "American internal imbroglio," a paper in Israel calls it. Not yet a crisis, it's nonetheless a steady drumbeat echoing down the days.

ARI BEGINS TO CRACK DOWN. HE REPORTEDLY MOVES HIS wife's accounts to his Monte Carlo office so he can watch them more closely. Openly, he begins to complain.

•

She had always liked shopping, and Ari's complaints about her expenses echo Jack Kennedy's. Much like decorating, shopping seems to have given her a sense of control. It was a way of refining and perfecting the world around her; her letters to decorators and couturiers reveal how precise she was in her desires, through the purchase of a table intended to fit a very specific corner of a certain room or a yellow chiffon dress in an exact shade of lemon. Her White House fashions would later be described as a form of emotional armament, a means of protecting herself amid circumstances beyond her control, and while there was a precision to her shopping, it also seems to have represented a relaxation of that same exactness.

In the contemporary press reports, she was buying all the time in "wild shopping sprees"—"purchasing armloads of dresses, hats, and handicrafts" during an "annual shopping tour" of Athens; going through Ungaro "like a hurricane," she "cleaned it out." According to Fred Sparks, she was "the fastest shopper in the West." The gossip Jack Anderson reports, "She walks into any store of her choosing, helps herself to whatever she wants and strolls off. . . . She pays no cash, signs no bills. Her face is her credit card. . . . She buys $1,000 and $2,000 gowns by the dozens." A Washington matron asks Helen Thomas, "What does Jackie do when the stores close?"

In the biographies to come—largely thanks to the testimony of Ari's friend Costa Gratsos—she will be portrayed as "a speed shopper," who "could be in and out of any store in the world in ten minutes or less, having run through $100,000 or more. She didn't bother with prices, just pointed. She bought anything and everything." But the restraint of Ron Galella's contemporary account is notable. "Jackie loves to shop as much as any woman—maybe more!" he writes. Significantly, he portrays her as an exceedingly normal shopper: "She didn't demand any special attention or get mad when other customers looked over her shoulder to see what she was buying. . . . She looked at different shoes and then asked, like any other woman would have, if she could try on a pair."

She begins complaining too. Calling Ari a "tightwad," after he refuses to fund a lawsuit against the photographers who took the pictures of her naked on the beach, she reportedly tells a friend that her husband is "cheap."

There were ways around this. And she wasn't the only one putting them to use.

•

Since it opened in 1954, Florence Barry's resale shop, Encore, did a brisk trade in the "rarely or never-worn extravagances" of New York's wealthy women. "I started out," Mrs. Barry told a reporter, "because I married late, had no children, a busy-busy husband and an apartment that couldn't keep me occupied. In short, I was bored." After years of volunteering in charity thrift shops, where she'd invariably been disappointed by the quality of the merchandise, Mrs. Barry decided to open her own shop. It was premised on the notion that women would rather have cash in hand than take tax deductions from their donated clothes. She was right.

The downside of her starry clientele was that she couldn't trumpet their names because discretion was paramount. However, Mary Gallagher had blown the whistle on Jackie's reselling in *My Life with Jacqueline Kennedy*, making her the one client Mrs. Barry could identify. "Mrs. Onassis likes money or she would give her clothes to charity," maintained Mrs. Barry. "All these women see this as a little extra income." Mrs. Barry reported that up to 25 percent of the garments coming through her door had the sales tags still attached.

For well-to-do New York women who had limited access to money outside of charge accounts, and whose husbands expected them to be seen in new outfits lest a repeat make it appear business was down, this was standard practice: buying clothes, maybe wearing them once or not at all, and consigning them, for quick cash, to Encore, around the corner from 1040 Fifth. But based on Galella's complaints about her re-runs, the problem of repeating outfits seems not to have been her motivation. Perhaps she's obsessed with buying and owning clothes, Liz Smith acknowledged, "But certainly not by wearing them . . . she is just as apt to turn up for days in a row wearing the same slacks, the same turtleneck sweater, the same Gucci loafers, and the same old trench coat."

In 1996, her friend Gloria Emerson offered a new angle on the story of Jackie's shopping to historian Carl Sferazza Anthony. In the early '70s, Emerson was opening a clinic in Vietnam intended to treat children disabled in the war. According to her, when Jackie asked Ari to donate, he refused and also denigrated the effort.

Jackie was livid. As was her husband when he received a bill from a Parisian fashion house for a collection of couture gowns he'd never seen his wife wear. "What the hell does she do with all the clothes she buys?" he asked Costa Gratsos.

It shouldn't have been such a surprise, as she'd been selling her used dresses for decades now. So why not new ones? He'd curtailed her discretionary funds, but her credit accounts at various stores were still active and she made good use of them. Maybe Ari wasn't on to her yet, but, as Emerson told Anthony, Jackie made a sizable donation to help her hospital. A donation received in cash.

•

"Don't know why everybody's in such a dither about Agnew, and Watergate and the Reds losing," opines one columnist, suggesting "the really big news is that Jackie Bouvier Kennedy Onassis has cut

down from $20,000 to $10,000 a week on her clothing allowance.
Without Ari telling her to, even."

"You didn't hear much about how that Leo of Leos spent her
44th birthday this year," the gossips note. "That's because Jackie
and Ari celebrated quietly on the island of Skorpios—no big gifts
of jewelry, parties or whoop-to-do." Things are going to be quieter
this birthday, reportedly, and "Onassis is happy as a clam that his
wife is spending some time with him for a change."

Fred Sparks is still penning his fan-fic and he's decided Jackie
and Ari are okay. Sparks reassures readers that, really, "all these
petty indignities" of the books and the rumors of divorce ultimately
only strengthened the Os' relationship, and that, "When they're
alone they laugh at the curious, they laugh at themselves, they
laugh at the world press that puts them, like microbes under the
microscope, on Page One, they laugh at the millions and millions
of people who want, through them, to live, vicariously, the life
glamorous."

Galella claims to be over it. "I'm not going to bother her anymore," the *paparazzo* informs reporters as he readies a book on
her for publication the following year. "She's not that hot a news
item."


ON OCTOBER 10, THE VICE PRESIDENT OF THE UNITED
States resigns, pleading no contest to a felony charge of tax evasion.
A "historic decision" announced by a weeping secretary. The White
House has no comment.

Through the reporter Laura Bergquist, *McCall's* reaches out to
Jackie and asks for a personal statement on the occasion of the tenth
anniversary of President Kennedy's death. They're stunned when she
offers to write something for publication. The result is a 350-word
handwritten essay, which the magazine entitles "The Bright Light
of His Days." It appears in the November issue and is excerpted
throughout October 1973 in news reports around the country.

In mid-October, the article "Jackie Breaks Silence, Writes About JFK" appears alongside the news that Elvis is in the hospital with pneumonia and President Nixon made a "conscious, concerted effort" to find a qualified woman to fill the vacancy left by Spiro Agnew's resignation. Finding none, he went with Representative Gerald R. Ford, the House Minority Leader, instead.

In her essay, all the old themes are present. "When he came to the presidency it was a time when the world seemed new—when it was right to hope, and hopes could be realized," she writes of the New Frontier, returning to that old idea of JFK as a Greek. If "He gave everyone around him a desire to excel," it was "not in the harsh competitive sense, but in the ancient Greek sense, that a life is not worth living unless all one's faculties are used along lines leading to excellence." The essay is short, and it has the restless wandering quality of so much of her writing—at times drifting into seeming non-sequiturs, introspections like "One must not let oneself be numbed by sadness. He would not have wanted that."

It's romantic, an elegy. She never once mentions Camelot, but she does indulge in the game of *What if?* Admitting she doesn't know "how he would have coped with the problems that lay there like sleeping beasts," the problems that were "so huge now" while men appeared "so tiny in this technological age." But she knows he would have confidently solved them, sure in "his deep belief that problems can be solved by men."

•

Nixon refuses to surrender subpoenaed tapes to the special prosecutor. He says the White House will prepare summaries of their content.

October 20, Saturday night, Washington, D.C.: The president orders the abolishment of the Watergate task force. He accepts the resignation of the attorney general, who disagrees with the legality of this order. The president orders the firing of the special prosecutor. He fires the deputy attorney general for refusing to carry out his order to fire the special prosecutor. The special prosecutor is, eventually, fired too.

"Impeachment fever mounts," the papers report. "President Nixon is a law-breaker. It's that simple," announces a senator from New York. Consumer advocate Ralph Nadar says, "He is acting like a tyrant, a madman, or both. This is the most serious political crisis in American history."

Senator Edward M. Kennedy calls it "a reckless act of desperation by a president who is afraid."

•

Three days later, Ari's nude pictures are published. No one pays much attention. It's passé now, this violation, "In these days of bugging, spying, data bank-keeping, scandal-mongering and too many additives in bread."

The Os are curiously stationary that autumn, primarily staying in Paris. Out at Maxims and Le Coqu Hari, dining with Rose Kennedy. No big dramas, no big stories or scandals. The same old rumors power up again around their anniversary, but they're met with skepticism. Earl Wilson flatly declares, "The split rumors are wrong."

•

Galella may claim to be over her, but their case is still winding its way through the courts and has landed in the docket of the U.S. Court of Appeals, which warns the photographer "not to touch" Jackie and then cuts the maximum distances by more than half. Her lawyers react swiftly, noting that the ruling freed Galella "to leap around her and hurl verbal taunts as he follows her up and down the streets of New York." They request another hearing, to produce a "clear workable decree that will protect Mrs. Onassis."

On November 15, in a six to two decision, the justices determine that her problems do not "rise to the threshold of importance" required for consideration by the court.

•

Two days later, speaking to 400 newspapermen and their wives and children, in a nationally televised hour-long press conference at a media convention at Walt Disney World, the president of the United States admits that "because of mistakes that were made . . . there are those who wonder whether this republic can survive." He vows "to restore confidence in the White House and in the president." The "facts will show that the president is telling the truth," he says. "'72 was a very busy year for me . . . frankly, I didn't manage the campaign. I didn't run the campaign. People around me didn't bring things to me that they probably should have, because I was just, frankly, too busy trying to do the nation's business to do politics. . . . My advice to all new politicians, incidentally, is to always run your own campaign."

By this point there are allegations about his personal finances, too, that he had shady investments. Those are the allegations he's responding to when, after explicitly accounting for all the money he has made in his career by counting one-two-three on his fingers, he speaks directly to the camera, "to the television audience," and declares: "I have made my mistakes. But in all my years of public life, I have never profited. In all my years of public life, I have never obstructed justice. But I welcome this kind of examination because the people wonder if their president is a crook. I am not a crook. I've earned everything I've got."

•

On November 21, reports break that an eighteen-minute segment is missing from a recorded conversation between the president and H.R. Haldeman, the White House chief of staff, three days after the break-in. The National Democratic Party chairman, speaking in Texas, says the president's staff who were involved in Watergate were "the most lawless gang since Bonnie and Clyde." It is, says one senator, "like a national funeral that just goes on day after day."

As of Thursday, November 22, "43 per cent of the entire adult public" think the president should resign. In Memphis, at a convention of Republican governors, Nixon reassures the governors that there are no "ticking bombs." Says one attendee, "He told us, 'You can take it from me that I would not pull the rug out from under you. There is nothing in Watergate that would embarrass you.'"

# THANKSGIVING DAY 1973

LET US GIVE THANKS FOR THE BOUNTY OF THIS GREAT LAND

November 22 is Thanksgiving Day in America: the "most American of holidays," a holiday where Americans give thanks for the blessings of the previous year.

"In a nation so torn and shaken by political and social upheaval, is it possible to celebrate a reverent and joyous Thanksgiving?" a columnist asks. "In this republic of alarm, concern, and division, is there any legitimate place, any deep yearning for Thanksgiving?"

"Certainly there are problems," an editorialist responds. "But we have the capacity to solve them. . . . What the country needs—and it is particularly apparent because of this year's linking of Thanksgiving with the 10th anniversary of the assassination of John Kennedy—is leadership that can take our innate confidence and inspire us to new heights of achievement."

Ten years. In Maryland, a reporter interviews seventh and eighth graders—who would have been toddlers approximately the same age as John Jr. at the time of John F. Kennedy's death. The reporter is shocked to find that to these kids "Kennedy was significant only for being killed while in office." A thirteen-year-old boy declares, "I kind of liked him from what I've heard," citing as JFK's greatest accomplishment: "Putting men in Vietnam." A seventh grader summarizes his life: "He was the President. He was assassinated in a parade in his car with the top down.

Someone said ride with the top up and he didn't and he got shot."

The kids, probably parroting language picked up from their parents, call Jackie "immoral" for marrying "so soon" after JFK was killed and condemn her for marrying for money.

·

Camelot, 1973. For those who remember, it looks different, not just because of all that happened in the interim, but also because of what is happening now. "Look, here we are talking about Camelot, and once again this country is crying out for leadership," JFK's former aide Larry O'Brien exclaims to a reporter. It wasn't fairy stories people needed, but leaders. Yet, the magic held. In Pennsylvania, when the Democrats encourage new local leaders to rise up, their criteria are incredibly specific. The nation needs, they say, "a young man, in his 40s, preferably, who is a dynamic individual so we can again have pride in government like we did 10 years ago."

"How many people will remember the magic?" a columnist asks, recalling Kennedy as "the first president to carry on a successful love affair with the American people." Whether you loved or hated him, "we were all personally involved with this man," and his memory "offers us hope today, when our government is shaken by divisiveness, hatred and suspicion."

"John Fitzgerald Kennedy was going to lead us to a 'New Frontier' and I for one wanted to go on that ride," writes a local columnist in Illinois. Many people shared that belief, and that was what was lost with his death. Some critics said he prepared the way for the "disillusionments" of the 1960s, but you could never know that for sure—and so there was always the possibility America would have been better. There is always hope, and that's what they want to remember in 1973.

All this talk of hope puts a rosy veneer on something darker; within the chorus of remembrances, a few critical voices emerge to analyze JFK's place in American life and the broader scope of

American history. *Newsweek* suggests "he presided at the highwater mark of empire," a notion an editorialist develops further, expounding upon the idea that JFK's appeal for the American people is "not some vague Camelot," but rather rests "on memory of a time of U.S. imperial greatness": a moment when the nation was recently victorious in war, with a booming economy and clearly defined communist enemies.

Kennedy hailed himself as the future, as the man to lead America into the '60s. He had said that, without him, America would be left wandering the wilderness. In his speech at the Democratic National Convention, he declared that "we stand today on the edge of a New Frontier—the frontier of the 1960s," a "frontier of unknown opportunities and perils—a frontier of unfulfilled hopes and threats" from which "It would be easier to shrink back" and "look to the safe mediocrity of the past." John Kennedy proposed this frontier as "a turning-point in history" and, appealing to America's own sense of supremacy, contended that "All mankind waits upon our decision. A whole world looks to see what we will do."

A week before the 1960 election, in a speech in Scranton, he warned "the 1960s can be . . . the best of years or the worst of years," implying that, with him, they would be the best. And without him, possibly the worst. An editorialist observes: "It is as if Nov. 22, 1963 marked the end of an America that was and the emergence of an America whose character we cannot yet perceive."

•

From Memphis, President Nixon declares, "As we give thanks for the bounty and goodness of our land . . . let us also pause to reflect on President Kennedy's contributions to the life of this nation we love so dearly."

IN EARLY DECEMBER, MAUDE CHAMBERLAIN, AN EIGHTY-two-year-old widow in Las Vegas, is in the hospital recovering from a broken hip sustained in a fall. Taking heed of the president's plea that Americans reduce their energy usage, Chamberlain was switching out her 100-watt light bulbs for 60s when she fell from a ladder.

She receives a letter from the president: "Today I learned of the accident which you suffered as a result of your intentions to help our nation's energy crisis. . . . Mrs. Nixon and I want to join your many friends in sending you our warm wishes as you get well." The papers call her "a real patriot" when they print her picture on page one.

•

The following day, December 6, Senator Gerald Ford is sworn in as vice president of the United States.

•

The day after that is the thirty-second anniversary of Japan's attack on the United States military base at Pearl Harbor in the U.S. territory of Hawaii. Events that, according to an editorialist, "reshaped the lives of all who remember them." An attack from which the United States learned "that the desire for peace is not of itself a guarantee of peace," which is why "Americans today continue to invest heavily in the weapons of defense, for in the age of the atom bomb we dare not risk again that our current dedication to peace be misread as weakness."

"A date that will live in infamy," President Franklin Roosevelt declared it in 1941. In 1973, its infamy will compound.

In his testimony before the Watergate committee, the White House chief of staff suggests that the eighteen-minute gap had a "fairly traumatic" impact in the West Wing and that, during the November 22 governors' meeting in Memphis, there'd been speculation among Nixon's staff that "some sinister force" was at work. The chief of staff believes the erasure was "totally innocent . . . an accident," most likely committed by Nixon's secretary Rose Mary Woods, who'd already taken the blame in her own testimony. That was shocking enough, for, "To anyone who knows her, the idea of Rose Woods' involvement in the Watergate mess brings an almost galactic chill," wrote Jeffrey Hart. A "tough-minded, utterly straight and self-possessed red-head . . . if Miss Woods could be sucked into the Watergate whirlpool, then absolutely anyone connected with the White House could be too . . . now the whirlpool . . . reaches, practically, into the Nixon family."

It was one blow after another, and this "sinister force" business was equal parts catchy and trippy: the revelation that there had been "finite discussion" among the presidential staff of these so-called "devil theories" that "perhaps some sinister force had come in and applied the other energy source and taken care of the information in the gap."

"That clears up a lot of unanswered questions about the Watergate scandal," wrote one reporter. "The devil made them do it."

•

The year goes out with an odd report. First appearing on December 22, it says Jackie's lawyers are filing suit against Ari for not paying his bills. He's been billed for 400 hours of work done on his wife's behalf in her 1971 suit against Ron Galella, work for which he now "arbitrarily refused" to pay. In their suit, her lawyers ask that the assets of Aristotle Onassis be frozen pending the outcome of their case.

A strange story, buried in the back pages just a few days before Christmas. She says nothing about it, nor does he.

And then, on December 29, comes the headline: "Jackie Drops Suit Against Her Husband." The law firm makes no comment on the settlement, but it's reported that she used $235,000 from her own funds to pay off the debt. And Ari is quoted in the papers saying that of course his wife is paying with her own money because, he says, "I had nothing to do with the damn thing."

It's unclear how she came up with $235,000 on short notice, but there appears to have been no breach between them. Two days later, they're off again, "vacationing" in Acapulco.

•

December 31, 1973. Melvin Cohen of Milwaukee wins the 1973 World Champion Liar contest with the following joke: "Aristotle Onassis is planning to get Jackie a small plant for Christmas. The name of the plant is General Motors."

•

Nixon is in California for the holidays. According to his chief of staff, the president feels a "sense of satisfaction" about his achievements and is looking forward to 1974. "This guy is strong and hearty and well balanced," his aide reports. "This is a time for all of us to try to get into a different environment . . . to get away from the pressures. It's a stock-taking period . . . to see where we have be[e]n and where we are going." The attitude is, he reports, "damn the torpedo[e]s, full speed ahead."

# 1974

*SCOOP: WE FIND CHER'S HIDEAWAY LOVE NEST! *

# MOVIELAND

MOVIELAND
31st YEAR
50¢

## and TV TIME

JUNE 1974
32793-IND - 50 ¢
a **LOPEZ**
publication

New
Tragedy
For
JACKIE
"Ari Going
Blind"

RICHARD THOMAS
& SARAH MILES
"She Swept Me
Off My Feet!"

Shirley Jones Battle
Against Leukemia!

New Year's Eve, 1974. The Os arrive in Acapulco to hold a meeting with a British industrialist, a meeting in which Ari mentions wanting to live there. But that's business. He seems never to have made a trip anywhere for business purposes without confiding to someone along the way his hopes to move to whichever city he's in. More and more these days, the business opportunity falls through and the promise of relocation vanishes with it.

But she seems to think this is a real possibility. She'd come to Acapulco on her honeymoon with John Kennedy, and the house Joe Kennedy arranged for them to stay at was a pink one she'd remembered from an earlier visit as a teenager. Now, here she was with her second husband. Maybe it seems a perfect escape: a pink house set up on a white beach against the blue ocean, like something out of a dream. Another new beginning, or a new way of avoiding what appears, increasingly, to be the end.

They look at the house she wants and at other villas, but he backs out. By all accounts, the resulting fight is epic.

At one point she reportedly calls him an ingrate and tells him she doesn't want his "goddamn money." To which he replies, "In that case, you won't be disappointed." As they fly to New York on January 3, he begins rewriting his will. When they stop to refuel at the Palm Beach airport, they're seen eating bacon and lettuce sandwiches together but, upon re-boarding, he goes back to writing his will.

He's been drafting wills for months now. She knows he made adjustments after Alexander's death—he's developed a charitable foundation in his son's name—and that he's trying to figure out how to best dispense with his fortune in the event of his death. But she couldn't have imagined the solution he's settling upon.

Ari is taking steps to change the Greek law so that she won't be entitled to his money. He's mad: at her, for her Kennedy life and her failure to be the wife he needs her to be now; at the fates, for taking Alexander and leaving him hollowed out. He's no longer the powerful force he'd been, a fact he knows and about which he can do nothing. Everyone sees it coming: with Alexander's death in 1973, he aged instantly; they fear he will not live long.

How bold of her to try, even if it is misguided. How curious that she comes back, ten years after Jack's death, twenty years after her wedding to him—that she's returned to Acapulco, bringing her increasingly troubled marriage here now in an effort to repair it.

Maybe it's a last-ditch effort at escape: another new life, another new house, another . . .

They seem to be going in circles: Athens, Paris, New York, Palm Beach, Athens, Paris, New York, Palm Beach, why not Acapulco? Somewhere else, anywhere else. So long as she can escape and feel she is free.

HER HUSBAND IS ILL. HE'S LOSING WEIGHT, HIS SKIN IS pallid, and he's having problems with his eyes. He seems suddenly frail. Jackie, Kiki, and Artemis worry he will catch a chill during his nighttime walks. They scold him for being insufficiently dressed for the cold, but he pays them no mind. Kiki later writes that his diagnosis came in the spring of 1974; other reports suggest he was briefly hospitalized in Lenox Hill back in December 1973, at which time he received a diagnosis that he shared with no one, not even his wife.

•

Back in New York, Jackie goes with Lee and her children to see Liza Minnelli's one-woman show. Police are on hand to control the crowds. During intermission, members of the audience walk down to the sisters' seats and stand before them, staring. A gossip observes: "Public interest seems not to have diminished at all."

·

The following month, in an interview appearing alongside her recipe for "Chicken in the Pink," novelist Jacqueline Susann—"queen of the glamor-sex novel genre" and the other famous Jackie of the day—worries, "There are no more beautiful movie stars. We need more beauty. Who's on the covers of movie magazines? Jackie Onassis. We are in a period of searching for past glamour now. . . . Deep down we're longing for it." Word on the street is, Susann is hard at work on a roman à clef about the beautiful wife of a dead president. "Her characters are always somebodies," a columnist notes, "they are always possessed with something that sets them apart." And they always live in "glamourland."

Glamourland royalty in her heyday, by this point Alice Roosevelt Longworth is, in her own words, "crumbling with age" but still sharp as a tack and about to turn ninety. "This goddamn birthday is driving me crazy," she complains to a journalist. "It will be a marvelous and horrible scene." When reporters come calling, they find her seated on a couch with an embroidered pillow that reads: "If you haven't got anything nice to say about someone, come and sit here by me." Pressed for an interview, she instructs them, "Tell your wretched people I send them my curses," then replies with a candor long since missing from American political life.

She dismisses the New Deal as "a pack of cards thrown helter skelter and then snatched in a free-for-all by the players." She feels the Watergate business is an overblown "intemperance of feeling," but concedes it is "fascinating to watch." After declaring Nixon an "old friend," Johnson "a lovely rogue elephant," Eisenhower "a nice boob," and FDR "90 per cent Eleanor and 10 per cent mush," Princess Alice says of Jackie Onassis: "I like Jackie very much. But I've always wondered what on earth made her marry Onassis. He's a repulsive character. He reminds me of Mr. Punch."

Many agree. They still can't get over it, how bad this marriage looks from a purely aesthetic point of view, even after all these years and all those magazine covers. "We want the Beautiful People," Jacqueline Susann says. Beauty is a prerequisite for glamourland admission. When a reader asks the gossips about the response to Ari's naked photos, the reply is: "Now you can see it wasn't his body she was after!"

But beauty, along with that old-school glamour Princess Alice and the characters of Jacqueline Susann, no longer looks as it once did. Jeans are all the rage, so much so that "the style can hardly be called a fad anymore—denim is a way of life." Denim was nothing new, to be sure, but it's moved from France "to the western plains of the U.S. and spread to college campuses today" to be "flaunted by everyone from Jackie Onassis to baby brother." Featured on bedspreads, curtains, and Bible covers, denim has become "an institution both in the U.S. and abroad."

Presumably Jackie's jeans were more expensive than baby brother's, but there's a leveling here: a feeling that no one is in charge, there are no leaders. "I feel that part of the problem is that we don't have anyone to lead the way," a fashion buyer complains. "Look what Jackie Onassis wears—blue jeans and sweat shirts." The women of glamourland no longer look glamorous. They spend thousands of dollars on couture they don't wear.

HE'S KEPT HER OUT OF HIS BUSINESS DEALINGS, TOLD HER SHE should read a book or leave the room. Now, he needs her. "Nobody thinks Onassis is down to his last penny," *Forbes* observes. "In fact, the Onassises are not even down to their late [*sic*] island or townhouse," but "the big question is: Can Onassis be slipping? Some suspect so." It's a circumstance betrayed through subtle shifts in his dealings, as he attempts to move from shipping into oil refinement. "Can it be that he needs a captive market for his ships, that his old role [as] a shipper is becoming obsolete?" *Forbes* wonders, noting "there is no more talk of giant deals in Greece."

He's at his best when he's busy. Now, the game is changing, and he feels beaten and bored and old, three feelings with which he's unfamiliar. He wants a proper job to do. He's been working on a deal in New Hampshire all autumn, but it's not going well. He draws pleasure in spending that same energy he used to put into business deals in the effort of trying to divorce his wife. It's a tactic that helps him save face publicly—all along everyone thought she'd married him for his money; maybe they'd been right, but now he'd show them—while also giving him an opportunity to wield in private the power he's losing in the business world.

Olympic Refineries plans to open an oil refinery, and Onassis is working with New Hampshire's governor. Their proposal sparks a massive public outcry. A letter to the editor: "If such a plan is fulfilled, the wishes of the people are once again a travesty, and Democracy once again a political whim." But when the city council votes six to one against the plan in early March, it isn't the outcry of the locals swaying their votes so much as the disorganization at Olympic. The "whole operation smacks of slapdash," announced one of the councilmen, while a councilwoman says she's "appalled" by the company's lack of planning. Olympic has, another councilman notes, a "credibility gap."

It's a verdict that essentially keeps "the new husband of Jackie Kennedy" from building a refinery anywhere in America. According to Costa Gratsos—billed by the local papers as Ari's "Man in America"—Olympic has been "bombarded with letters from various lovers of nature" in Rhode Island too. "We have more important things to do than to be abused by ecologist groups," Gratsos, rebuffed, tells reporters. "Unless we are invited, we are not going to set foot in Rhode Island again." An especially awkward circumstance since Onassis's mother-in-law lives there.

This proposed deal and the vehement responses to it are tied up in the 1973 energy crisis and the oil embargo. It's a time of shortages in the land of plenty. "This does not mean that we are going to run out of gasoline or that air travel will stop or that we will freeze in our homes," Nixon reassures his fellow Americans in November 1973, for "The fuel crisis need not mean genuine suffering for any American. But it will require some sacrifice by all Americans."

Elvis is back in Vegas, "a noticeable bulge at the midsection," his face "a bit peaked," some of "the baby-faced softness" gone and his act "ever so subtly" toned down, but the show goes on: "Not even the energy crisis disturbed the Presley hoopla." When the billboard lights of Vegas are shut off to conserve power, Presley's tour manager puts luminous paper on all his signs, so they'll be visible in the desert night. When the crowd shouts, "Presley for President," The King yells back "Don't put that on me, man." The president has a lot of problems.

"Wasn't anybody smart enough to notice until right now that we were running out of oil?" The answer: "Of course! Children of the 1930s—and they are running the government today—were aware of it. 'What will happen when we have used up all the oil?' They used to say. 'What a silly question!' Their parents used to reply. 'Before that can happen science will come up with something new to replace oil.'" Of course, they'd known all along—a reality that only deepens public suspicion.

In October 1973, a coalition of Arab countries initiated an oil embargo targeting nations who provided Israel with military assistance during a month-long war, led by Egypt and Syria, to recover stolen lands. The embargo was still in effect when Onassis tries to cut this deal and there's a lot of xenophobia and anti-Arab bigotry connected to it. Rumors swirl that he's offered "the Arabs"—always portrayed as a monolith—a part-stake in the refinery, talk that spurs the vice president of the Senate to warn New Hampshire's governor that "not one foot of this great state" should be offered to "the Arabs." For there are racist worries an Olympic refinery will be the gateway through which an "Arab Takeover" will commence.

AGAIN BERNADETTE CARROZZA, EDITOR-IN-CHIEF OF *Photoplay, Motion Picture,* and *Radio Mirror,* announces she has "banned all mention of Jackie." The cited reason: "Over-exposure."

"We'll do a story on Jackie when she makes a movie," Carrozza tells columnist Jack O'Brian, who wants to see this as a sign "of less exasperating times" but assumes it is hopeless, that "she'll be mentioned long before she makes a movie."

According to the gossips, everything is okay: "You are always reading about the trouble in the marriage of Aristotle and Jackie Onassis, but if you had been in Cadiz, Spain, the other night you wouldn't have believed a word of it," because the Os were "whooping it up at a rich American's villa like a couple of lovebirds." But when he sees them in Madrid, a former beau of Jackie's has a different impression. When she dances with her husband, he thinks, Ari performs like "a wounded beast": "She was the master; he was clearly her slave."

•

In mid-April, NBC's *Today Show* airs an interview with Maria Callas by Barbara Walters. Ever one for a provocative comment, Callas appears relaxed and content as she declares, "Love is so much better when you're not married . . ." and "There are no chains for love." She admits to never having met Mrs. Onassis but maintains that this isn't her fault. "I hold no grudges," she announces. "I don't think it's necessary . . . it's tiring, and I don't think that, in the long run, it helps in life." As with most everything she says in relation to Ari, this implies that the opposite holds true with his wife.

Asked if she has bad feelings toward Jackie, she swears she doesn't: "Not at all, not at all. Why should I? Of course, if she treats Mr. Onassis very badly, I might be very angry."

This interview is given in advance of what is billed as her comeback tour. It's a return to a career she largely gave up because of Ari. "I thought that when I met a man I loved that I didn't need to sing," she tells Walters. "The most important thing in a woman is to have a man of her own, to make him happy . . . naturally, any man who is in love with you, the way he was, I'm sure he was, did not want me to sing."

The tension Maria describes is present in Jackie's marriage as well. She wants to *do* something, and increasingly she's looking for ways she might. When the columnist Aileen Mehle confides she wants to write a book about society women in New York, Jackie tells her, "Write about them, their lives, their ambitions, their lies. Write how nothing really is the way it seems. How these women who seem to have it all, are really desperate and trapped." It is advice, Mehle feels, that holds personal resonance for her.

If she married looking for freedom, she no longer feels she has that. She seems to be, during this time, searching for a new role or, at the very least, experimenting with the possibilities available. But she does so hesitantly. There is a tension between her desire to do something and her insecurity that whatever she does might be excoriated. There are, it seems, also tensions within her marriage around the idea of women and work.

Lucy Jarvis, a documentary producer, approaches her about doing narration for a film on the Sistine Chapel, but the conversation abruptly ends when Ari announces: "Greek wives don't work." Ari tells Jarvis, "Grace Kelly was a working girl when she married a prince and became a princess. You want to take my wife, whom I consider a princess, who was the wife of a head of state, and turn her into a working girl?" He had, Jarvis felt, "a marvelous ability with words that influenced her," and Jackie was "totally devoted to him."

When the producer Karen Lerner offers her the opportunity to work on a documentary about Cambodia's Angkor Wat, she discusses it with the president of NBC News, but she ultimately turns that down too. She hesitates to seize upon a new direction but, increasingly, she explores the possibilities.

IN 1967, EGYPT SUSPENDED DIPLOMATIC RELATIONS WITH the U.S., due to U.S. military and financial support of the Zionist state of Israel and its seizure of Egyptian, Jordanian, Syrian, and Palestinian lands. Egypt has only just resumed diplomatic relations with the U.S. on February 28, and she's eager to go. The plan is to tour the pyramids and other ancient monuments in Luxor and Aswan. According to the papers, it's a "vacation" for "Onassis and his party of millionaires" —a group that's apparently just Caroline and John and some of their friends. Surprisingly few details emerge, no indications that Ari's conducting negotiations or planning to move there. Either it really is a pleasure trip or he's conducting his business far more quietly than he did in the past.

A few photographs surface, far fewer than usual. A belly dancer atop their table in Cairo. Jackie and Caroline pouring sand out of their shoes in Aswan. Jackie and Ari on a riverboat floating down the Nile, relaxed, serene. Jackie on a camel. The whole family on camels, smiling, looking strong and eager and well.

•

It's a time of relenting and revelation, a time of reckoning.

To reduce gasoline and fuel consumption during the energy crisis, a fifty-five-mile-per-hour maximum speed limit goes into effect countrywide. By late April, if Americans keep carpooling, remain thoughtful about using their cars, and adhere to the new speed limit, the new head of the Federal Energy Office assures them "there will be enough fuel for vacations" come summer. Scientists, in contrast, warn that Americans are living in "an energy dream world."

•

In New Jersey, Little League baseball claims girls are likely to get breast cancer if struck in the chest by a ball and that their "bodily privacy" will be threatened if they are permitted on its teams. In a two–one ruling, the circuit court rules in favor of the girls.

It's a ruling that comes amid what appears to be a turning tide of American attitudes toward women. The Equal Rights Amendment is winding its way through the country. In late April it requires the approval of five more states, approval that can come from any of the seventeen states yet to ratify.

"Every president since Eisenhower has supported the Equal Rights Amendment," the ERA chairman and president of the League of Women Voters of Sterling, Illinois, writes the local paper. "The Equal Rights Amendment is frequently discounted by calling it a 'Communist plot' or a 'Women's Lib' proposal. In fact . . . the Equal Rights Amendment was initiated in 1923! . . . We urge you to consider this amendment on its merits and not be persuaded by the current circulation of inaccuracies describing it."

And then something goes terribly wrong. First, Nebraska rescinds it ratification, followed by Tennessee. The legality of this is unclear, and the question is, as the UPI puts it, "whether a state, as sexist folklore says of women, always retains the right to change its mind." In Nashville, women and children watch from the balcony above as the amendment's sponsor, Gwen Fleming, declares it "a sad day for women, men and children of this state" from the state capitol's floor.

·

It's a sad day in Hollywood when, on April 25, Richard Burton and Elizabeth Taylor announce that they are divorcing.

But there's an emergent cynicism as well. "So what else is new?" Linda Deutsch of the AP asks. Their marriage, the papers report, was "a 10-year spectacle of lavish living, stormy quarrels and loving public reunions." In York, Pennsylvania, asked about her reaction to the news of this divorce, a young woman says, "I've heard so many rumors and stories for so long that I find it is hard to believe that report is true."

·

In Washington, Vice President Gerald Ford warns, the "erosion of confidence in our federal government . . . has reached crisis proportions," creating "a grave situation." The time has come in this "sorry mess," Ford believes, "for persons in public life to face the truth and to speak the truth."

The White House tapes are subpoenaed. Following much back-and-forth, the Nixon administration gives in with a deluge of transcripts. It is, Helen Thomas believes, a "gamble against impeachment." Nixon maintains it's an effort to put to rest all the nonsense about this jack-ass crime and return to the real work of the country, because, as he tells Americans, "every day absorbed by Watergate is a day lost from the work that must be done . . . with the great problems that affect your prosperity, affect your security, that could affect your lives."

•

May Day. The transcripts total 1,308 pages and it's reported "President Nixon himself put the final pencil" to them. As an editor, his choices are baffling. Curiously, "The White House permitted numerous 'hells' and 'damns' to remain intact, but anything harsher was censored for public consumption," giving rise to the notation "(Expletive Deleted)," a phrase that "occurs most frequently in President Nixon's conversations."

The president's editing doesn't have the effect he hoped. "(Expletive Deleted) Sweeps Land Like the Hula Hoop," according to the headlines. For the most stunning revelation in the transcripts is the fact the president of the United States so often resorts to what the evangelist Billy Graham calls "salty language." There will be a rush to claim this isn't unheard of in the White House, that prior presidents also had foul mouths, but the transcripts are disillusioning.

The Government Printing Office produces 15,000 copies, while 700-page paperbacks are rushed through commercial publishers. All of them sell briskly.

One of the president's advisors, Pat Buchanan, observes wryly: "We didn't think it was going to get the reception of 'Gone with the Wind.'"

A bumper sticker in D.C.: "Impeach the (Expletive Deleted)."

•

From New York, Jackie endorses her old friend John Glenn who's in a tight primary race to be the Democratic nominee for an Ohio Senate seat. In a message for broadcast on radio and TV commercials, she says, "I have never done anything political for anyone before, but I feel that both I and the country have an obligation to John Glenn."

When he orbited the earth in 1962, he "made us feel pride in America that we had not felt for a long time," she remembers, suggesting he could do it again now. In the Senate, she says, "John Glenn's leadership would be a shining light."

Glenn wins.

•

A week later, a thirteen-year-old boy is cycling into Central Park one late afternoon, on his way to his tennis lesson with a friend, when an older teenager comes up to him and says, "Get the hell off the bike." The thief pushes the kid off the ten-speeder, mounts the bicycle, steals the kid's tennis racket, and then pedals away into the park. He has just stolen John F. Kennedy Jr.'s bicycle.

John, who had slipped his Secret Service detail, informs the police then rides through the park with them in a patrol car looking for the thief, whom the AP describes as "A teenaged Central Park marauder."

Publicly, she appears nonplussed. The robbery occurred in New York on Tuesday, and on Wednesday, she is photographed at a Democratic Study Group fundraising dinner in D.C. She poses willingly for photographers and appears "amused." When reporters ask if she's missed the American press, she smiles and says, "Yes." The next day, she's photographed while viewing the "African Art and Motion" exhibition at the National Gallery of Art. In its caption for one of these photographs, UPI declares her "possibly [the] world's greatest human tourist attraction."

Back in New York, the NYPD revives its bicycle theft unit in direct response to the theft of John F. Kennedy Jr.'s $145 ten-speeder. A dozen police officers with rented bikes assemble before TV cameras in Central Park. As they practice what the AP characterizes as "tactical maneuvers intended to strike trepidation in the hearts of would-be bicycle thieves," two youths from the crowd climb aboard unattended police bikes and cycle away.

•

Caroline is interning in her uncle's Senate office that summer, answering telephones and sorting mail. One afternoon, she sits in the audience of a debate by the House Judiciary Committee on impeachment.

•

In Rome, Jackie is all the rage: the hottest, newest nightclub is called "Jackie O," and Pier Carpi's play *Vieni Tutti* is astonishing Romans with its suggestion that Jackie was involved in her husband's murder and felt an unrequited passion for Bobby, her late brother-in-law.

•

Back in Greece, on July 23, the junta hands control of the government back over to civilian political leaders. The collapse was preceded by the junta's brutal quashing of a protest at the Athens Polytechnic the prior November and then precipitated by events in Cyprus, which had been invaded by Turkey earlier in the month. The first free elections in over a decade would be held later that year.

•

That month's *McCall's* magazine features an article entitled "Jacqueline Onassis at 45." Jackie has a good relationship with both Gloria Emerson, the writer of the piece, and *McCall's*, and she reportedly authorizes Emerson to speak to some of her friends. If Emerson does so, she puts precious few of their quotes in the published piece. Instead, Emerson explores the difference between the public perception of Jackie and the woman she knows.

When a friend of Emerson's asks what Jackie is like, Emerson writes, "My friend, as do many other women, sees Jacqueline Onassis in rooms with huge chandeliers, furs strewn everywhere, and all those hundreds of dresses." She goes on to write, "None of it is true, of course. . . . Yet my friend does not really want to hear that. . . . It makes my friend feel cheated," because "we wanted her to help us, to make things nice again, to make us feel less frightened. It would not do for her just to look pretty and pay attention to the children and go to the theater, you see."

"It would be foolish to pretend that Jacqueline Onassis has a run-of-the-mill life, worrying about grocery bills or rent," Emerson writes. "But the point is that she is not as removed from the realities as many people prefer to think. She does not choose to be." Jackie is, in Emerson's estimation, an artist who despite "genuine gifts" no longer paints, a "restless, original woman who cannot see too many ruins." Emerson stresses her normalcy, establishing that she answers her own phone and clarifying that "Her voice is not really that of a little girl. . . . It is not the voice of a babyish woman or one who tries to be cute."

Emerson is the *New York Times* correspondent in Saigon, and with "Jacqueline Onassis at 45," she's writing an article about a friend for a publication traditionally considered a "woman's magazine." In Emerson's account, Jackie has choices, as do the women reading it: they can continue to see her "only as thrilling theater lived by the very rich," which is "to cheapen and cut off our own past." Or they can choose an alternative: a more complex woman, "often generous, kind and sensitive . . . temperamental, impatient, too fussy, stubborn and sharp." Not a "woman of wild extremes," but a woman whose full humanity is realized, a woman with moods and choices and depths, not stuck in a soap opera but living her life.

"Not many women I have known have been driven back upon themselves as she has. It is a long and hard journey none of us need envy. She is a survivor . . . free now to be what she wishes,"

Emerson writes. "It would be easier to be removed from things, but she does not choose to: She remains curious and alive."

"She had never chosen to be our heroine," but she is, and Emerson concludes, "It is not history we want so much as more gossip."

HER HUSBAND IS NOT WELL. THE SITUATION GOES PUBLIC when, in an effort to keep Ari's sagging eyelids open, Christina resorts to Band-Aids. Looking at photos, neurologists who've never treated him diagnose myasthenia gravis, a chronic disease that involves wasting of the muscles.

The neurologists who diagnosed him sight unseen were right, and the cause seemed clear. "You don't catch myasthenia gravis from anything," according to his doctor, Isadore Rosenfeld. "It's an autoimmune disorder produced by the body itself in the later years and often following an overwhelming emotional crisis. That was the case with Onassis after the death of his son."

A "bloody nuisance," the patient calls it. He's supposed to accompany his wife on safari in Kenya, but reportedly "he stayed behind at the last minute," though it seems likely this is due to business rather than health.

•

His wife is on what's billed as a "photographic safari," where she, her children, and their friends view elephants, lions, rhinos, and giraffes in their natural habitats. It's a good time to get away from America.

The impeachment hearings have picked up momentum and, on July 24, a ruling comes down from the Supreme Court compelling the president to surrender more tapes. Upon reading the transcripts, one of Nixon's "most vocal supporters" on the Watergate committee, a Republican, changes his mind and comes out in favor of impeach-ment, citing the transcripts as "the body blow" to his faith in the president. From there, it's a mass exodus as Republicans abandon him. "Watergate is our shame. . . . There are frightening implications for the future of our country if we do not impeach the president of the United States," says a Republican congressman from Virginia. "I think we are at the point frankly where it may be in the national interest and in the president's interest that he resign," suggests the second-highest ranking Republican in the Senate.

Ted Kennedy is conspicuously silent, as the president's troubles seem to only remind everyone that Teddy might not have told the whole truth about Chappaquiddick and that he got away with something too. The fifth anniversary of the accident passed with a flurry of newspaper articles and magazine retellings the previous month. "President Nixon's removal from office would effectively end the 1976 presidential candidacy of Sen. Edward M. Kennedy," hypothesizes one commentator, because Nixon's removal "would uncork a backlash surely aimed at Kennedy," and the "the burden of Chappaquiddick during the immediate post-Watergate, post-impeachment period" would be "too much of a drag for Kennedy to overcome."

•

Events accelerate.

Sunday, August 4. The president is ordered to surrender another set of tapes. "All hell will break loose when they come out," an unidentified source informs the *Washington Post*.

On Monday, the tapes come out, revealing that six days after the break-in the president indirectly ordered the FBI, "Don't go any further into this case, period!"

"It's bad," a White House official tells a reporter. "This is the end," says a senator. Another says simply: "He's gone."

The Republicans begin pressuring the president to resign as the headlines scream: "NIXON'S HOLD ON PRESIDENCY SLIPS."

Tuesday's *Atlanta Constitution-Journal* predicts, "At the rate things are going now, President Nixon isn't going to have the American public to kick around much longer."

On Wednesday, "Appearing more alone than ever," Nixon con-
venes his cabinet and swears he will not be hounded from office,
but the bravado is short-lived. That same day, a Rhode Island paper
reports that, in "great anguish," he's made an "irrevocable" decision to resign, "irrespective of the massive injustice committed
against him."

"How could a smart politician permit the Watergate burglary,
which seemed safely consigned as a footnote to history in early
1973, to mushroom into the most shattering disaster ever to over-
take an American president?" a columnist in Missouri wonders.

At 9:00 p.m. on Thursday, August 8, 1974, in a televised address
broadcast across all three networks, Richard Nixon announces that
he is resigning the presidency effective at noon the following day.
NBC estimates that 130 million Americans—over 60 percent of the
country's population—watched the sixteen-minute speech. "We are
not likely to see this again in our lives," NBC's broadcaster notes.

"Television, which has brought this nation its share of assassina-
tions and funerals, presented a soothing effect," observes the UPI's
reporter. "One only had to look into [the news anchors'] eyes and
know that all will be well. There will be a United States tomorrow."

After taking the Oath of Office, President Gerald R. Ford sighs
in relief: "My fellow Americans, our long national nightmare is
over."

That same day, Jackie Onassis arrives in Kenya. She says nothing,
publicly. Privately, according to a relative, she says she feels terribly
for Richard Nixon, that he had wanted the presidency so badly and
then it all ended so ironically, so sadly.

A MONTH LATER, IN BOSTON, TED KENNEDY APPEARS AT A
rally staged by local white parents protesting a federal school deseg-
regation order set to go into effect later in the week. As Kennedy
enters the building, the crowd pelts him with eggs, tomatoes,
and garbage. They turn their backs to him, so that they are facing

the John F. Kennedy Federal Building as they sing "God Bless America."

Three days later, the family receives a serious and credible kidnapping threat in Boston against "all children of Kennedy blood." The FBI believes it's part of an organized plot and takes it more seriously than the usual sixty or so threats Ted Kennedy routinely receives each week.

The next day, Kennedy meets with his advisors at his home on Squaw Island and decides he will not run for the presidency in 1976.

•

Former President Nixon is resting in Long Beach, California, and is expected to remain hospitalized through the week, recovering from a blood clot. A "potentially dangerous situation," his physician says, "but not critical at this time."

•

In Athens, Christina overdoses on sleeping pills and is secretly admitted to a hospital in London. Tina flies in from France to care for her daughter. The event is kept out of the papers and even Ari isn't told until Christina is out of danger.

But Tina isn't well either. She and Alexander hadn't been on speaking terms at the time of his death. He'd not wanted her to marry Stavros Niarchos; she'd not wanted him to marry Fiona Thyssen. They had a falling-out in the autumn of 1972 and hadn't reconciled before his sudden death, leaving his mother griefstricken and remorseful. Ari and Niarchos tried to help her, but she increasingly relied on barbiturates and suffered ill health. Phlebitis—an inflammation of the veins and a disease shared by Richard Nixon—became problematic, aggravated by a pair of skiing accidents in the winter of 1974, and so she'd spent the summer resting on Niarchos's yacht. "I'm *suddenly* forty-five years old," she says. She can't quite believe it; time goes so swift.

When a maid finds Tina's body in her room at the Niarchos mansion in Paris on October 10, rumors circulate that Tina's abuse of barbiturates further aggravated her condition and led to her death. Christina, suspicious after her aunt Eugenie's death, requests an autopsy to rule out foul play. The coroners do nothing to ease her mind: the autopsy reveals no signs of violence, but they also can't identify a cause of the lung swelling that killed her. Christina is so distraught that Ari fears she will try to kill Niarchos.

"The death of Tina Niarchos marked the third to strike the clan in four years," notes the UPI, declaring it "a modern Greek tragedy." It's too much. At the funeral, Christina's heard to say, "My aunt, my brother, now my mother—what is happening to us?" She blames Jackie.

Ari doesn't attend his ex-wife's funeral. He's "too old, too sick," one of his aides tells the press, but according to an Olympic executive, "the psychic wounds inflicted by the tragedy in Paris and the renewed bitterness between the families exacted a dreadful price."

In early November, Ari checks in to a New York hospital for what is described as a "routine physical checkup." He remains for a full week. Upon his release, there are no comments.

His wife is in New York then. In the hospital, he was put on cortisone—a medication known to prompt mood swings and uncontrollable anger, particularly in people with short tempers. During one of her visits, he experiences what one of his doctors describes as "a cortisone rage." Distraught, his wife leaves the room.

But business continues as usual, though things are not well in that realm either. A letter to the editor of the *San Mateo Times* had noted of the current financial crisis, "Things are so bad that legendary money maker Aristotle Onassis has sought to end operations of Olympic Airways." A few days after he discharges himself from the hospital, he learns about Olympic's cash flow problem, the full extent of which had been kept from him. The company can no longer sustain itself. Efforts to ease the financial strain by firing employees result in a strike by the company's entire work-force. Onassis is also, at this time, building the Olympic Tower, a residential-commercial property featuring apartments primarily intended for international businessmen like himself who need a place to stay while they're in New York. "They're the first apart-ments of their kind," says the president of the real estate group han-dling their sale, "designed more as weekend cottages than primary homes." It's a business decision that appears out of touch given the current economic realities.

"He was visibly going downhill, yet the people at Olympic, even Johnny Meyer, were insisting that it was something that was going to be fixed," remembers a journalist at *Paris Match*.

For Jackie, there's a re-entrenchment. Skorpios no longer feels like a refuge—too many photographers buzzing around—and so she avoids it and stays in New York. Ari is in and out of the city, in and out of the hospital, but it seems they go on as usual.

She quietly attends a Thanksgiving dinner for seniors at Lennox Hill Neighborhood Association, a social service agency on Manhattan's Upper East Side. This doesn't make the papers. The only evidence of the visit is a pair of photos in the organization's archive at Hunter College of the City University of New York, where she stands in the middle of an ecstatic crowd, smiling and shaking hands.

## Friday Morning. November 22. 1974

Her attention is increasingly drawn to issues and causes at home, specifically in New York, and she's putting down roots in the area. News hits the papers that she's spent $200,000 on a two-story frame house in the New Jersey horse country she's loved for years—a part of the U.S. that, so go the rumors, Ari does not enjoy.

There's more than a little irony to her support of the International Center for Photography and in that, at the museum's opening, she doesn't avoid the press. She also delivers a statement to a reporter praising the Center's purpose, saying it is "something we should all be grateful for," not only because it "preserve[d] a landmark—a gracious, old building," but because photographs—which "have terribly moving moments in people's lives . . . the things that touch people most"—"can be an instrument of change."

"Photographers can affect people," she says. "Maybe people will see things differently now—you know, care."

·

People care a lot. The humorist Erma Bombeck runs a column describing the violent symptoms she experiences after missing her beauty shop appointment. "You are having withdrawal symptoms from not having read anything about Jacqueline Onassis for a week," her hairdresser informs her as Bombeck realizes that a "little Jackie news calms the nerves."

"I cannot remember when I became addicted to Jackie or why," Bombeck writes, but she knows her loyalty has become "habit forming."

Jackie isn't the only habit-forming personality around. Why all the interest in Secretary of State Henry Kissinger? a columnist asks. The response: because "Kissinger, like Jacqueline Kennedy Onassis, is a representative figure of a certain American culture," and, therefore, "one of those people about whom a certain group of Americans will read even when there is nothing to read about them."

They're different cultures—Jackie's far more low-brow than Kissinger's, the columnist thinks—but he wonders if perhaps the interest in these people reveals that America is, in effect, many cultures, and whether "Sociologists could . . . catalog us all into our distinctive cultures by studying the people we are willing to read about on days when there is nothing worth reading about them . . . what you think is important enough to care about when there is nothing going on worth caring about."

But it's not that there isn't anything going on. It's precisely because so much is happening so quickly that these people, whom other people are willing to read about when there is nothing worth reading about them, matter so much. Jackie's star appeal was, in some ways, self-perpetuating once it began. There was always something more, so that the story kept on going and it kept you wondering and reading because you did not know what might happen next.

There is always something else to read. Ron Galella is still kicking about, publicizing his book of photographs and talking about his favorite subject. "Jackie. Jackie. Jackie. Everything depends on Jackie," he writes, "the biggest star all over the world." She has "every ingredient of ultraglamour," he muses to a fashion writer. "Jackie has power and great magnetism. She has physical beauty. She has social charisma. She's intellectually wealthy. She's culturally advantaged. Jackie is the composite Super Woman who possesses every desirable trait."

IN ALL THE YEARS OF ALL THE RUMORS, THEIR LIVES HAVE never been so clearly divergent as they are during this period. She's bought the home in New Jersey. In New York, apparently at Costa Gratsos's suggestion, Ari summons the columnist Jack Anderson. In his column that December, Anderson reports that Onassis has "the fierce look of a Mediterranean pirate, but the harsh features are softened by a quiet, gentle charm." In their conversation, Onassis discusses the economy, oil, the CIA, Watergate, and his wife. Jackie is in horse country, he says. He "scoffed" at reports of a divorce.

At this meeting, according to Anderson, Ari says nothing derogatory about his wife, expressing only "a mild complaint about her extravagance and her horsey friends," but Gratsos later tells Anderson and his colleague Les Whitten about "the total

incompatibility of Jackie and Ari . . . and Jackie's faggoty friends."
It is through these discussions that Anderson gets the Onassis-
authorized story of how "Jacqueline systematically converted
gowns, gifts and other indulgences of Onassis into cash by selling them off at fashionable New York City resale houses." It is a
story orchestrated to make her appear selfish and greedy before the
American public, at a moment when she is expected to be contest-
ing Ari's will.

•

He complains about her spending to anyone who will listen, but
beneath such complaints lies another: he's saying she doesn't
want to be with him. "I cannot understand her. All she does is
spend, spend, spend—and she's never in the same place as I am,"
he tells an acquaintance. "If I'm in Paris, she's in New York.
If I go to Skorpios, she goes to London . . . She's never with
me. . . . Anywhere I am, she is somewhere else. . . . She wants my
money but not me." The acquaintance believes the problem is "her
coldheartedness," though Ari claims her expenses are the bigger
issue. But he would say that. It would be harder, in the end, to
admit he's lonely and misses his wife and wants her to be there for
him in a way that it seems he cannot ask her to be.

When she's away, she has Nancy Tuckerman call to ask when she
should return. He reportedly replies to Tuckerman, "Tell her to
stay indefinitely." He makes it seem as though he's done with her.
Perhaps he is, perhaps he isn't. Maybe even he doesn't know.

His frame of mind is betrayed by a front-page advertisement
he places in an Athens newspaper on Christmas Eve: it offers an
$830,000 reward to anyone who can bring proof that "sabotage
rather than negligence . . . caused the death of Alexander Onassis."

# 1975

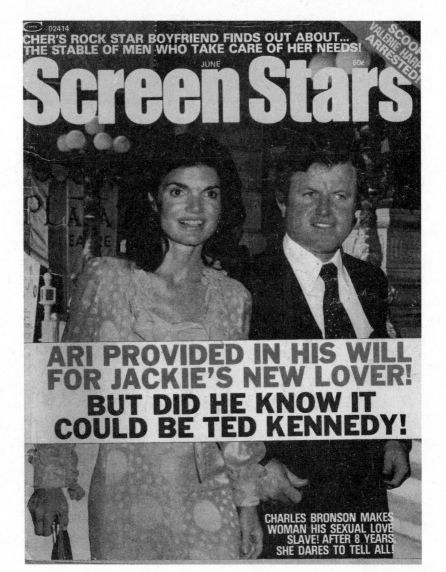

02414

CHER'S ROCK STAR BOYFRIEND FINDS OUT ABOUT...
THE STABLE OF MEN WHO TAKE CARE OF HER NEEDS!

JUNE          60¢

# Screen Stars

SCOOP
VALERIE HARPER
ARRESTED!

## ARI PROVIDED IN HIS WILL FOR JACKIE'S NEW LOVER!
## BUT DID HE KNOW IT COULD BE TED KENNEDY!

CHARLES BRONSON MAKES
WOMAN HIS SEXUAL LOVE
SLAVE! AFTER 8 YEARS,
SHE DARES TO TELL ALL!

AFTER NEW YEAR'S 1975, NEW YORK IS ABUZZ WITH THE revelation that an anonymous 1,500-word piece in the *New Yorker*'s January 13 issue was written by "Jacqueline Kennedy Onassis, long the most-publicized woman in the world."

"It's a straight little piece of reporting, very good and very usable," the *New Yorker*'s editor-in-chief, William Shawn, reveals. "Jackie Writing Again" read the headlines, reminding everyone—as if they could forget—"she writes from a background of a trained newspaperwoman who understands photography first hand." Technically, she's been writing all along, penning short essays in memoriam to John Kennedy for *Life, Look,* and *McCall's*. What's different about her writing for the *New Yorker* is that it has nothing to do with JFK.

"We treated it like any other contribution," the editor-in-chief informs the press, earnestly if not convincingly. In reality, she telephoned Shawn in late 1974 and said she wanted to do some writing for the *New Yorker*. Shawn, just as eager to have her, discussed the possibility of regular contributions to the magazine. According to Shawn, she said "she knew about a lot of things but she especially knew people—had met lots of them, from all walks of life." A few weeks later, she submitted a manuscript for the *New Yorker*'s anonymous "Talk of the Town" column. But the idea of regular contributions fell through, possibly due to events to come and her own shifting ideas of what kind of career she might have.

•

A week later, the Greek government announces it is assuming operational control of her husband's airline. Ari's only public comment after the negotiations: "Amen."

Then he pulls the rug out from under them, upping his price and refusing to sign the final documents. An official tells the AP that Onassis "still has a number of powerful cards in his hands which could cause difficulties for the government," but that isn't enough to keep people from wondering if "the Greek Midas with the golden touch is losing his luster." His confidence is shaken, his thinking clouded. He's "lying low," a spokesman says. With his counterdemands driven by his "realization of his mistake," the papers report he is now "back-peddling to save as much as possible."

It will be his final major business transaction and it's far from elegant. "He'd lost touch completely," an aide remembered. "He was played out."

He's old, he's ill, and he's angry. "After a certain point, I never saw love on his side when it came to Jackie," remembered the columnist Aileen Mehle, who moved in the same social circles. "I never heard him say anything nice about her. Now, *she* was sweet and warm and affectionate. He was aloof." He'd taken to calling her "The Widow" and, Mehle recalled, though she "tried to keep up appearances . . . he was obviously mad at her. And I mean all the time."

Amid his November hospitalization, during the "cortisone rage," he reportedly screamed at his wife and berated her. When he left the hospital against doctor's orders, she retreated to New Jersey.

"He was angry that Jackie was away so much," remembered his personal attorney. "He felt that she was not around as much as before. Whether that was true or not—and, in my view, it was not . . . he was feeling abandoned. . . . He was used to abandoning people. Now, for the first time, he was the one abandoned."

When he flies back to Athens in late 1974, she doesn't follow. And she remains in New York throughout January, as his empire crumbles in Greece. A friend who'd been struck by her happiness during a 1969 visit to Skorpios said of her in 1975, "The change was like day to night. She seemed apprehensive about the future. I don't think she mentioned Greece at all. She seemed to be in one black mood after another." But she kept busy during this period. In particular, she got involved in the effort to save Grand Central Station from the wrecking ball.

UPON OPENING IN 1913, THE STATION WAS DECLARED "A Glory of the Metropolis," "The World's Greatest Railroad Station," a "possibility . . . fraught with tremendous importance to the City of New York." By 1975, it's in total disrepair: grimy, cluttered, and dark—the soot and ash of the trains combining with the nicotine and tar of patrons' cigarettes to create a film that obscures the zodiac on the Main Concourse ceiling, which will ultimately take experts twelve years to remove.

The building's landmark status has just been revoked, leaving it vulnerable to corporate development, and its owners are threatening to erect a fifty-nine-story glass and steel office building above it, capping the Beaux Arts exterior.

She's read an article about it in the *New York Times* and calls the head of the Municipal Art Society, who remembers, "She'd heard all about it, and wanted to be helpful. She said she wasn't working. I tried to ask for something modest, and told her we were having a press conference, and perhaps she could appear. . . . And she said, simply, no problem."

At the press conference on January 30, she appears relentlessly optimistic. "If we don't care about our past we can't have very much hope for our future," she says. "We've all heard that it's too late, or that it has to happen, that it's inevitable. But I don't think that's true. Because I think if there is a great effort, even if it's the eleventh hour, then you can succeed and I know that's what we'll do." Asked why she joined the committee, she replies, "Because I care desperately."

•

A few weeks later, in Athens, her husband is reportedly ill with the flu. Friends tell the AP that he called his wife on February 2, "complained of being lonely and depressed," and that she flew from New York to be with him.

There are rumors he's battling a muscular disease, but his spokesman scotches those. "Mr. Onassis went to the airport without a coat and caught a cold" is the official story. But the family has a different version of events. They mention myasthenia gravis, saying the disease was to blame for his hospitalization back in November and he was experiencing a flare-up now.

Bullshit, says his aide Johnny Meyer, back in New York. According to Meyer, the reports are "exaggerated" and, though Ari is "feeling unwell," he's "on the phone as usual."

Rumors of his death are rampant. Relatives take turns manning the telephone in order to deny them. Finally, his wife insists—apparently over the objections of his family and Greek doctors, but supported by a French specialist—that he be transferred to Paris for better care.

Arriving in Paris, he goes against doctor's orders and stays in his own home for a night before checking into the hospital. Though he has difficulty walking, he refuses assistance from his wife and daughter, telling them, "I don't want those sons of bitches to see me being held up by a couple of women." And so he arrives at 88 Avenue Foch by himself, looking weak and weary, says "good evening" to the gathered photographers and newsmen, walks across the garden, and into his home.

When he goes to the hospital the following day, photographers rush him, and three bodyguards shout "Assassins!" then link arms to keep the *paparazzi* at bay. Of Ari, reporters note, "He looked tired and had deep circles under his eyes." It is the last time he's seen in public.

A few days later, he's said to be "all right," and his wife is reportedly visiting daily. But a friend who sees him in the hospital senses he no longer wants her there. The friend, a Greek, sees Jackie lounging on an adjacent hospital bed and thinks to himself that no Greek wife would behave like that. "As soon as Onassis saw me," he recalled, "he motioned me to come in, and he turned to Jackie and said, 'Why don't you go home now?'" Ari couldn't wait to get rid of her, he thought.

Ari's problems compound, the complications from myasthenia gravis aggravated by jaundice, pneumonia, and cardiac issues. He's stricken with influenza and placed in an oxygen tent. He undergoes a gallbladder operation. He keeps rallying. An aide tells the press that he's seriously ill, but not in danger.

And he's cantankerous as ever. He doesn't like being seen as weak, doesn't want everyone standing around, staring, watching him get worse and worse. He hadn't wanted to be seen propped up by women when he arrived in Paris, and he doesn't want them around watching him die now.

She seems resigned to this. When she's in Paris, she dines with friends, who endeavor to keep her spirits up. After a dinner with Mona Bismarck in mid-February, she updates Mona on Ari's progress, writing: "Today the doctors say I may go to New York for a few days to see my son John who is alone there and anxious. So that shows Ari is better—They won't let us see Ari for the rest of the week because it agitates him—so that is a blessing which makes me feel less guilty about longing to see John so much."

It's unclear what her relationship is with Christina. By most accounts, Christina hates her and blames her for the tragedies that have befallen the Onassis family. But Christina is nonetheless in her thoughts. In the same letter, she mentions her intention to find "Fra Giovanni's prayer," because "I know it will strike a chord in Christina—and help her in the weeks ahead." What she refers to is most likely the prayer written by Fra Giovanni Giocondo to Contessina Allagia Dela Aldobrandeschi on Christmas Eve 1513, which reads, in part:

> The gloom of the world is but a shadow. Behind it, yet within our reach, is joy. There is radiance and glory in the

darkness, could we but see; and to see, we have only to look. . . . Everything we call a trial, a sorrow, or a duty: believe me, the angel's hand is there; the gift is there, and the wonder of an overshadowing Presence. Our joys, too: be not content with them as joys, they too conceal diviner gifts.

All sentiments in keeping with her philosophy that the good and bad in life must be taken together, as she'd said in Tehran.

•

That she doesn't appear prostrate with grief doesn't mean she isn't grieving. "I was in Paris with Jackie at the time," remembered Niki Goulandris. "She visited him in the hospital daily. . . . We went to Notre Dame together, and she got down on her knees and prayed for Ari, even though she knew his condition was hopeless. She knew it was the end." But she refuses to put her life on hold. Her children need her and so she shuttles back and forth.

•

From New York, she continues lobbying for Grand Central and writes Mayor Abraham Beame "with the prayer that you will see fit to have the City of New York appeal" the Supreme Court's decision. "Is it not cruel to let our city die by degrees . . . until there will be nothing left of all her history and beauty to inspire our children? If they are not inspired by the past of our city, where will they find the strength to fight for her future?"

BACK IN PARIS, ARTEMIS IS AFRAID THE PRESS WILL REPORT any visit Maria makes and it will be a dreadful affront to her brother's wife, and so she forbids it. According to Kiki, the family's orders were followed. But Maria reportedly calls every day and also gets updates from a friend whose mother is hospitalized on the same floor. And she tells at least one acquaintance that she did see Ari before he died: that "he was calm and I think at peace with himself. He was very ill and he knew that the end was near, though he tried to ignore it." As she was leaving, she says, "he made a special effort to tell me, 'I loved you, not always well, but as much and as best as I was capable of. I tried.'" Given that he was intubated in mid-February and so incapable of speech, it's unclear how this was communicated.

On February 27, the American Hospital in Paris indicates that Ari is "improving slowly but steadily." But he isn't.

Unable to speak, according to one source, he seizes a pencil and writes to Christina: "PLEASE, Let me die!"

On March 10, Maria removes herself from the situation, fleeing Paris for Palm Beach. That same day, Jackie returns to New York. She leaves Paris reassured by Ari's doctors that his condition will continue indefinitely and it's okay to go. The "doctor advised her that Ari could hang on like that for weeks, perhaps even months," remembered Niki Goulandris. "Jackie felt that she could be of more use in New York to her children than she could be in Paris with Ari. So she left." Johnny Meyer, who was no Jackie fan, concurred: "Jackie and I both talked to the doctor. He told us that Ari was going to get better. . . . All [Ari] could do was give me a little wave with his hand. But the doctor said he was getting better, so Jackie and I got on the plane and flew home." As Meyer himself jokes to Ari, "Who ever heard of anybody dying from droopy eyelids?"

Two days later, a spokesman at the Onassis apartment informs the UPI that Ari remains "not too well," and that his wife is expected back after the weekend. She's keen to be in New York that weekend. Caroline's senior project for school was a month-long unsalaried stint at NBC; she spent the time working on a documentary, which is set to air on Saturday, March 15. Her mother wants to celebrate her accomplishment properly and plans to host a viewing party in Caroline's honor.

She's calling every day to check on her husband's condition and is told that it has not changed. By some accounts, the Onassis family can't reach her by phone to alert her of Ari's decline. By others, Christina orders the doctors not to tell her. Still others contend Artemis notifies her, and she's packing when she receives word on March 15 that her husband has died.

The press get their first look at the new widow that night when she leaves 1040 Fifth, pushing through a crowd of nearly 100 bystanders, and heads to John F. Kennedy airport for a nonstop flight to Paris. According to the *New York Times,* she wears "sunglasses, a black coat, black turtleneck sweater, black shoes and black stockings."

THERE'S TALK THAT SHE ABANDONED HIM IN HIS FINAL HOURS AND the notion sticks. On both sides of the Atlantic, people are talking, trying to get their version of the story out. The day of the funeral, the *New York Daily News* quotes "unnamed sources"—Johnny Meyer?—who suggest that the Os' marriage—a "glamorous union" but "no big love deal"—had been headed for divorce: "there was a time when they were not getting along well at all—it was all over but after Ari got sick, they decided to stay together." And, according to this source, Ari married her only "because he was fascinated that he could capture the Kennedy widow." It had all been a power play.

As a named source, Meyer is in the process of lowering expectations. Asked about Ari's will, he tells reporters the widow will get far less than the $170 million being reported in the press. More like $2 million, he thinks.

Conspiracy theories abound. A French friend of Jackie's suggests Ari's relatives conspired to keep her away from her husband's deathbed: "She was the outsider. They always resented her. They hated the idea she was getting the money. They kept her away from her dying husband." Lee Radziwill seems to back this up when she tells a journalist that "whenever Jackie phoned Paris this week to ask about Ari's condition she was told that he was still very sick but it looked hopeful. She was given no hint he was critical."

"Nonsense!" contends an observer in Paris. "It was common knowledge here that Onassis had only a few days to live."

According to Fred Sparks, Lee haughtily told his friend, "One cannot expect the AVERAGE person to understand why Ari ORDERED Jackie out of Paris. But that was his nature. He wanted to always bring Jackie laughter and love—not sorrow and death."

Regardless of the circumstances of her being away, upon receiving the news, Jackie immediately returns to Paris where a hospital attendant says, "She seemed like any other grieving wife who had just seen her dead husband." Greeting Kiki at the airport in Athens, she asks, sorrowfully, "What has happened to all of us?"

But this is not what everyone sees and the footage of her arrival in Greece appears particularly damning. According to the papers, when it airs on the nightly newscast of a local station, the "phones started ringing before the newscast had even ended," as "A broad cross-section of the Greek public . . . expressed both shock and resentment" over the demeanor of Onassis's widow. The director-general of the state-run station admits, "It's embarrassing for me to have to make this comment," but "Mrs. Onassis's manner at her husband's funeral has caused a wave of public indignation in Greece."

The problem is this: it appears she's smiling.

Kiki Moutatsos notices it at the airport, that "For one second, a smile crossed over Jackie's face . . . her usual expression, an attempt to mask the pain within. Yet I knew what others would think when they saw the photograph of that famous smile." It's the same look as when she walked in the funeral procession of John Kennedy, and the American commentators make the connection. They note that, "to most Americans over 25, that fleeting half smile, the erect head and almost savage composure were wrenchingly familiar." But in Greece it doesn't strike the right tone: she is too calm, too collected.

It's an impression exacerbated by an unfortunate series of photos where, while the Onassises appear devastated, every member of Jackie's family grins. But what appears inappropriate levity is more

likely the family distracting themselves as they power through emotionally grueling events, all of which must be endured in public.
Ted Kennedy, her mother, and her children are all present and providing emotional support. For, in truth, the situation is unnerving
and extraordinarily uncomfortable, especially for her.

At the funeral, the widow is repeatedly shunted to the back,
Christina walking in front with her aunts. Throughout the
ceremony, according to Kiki, the name of Maria Callas seems to
float on the air, along with the Greek word for "curse": "I shud-
dered to hear the dreadful word spoken and knew to whom it was
directed . . . his death had strengthened the numbers of those who
mistakenly believed that it was Jackie Kennedy who had brought
about the fall of the Onassis family."

During the funeral, she remains arm-in-arm with John and
keeps her sunglasses on, though the day isn't particularly bright.
In another photograph, she's arm-in-arm with two men, apparently
held up by them as she moves through the crush of mourners.

This is not a private event. Photographers are present throughout, shooting the funeral, and the other attendees audibly comment
on her looks and behavior. It is an upsetting and uncomfortable
situation. As one friend recalled, "Nobody gave her a chance to
grieve."

IN THE PRESS, THERE ARE TWO LINES OF INQUIRY: WHO WILL SHE
marry? How much money will she get? Conjecture is rife. "Before
the flowers had fairly wilted in the funeral chapel," a columnist
notes, "friends and compulsive Jackie-watchers were already spec-
ulating on who the next man in her life would be . . . the list of
'elligbles' [*sic*] would seem to be small." She's reported to be "heiress to a fortune variously estimated at anywhere from $2 million
to $125 million."

The money question is complex. In the Acapulco will, Ari left
her $100,000 per annum, plus $25,000 each per year for John and

Caroline until they reached twenty-one, at which point their payments would revert to her. He also specified that if she contested the will, she would forfeit everything. Under Greek law, she was entitled to one-eighth of his estate; however, he'd taken measures to prevent that. In October 1972, he had her sign the "Mutual Waiver and Release," a document in which she renounced her right to inherit, and which entitled her husband to leave her whatever he liked. She assumed he would make adequate provisions.

In reality, the "Mutual Waiver and Release" was a bogus document, legally unenforceable. And so he'd changed the law.

The Greek military government passed the "Regulation of Certain Matters of Greek Nationals Domiciled Abroad" in June 1974, a month before the dictatorship toppled. It was so specific a regulation, so clearly designed to do what Ari wanted, that her lawyers will call it "Lex Onassis." It decreed that if a Greek national (Ari) and a foreign national (Jackie) made an agreement while living abroad (in New York) wherein the foreign national waived her inheritance rights to the legally required 12.5 percent of the Greek national's fortune, the waiver would be valid in Greece. Under this law, Ari hoped his wife would be unable to contest his will. She would be forced to take whatever he gave her, and he would give her the bare minimum.

Christina thinks she's "greedy," but lawyers on both sides disagree. When they settle upon a cash figure, even Christina's lawyer observes that Jackie was hardly greedy and had accepted far less than she was entitled to under Greek law. But it isn't over. A month after the agreement is signed, another will surfaces, leading to a protracted legal fight that ultimately stretches on for eighteen months. In the end, Jackie gets $20 million, plus $6 million to defray U.S. inheritance taxes.

But for many, the money is the lesser of the two stories. According to the New York News service, "millions are wondering what the future holds for . . . the tragic heroine of America's favorite soap opera, 'The Life and Times of Jacqueline Kennedy Onassis.'"

"What in the world can Jackie do now?" Truman Capote asks.

"I expect she'll come back here and carry on life as it was," Lee Radziwill muses to a reporter. "After all, her children are settled here, and she has her life here."

Fred Sparks looks deep into her past to "do some educated guessing on Jackie's future now that she is once again the Best Known Widow on Earth." Will she "sink into the shadows in mourning for Ari" or do as Ari would have wanted and, "after a proper withdrawal . . . be reborn . . . in yet another romance"? Her husband has not been dead a month, and already everyone wants to solve the riddle of who she will marry next. Already she is a woman who must marry again, just as she had been throughout so much of the 1960s.

It is, in many respects, as if the marriage had never happened—another long nightmare, now over. Echoes of Lord Harlech's being "The Man Most Likely to Succeed with Jackie Kennedy" can be heard in Sparks's breathless exclamation that "'Queen Jackie' or even 'Princess Jackie' would not be bad, not bad at all. It's a shame Prince Charles isn't 30 years older!" It is, it seems, never too soon for love.

The columnist Kitty Hanson sees other possibilities, and suggests that "older, richer, and free from the constraints of national idolatry, she may be a much more liberated Jackie" and "decide not to remarry at all"—an interesting possibility effectively scotched by a school friend's assertion that, "For Jackie, men have always held the answers in life."

•

The shopping revelations Ari fed Jack Anderson in December 1974 appear in newspapers around the country in early May. "She is so avaricious, so greedy," says a "close friend of the Onassises." (Gratsos?) Her "favorite insignia is the dollar sign," Anderson writes. A "monetary monomaniac," he calls her, a woman who "raised pin money to the level of a six-figure tax shelter, and turned her clothing into a resale industry."

In response, Anderson receives "a Vesuvius of angry denials and denunciations" so intense that he writes a follow-up column establishing Ari as his source. Titled "Jackie: She Chose a Life of Uselessness," it criticizes the former First Lady for shirking her responsibility—the "staggering opportunity to serve mankind" that fate bestowed upon her—and "pursuing instead a life of luxury, languor, gowns, jewels and the wheedling of unearned wealth."

"There is always a vicarious curiosity generated by what famous and wealthy people do with their money," admits an editorialist in Minnesota. "But Jackie O. is something else again." The "enormous pride in her inspiring performance" at Kennedy's funeral contrasts with "a certain melancholy sadness to see her pictured as preoccupied with money, pure and simple, and living a vacuous life that involves flitting from continent to continent." It leads one to wonder: "Which is the real Jackie?" And "who would be a suitable partner to make her life interesting?" The only certainty in these uncertain times is that "Whatever Jackie does will make big headlines."

LATER IN MAY, SHE RETURNS TO GREECE FOR A MEMORIAL. There's a party at Artemis's house. After, she confides to her sister-in-law that she's feeling fragile, and she worries she's brought all this misfortune on herself because she'd told Jack he should be better protected, but he wouldn't listen. And she tried to get Ari to take better care of himself—to get more sleep and go to the doctor—and he wouldn't. "No matter what I did," she says, "I couldn't save either of the two men I loved." She is now, as she was when widowed in 1963, blaming herself.

While in Athens, she's interviewed. She tells the reporter she feels Aristotle Onassis "rescued me at a moment when my life was engulfed in shadows . . . he meant a lot to me. He brought me into a world where one could find both happiness and love. We lived through many beautiful experiences together which cannot be forgotten and for which I will be eternally grateful to him."

•

Nearly every day when she's in New York, she leaves 1040 Fifth at midday and crosses the street into Central Park, where she jogs around the reservoir that will later be named for her after her death. As she's cooling down one afternoon that June, a reporter approaches, and she consents to a conversation. She wears a dark blue sweatshirt, matching sneakers, and light blue jeans. Her hair is tied back in a pale blue scarf, and she has on sunglasses. Together, they sit down on a grassy bank.

She admits she's reluctant to give interviews because "if I give an interview to one paper, I'd have the whole world's press banging on my door." And she doesn't want to excite any more attention. Already, there is so much. But her pleas for privacy don't conceal some dark reality. "I want to keep my personal life private," she says, "but I certainly don't have anything to hide."

> Everyone thinks that I'm living it up all the time—but nothing could be further from the truth. I'm just trying to lead the normal life of any other American mother and be with my children. . . . After all, those poor children have been through so much over the past few years. I just want to be like any other mother with two children and lead an uncomplicated life.

She plucks a blade of grass and begins to chew it as she says:

> My life is very dull right now. I'm doing just very ordinary everyday things. Really, my life at the moment would make very uninteresting reading. Do you think it would be of much interest for anyone to know that I go shopping at the local A & P? Right now I have no trips planned abroad. All I intend to do is spend my time between the city and my

little old country home in New Jersey. Most of all, I want
to devote my time to being a good mother.

It's unclear whether she knows the reporter she's speaking to
works for the *National Enquirer*, but it's obvious that she's talking
now to combat all the bad press. It's frustrating—always seeing
yourself portrayed as someone else, people so certain of who you
are and what you're like when you can't even recognize the person
they believe you to be. She wants to bridge the gap, to clear up all
the misinformation. She's really not so awful as they say, and she's
still not entirely given up hope that, someday, people will see her
as she feels herself to be.

She shifts her sunglasses to the top of her head. "I'm sure I'm
going to be watched closely for the next year or so. Maybe people
will find out what Jackie is really like and write something different
for a change." She pauses. "I sure wish people would write something nice about me sometime."

•

As the stories swirl, she retreats to Hyannis, where she swims with
Rose Kennedy every day and reevaluates her situation. She later
says of this time,

> When I came back everything just hit me, because this was
> the only house where we really lived, where we had our
> children, where every little pickle jar I had found in some
> little country lane on the Cape was placed, and nothing's
> changed since we were in it and all of the memories came
> before my eyes. . . . And I found myself becoming so happy.
> Away from all that noise.

•

But the chatter continues. In July, *McCall's* runs a profile called
"Jacqueline: Behind the Myths." In it, Vivien Cadden writes, "She
is our national obsession. . . . We can't seem to get her out of our

consciousness and out of our conversation. . . . Why is it Jacqueline who continues to fascinate so many of us even though so many others claim to be sick and tired of her?" She wonders how Jackie will hold up in the American imagination after the death of her "unsuitable husband," concluding, "She will probably sink further in the nation's esteem," but noting "that is hardly the point." It hardly matters whether people like her or approve of her because "we are certain to be as involved with her as ever before," no matter what she does or who she is.

There's an awareness here that after all the stories about her, still they do not know her. And also an assumption arising that she does not even know herself. "Hope springs eternal that there is a real Jacqueline and that she will find herself," Cadden writes. "Let her go, let her go, God bless her. . . . If once she owed us something, or if once we thought she did, certainly she does no longer. We will have to invent another legend."

PRIVATELY, SHE'S EXPLORING, DEFYING THE DESTINY SHE'S always been taught to expect and having something of a feminist awakening. "I have always lived through men," she tells a friend. "Now I realize I can't do that any more." And so she does the most surprising possible thing for a woman who just inherited $20 million and, in autumn 1975, she takes a job as "consulting editor" at a publishing house, earning $200 for a four-day workweek.

It reads as inevitable now. At the time, the response was bemused astonishment. Clearly she did not need the money, and why else would anyone work? But she'd always doggedly pursued that Greek ideal of excellence that Jack Kennedy espoused, repeating it in her interviews with Schlesinger and in the piece she penned for *McCall's* in 1973, where she wrote, "A life is not worth living unless all one's faculties are used along lines leading to excellence." There are echoes of this in what she tells Steinem a few years later:

What has been sad for many women of my generation is that they weren't supposed to work if they had families. There they were, with the highest education, and what were they to do when the children were grown—watch the raindrops coming down the window pane? Leave their fine minds unexercised? Of course women should work if they want to. You have to do something you enjoy.

And she wants to do it on her own terms.

•

Just a few weeks after Jackie begins at Viking, Dorothy Schiff approaches her with the idea of running for the Senate from New York. When they meet for lunch to discuss the possibility, Schiff finds her more relaxed and exuberant than she has been at any of their meetings in the previous decade. Schiff is amazed to hear her tell stories about Ari and their dogs—about how the dogs would pee on the carpets on the boat and, before Ari awoke in the morning, she'd spray the living room with soda water to get the smell out so her husband would never know.

She's excited by the Senate idea and confident that, if she runs, she will win, but she's reluctant. If she's going to do it, it's got to be on her terms. She doesn't want to relocate and asks if it can be done with three days in D.C. and four days in New York. And she wishes that this opportunity weren't arising quite so soon because, she tells Schiff, she's only just reorganizing her life and she certainly hasn't decided yet what to do with the rest of it.

A week later, she decides against it and telephones Schiff, saying she realizes a campaign would be a total commitment and she doesn't want that. She says she would do it if only it were a year from now or a couple years later, but she needs to be free for the time being. A friend tells *McCall's* magazine that she wants "very much to do something on her own" at this time, and she must realize that—drawing on the old Kennedy connections and the Camelot memories—a political campaign wouldn't allow it.

"In retrospect, the most interesting thing about the barrage of directives and suggestions for her future was what they left out," Gloria Steinem writes a few years later: the fact that "no one even mentioned the idea that she might lead a life of her own" or "paid her the honor of considering her as a separate human being; as the person she was and would have been, whether or not she had married a future president."

Photographers line the entrance to Viking to get a picture of her going in. Jackie reportedly scoffs at these stories, calling them "Nancy Drew goes to work." According to her assistant, "She's out to prove herself an independent, working person." A coworker says, "She's told us she just wants to prove she can be a woman in her own right. . . . She says everybody here must call her Jackie. She's told us she's not here to play."

She's enormously proud of herself for having gotten out of that stifling world she grew up in and gotten up the nerve to go after work she enjoys. She brags that, now that she's taken a job, her son finds her so much more interesting, and she loves to tell the story of how a taxi driver once asked her, "Lady, you work and you don't *have* to?" To which she replied, "Yes," and he turned around and told her, "I think that's great!"

# PART III

# Afterlife

# MOTION PICTURE

DEC. Only 60¢

02782

**Was Marilyn Murdered?**
**Part II**

## Solving The Jackie Mystery
### By Dr. Elizabeth Thorne

A PSYCHOLOGICAL STUDY OF THE WORLD'S MOST COMPLEX WOMAN

ROBERT BLAKE:"DO YOU WANT THE TRUTH OR A BUNCH OF P.R. BULL?"–The truth,and nothing but...

HOW LIZ TOLD HENRY GOOD-BYE • WE WERE THERE!

"I'M SICK OF BEING A CELEBRITY," SHE REPORTEDLY TELLS A friend in 1976, though, like it or not, she is one. A 1976 article on Jackie's future admits that, after all these years and all that's been written about her, "Jackie as a person remains a blur . . . mystique mingled with mystery." Which is precisely what makes her so important—the fact that this blur enables her to be anyone. If "The death of John F. Kennedy fixed her, for history, in a kind of strobe light," it is distorting but also illuminating.

In the aftermath of Ari's death, she's portrayed as a regressive figure, dismissed as "a woman whose importance has been traced wholly by the men to whom she attached herself," a woman who "changed her wardrobe while other women changed their lives."

An acquaintance blabs to *McCall's*, "She *will* remarry—she will opt for marriage because she hasn't a strong enough view of herself or her goals . . . she remains a very dependent woman . . . unable to make the next jump that many women in their mid-forties are making: the decision to live their own lives, not necessarily without men but without marriage." Bess Myerson, a former Miss America turned consumer advocate, asks in frustration, "If one could just have her—and *program* her—can you imagine what a force for good and important causes she could be?" They think she is the same old Jackie.

She is, to be sure, convenient. "We don't leave her alone because she's there," the reporter Marianne Means suggests, though she notes, "It's easy to scoff at this [Jackie] phenomenon," because it's to do with gossip, emotion, and imagination—and because, as Means admits, "it's not a particularly attractive [phenomenon]." The interest, Means imagines, "is probably rooted, at least partially, in the secret thrill one can get from living vicariously." Still, in contemporary culture, "The legends of no queen—ancient, medieval, or modern—can quite match the extraordinary existence of Jacqueline Bouvier Kennedy Onassis," as a biographer will write in 1978. "She has become the world's leading celebrity," and her story, the story of her life, has become America's greatest drama and its most captivating myth.

.

"Celebrity" becomes a catchall word for her complex allure, but there is no agreement on what her life means, probably because it can mean anything: her story is not nothing, it is *everything*. It is not always the story America feels it needs or that it wants, but it is one in which Americans can see themselves: as they are and were; as they want to be and wish they were not. And so, when the writer Diana Trilling calls the marriage to Onassis "inappropriate," she quickly clarifies, "that is, inappropriate for the rest of us—what her own needs were was her own affair. She held such an extraordinary place in the public imagination. She was a figure who stood for a certain idealism in American life. It was one more thing of which the American imagination was robbed."

It's likely no coincidence that the interest in her life coincided with a historical period in which the American imagination felt it was robbed of much. And that much of what was taken away linked back to her in various ways.

In November 1960, Letitia Baldrige called her "a woman who has got everything, including the next president of the United States." In May 1970, Susan Sheehan, noting the D.C. gossip, observed that "the woman who has everything doesn't have a husband with an eye for other pretty women." But by then, Sheehan suggests, the needs of the press and the public had changed; if America was primed for glamour when Jackie arrived in 1960, later there was a distrustfulness of people in public life and "nowadays our attitude toward our celebrities . . . is properly cynical." But the existence of such a cynicism didn't obliterate the memory of that past innocence, and Jackie remained one of the few figures to straddle the divide: existing simultaneously as a memory, a living woman, and an image through which the needs of the moment could still be worked out. This gave her story an extraordinary nimbleness and flexibility, and also a special magic, which endured.

THE MAGIC ENDURES DESPITE ITS UNDERLYING UGLINESS. In 1975, based on evidence of wrongdoing that came out during the Watergate investigation, the Senate establishes a committee to investigate illegal actions within the CIA, NSA, and FBI. They are particularly interested in the subjects of domestic civilian spying and plots to assassinate foreign leaders. "Was murder part of the established foreign policy of the United States?" a *New York Times* editorialist asks. He notes that, though there is neither agreement nor clear evidence to determine whether murder was "Government-wide policy," the revelation of such a policy would have profound impact because "No other major nation since World War II has lost so many political leaders to the assassin's bullet as has the United States."

The investigators tiptoe gingerly through the unexpected field of horrors they've unsettled. Come December, a bombshell: a woman named Judith Campbell Exner placed seventy phone calls to President Kennedy at a time when she was also friendly with the mobsters Sam Giancana and Johnny Roselli. Exner holds a press conference and, though she coyly declines to say whether or not she slept with President Kennedy, when a reporter asks if, when they talked, it was "man-woman talk," she says yes. Exner also confirms that she had "a relationship" with what the AP described as "two underworld figures" at the same time she was seeing the president.

A shift is occurring in press attitudes. As the *New York Times* admits, during the Kennedy administration, "virtually all the reporters who regularly covered the President . . . were privy to rumors that he was having romances," though reporters did not investigate those rumors. It was felt that, unless the president's private life had an impact upon his public life, there was no need to report it and this was the prevailing ethical code. But in 1975, in its reporting of the Exner revelations, *Time* takes things a step further with an article linking the president to at least five other women without demonstrating how those romances affected his ability to lead. *Newsweek* concludes that, with this report, *Time* has broken "a kind of gentleman's code of silence that has long sheltered Kennedy's private diversions from public view." Now, everything is fair game.

"Camelot Tainted," blare the headlines. With these revelations, a columnist laments, "we naïve Americans, wanting and longing to believe that all is best in the best of all possible worlds, have lost our fondest illusions." The revelations, Mary McGrory writes, "added to the general feeling that all you can say about America now is 'more to come.'"

•

It keeps coming, as Jackie knew it would. Undoubtedly, she knew all along how bad it would be if the full extent ever got out. So much of her last marriage had been laid bare before the press, but it was her life with Jack, her life with the father of her children, that she'd fought fiercely to protect. Here it was slipping from her grasp, beyond her control. Caroline is eighteen and John fifteen, and she has spent all their lives trying to keep their memories of their father alive. Now, here are the ugliest parts of her life with him, on all the magazine covers and in the papers, featured on special commemorative publications entitled simply "Kennedy's Women."

She shows up at the apartment of her friend Karen Lerner on the day the New York papers first print Judith Campbell Exner's name. Lerner recalls that "she didn't seem to be seeing anything—she certainly didn't talk about that—she was just very kind of resigned and depressed." She knows there is absolutely nothing she can do.

These stories of her husband's other women are painful, and they will continue to circulate for the rest of her life.

•

In tandem with these revelations, her story migrates into the realm of biography. There's a spike in the number of books released, with three biographies appearing in 1978 alone. For many of the publications, the aim is, in the words of one, "to de-mythologise her without reducing her," to coalesce the existing stories into "one coherent whole"—a mission complicated by the fact that her intimates don't want to breach her trust and her detractors aren't trustworthy witnesses. And so the contemporary estimates of her filter into the books, where she is still, in the words of another biographer, "sphinx-like, Garbo-like, our greatest, most tantalizing, most exasperating celebrity."

The same old Jackie—frustrating, perplexing, bewitching, unreal. Marianne Means concludes her roundup of the trio of 1978 books with this observation: "No matter how tired we get of hearing about Jackie, we're stuck with her. And—she's stuck with us."

For all that everyone wonders who she is, which Jackie is real—maybe, in the end, it doesn't matter. What matters is simply that she's there, present, a star in the firmament of American life. In 1983, Norman Mailer writes in *Vanity Fair* that she is a "Prisoner of Celebrity . . . not merely a celebrity, but a legend: not a legend, but a myth—no, more than a myth: she is now a historic archetype, virtually a demiurge. . . . There are few people in the world whom the media have projected right out of themselves," Mailer writes. "Of this number, Jackie Kennedy may be the first, since history cast her as the leading lady in what must have been the greatest American drama of them all (at least, if drama has the power to make us all react as one)."

When he writes this, she is alive. And yet he uses the past tense when he declares, "She was ours. She did not belong to herself." Already it seems she is slipping away.

•

She does not disappear, though the spotlight pivots and she appears to recede in the shade of that shift, featured in the papers less and less, her story migrating to the bookshelf and the TV screen. "It seems evident to me that Jackie Onassis has been receiving less and less media exposure nowadays. Is this due to a desire on her part for less attention?" a reader asks the gossips. The answer: "So it seems."

She takes Ron Galella to court one more time, says she doesn't mind his taking her picture, but she's bothered "when he comes really close and bumps around me and makes other people stare at me." She wants to blend in. Which is impossible.

At an exhibition of African art in New York, she's standing in the corner as the question "Where is she, where's Jackie?" reverberates around the room.

Andy Warhol accompanies her to the Brooklyn Museum one afternoon and, as she pumps him for gossip on Liz Taylor, Warhol is distracted by how Jackie's name seems to float on the air.

When she leaves her wallet in a taxi, it's found and the fact that it contains a museum membership, an airline credit card, a Massachusetts driver's license, and $176.09 in cash is reported in the press.

In Gladwyne, Pennsylvania, when she uses the restroom at a gas station, a plaque is erected to commemorate her visit.

For $10, you can take a walking tour through New York that includes 1040 Fifth, the former First Lady's supermarket, florist, church, bank, drugstore, and the Encore resale shop.

She is, at once, an American myth and a real woman. When they see her, people might say, "Hi, Jackie," as they walk past. When they bump into her in airports and bookstores and theaters in New York and in convenience stores in New Jersey, they look, but out of respect, try not to be too obvious about it. Maybe they point her out to their kid, and say, *When you're older, you'll want to remember you once saw Her.*

# Tuesday, November 22, 1988

"[SHE'S] MOVED ON. YET AMERICA CLINGS TO HER AS ITS living link to Camelot, the days when hope and music were in the air," the *L.A. Times* notes upon the twenty-fifth anniversary of John Kennedy's murder. Still, "she endures as an object of fascination."

"By living a relatively normal life, raising two kids, by really making an effort not to get into the public eye, what it's done is to allow the old memories to remain and not be replaced by something different," suggests a friend.

"She stands for a time. She is the remaining familiar face from a time of hope in this country," Gloria Steinem contends. "And we have been led by fear ever since."

•

So much has changed. The movie magazines all folded and, more and more, stars open themselves up on talk TV and tell all to *People* magazine and, in the cacophony of all those other stories, hers falls from the fore as the magazines and the broadcasters rush to curry favor from the stars who give them access. "Many, many people were deeply troubled during this decade," observes a columnist. "How do we know? Because 50 percent of them admitted it in People magazine."

Eventually the novelty of her having gone back to work wears off and her life begins to resemble the lives of so many others. Privileged, yes, but *normal.*

She works in an office without a window. Quietly, with nothing near the fuss of her second marriage, the diamond merchant Maurice Tempelsman—whose wife refuses to grant him a divorce—moves his things into 1040 Fifth. Caroline marries and has children. They call her "Grand Jackie."

By the *Readers' Guide to Periodical Literature*'s count, she has more listings than any other living American woman. The columnist Ellen Goodman identifies it as "30 years of speculative, bitchy biography." Books on the bookshelves of my grandmothers and their friends: that name—*Jackie*—up there next to the newly published sequel to *Gone with the Wind*.

They are biographies wherein every receptionist or salesperson or chef who's ever encountered her has an anecdote and opinions galore. A mom with a son at John's school who feels the former First Lady was "unkempt" at a Field Day event two decades ago, when she sported "unwashed, stringy hair" and looked like "she'd just gotten out of bed." The nursing assistant at her doctor's office, who snitches that "she used to leave her dressing gown on the floor for me to pick up" and she "came in with dirty feet." The assistant tells the biographer, "I couldn't figure it out. She didn't seem to care what people thought." The owner of a bookstore doing brisk business in the Jackie trade says, "It's great trash reading."

And then there are the biopics: multi-night television movie events. A three-hour TV movie in 1981, starring the former *Charlie's Angel* Jaclyn Smith. A six-hour miniseries in 1991, starring Roma Downey. "Who will watch?" asks a reviewer of that one. "Everyone."

When her name comes up in conversation, Ellen Goodman notes, it's still just Jackie. "I do not ask Jackie Who? I know. Everybody knows." Hers is "the most private of public lives, the most public of private lives," the details of which many Americans know better than the lives of people they actually know. "How many know our own sister's shoe size?" Goodman asks. "We know Jackie's size: 10."

Younger women don't quite get it, but they've picked up pieces of the story and they also know the name. "I remember my mom and other mothers on the block talking about her," a twenty-two-year-old from Long Island tells the *New York Times*. Listening to the stories, she always assumed there were two different women. "Jackie Kennedy was the graceful, elegant hostess who gave White House tours and was the perfect mother and the perfect wife and the perfect feminine woman," while "Jackie Onassis did what she wanted. She was more aggressive. If she wanted to marry Onassis, she did. If she wanted to become a book editor, she did." This young woman says she was in high school before she realized that Jackie Kennedy and Jackie Onassis are the same.

## MONDAY, NOVEMBER 22, 1993

"[F]OR ALL THE UNAUTHORIZED BIOGRAPHIES," THE *GUARDIAN* asserts upon the thirtieth anniversary of John F. Kennedy's death— "at least twenty-five, by one count—we seem to know very little about her inner life." But maybe that never really mattered. Her life is a movie, a saga. Ultimately, it's a love story: the story of America's love for her, wherein what she really represents is America's love of itself.

And America is primed for magic again. "It's a curious thing, this notion of Jackie as nostalgia," suggests a fashion writer, surprised to find "the Jackie K. look, nestling in the glossy stock of Vogue. . . . It's Camelot—upscaled, updated, rescued from retro by an overload of faux pearls." A look that appeals because "In the 90s, women are ready to shed their mannish dress-for-success disguise and look like the women they are." Again, they look to Jackie because "Jacqueline Bouvier Kennedy Onassis has been to us most everything a high-profile woman can be—socialite, working girl, bride, grieving mother, wronged wife, widow, expatriate, proud mother, fashion plate, career woman, grandmother."

Camelot still means something, then, though perhaps it has corroded to such an extent that it just means *her*. "What does Onassis touch in the American psyche that makes her appeal so lasting?"

the *Guardian* asks, offering no answers. Only the acknowledgment that "The only thing she has ever done that was questionable in the minds of Americans was marry Onassis."

She has, at this point, less than six months left.

•

In February 1994, she's diagnosed with non-Hodgkin's lymphoma. Nancy Tuckerman releases the news in an announcement along with the fact that she's going to get better. She's hospitalized a few times with complications, but she's only sixty-four and the prognosis seems good. They caught it early. All will be well.

In April, she's hospitalized again. She and the dying Richard Nixon are in the same hospital on different floors. She says she will get better, or else all those push-ups would've been for nothing. She writes friends of how, after such a long, bitter winter, she's looking forward to spring. All will be well, she says.

"She knew," a French friend believes. "She knew she was lost."

On Monday, May 16, she's back in the hospital for a "routine visit." Nancy Tuckerman says she's fine, that she will be fine.

Two days later, she chooses to leave the hospital. She goes for a walk in Central Park with Maurice.

Thursday morning, May 19: there are reports of "serious complications." Ted Kennedy tells reporters the family is "distressed." Nancy Tuckerman does not return reporters' calls.

Thursday night, around 10:00 p.m., as Tuckerman tells reporters: "She just sort of slipped away."

"WHEN WAS THE LAST TIME ONE WOMAN SO AFFECTED THE world?" *People* wonders. In the magazine's 238-word eulogy, the refrain "We were not ready" repeats three times.

A few weeks later, Frank Rich writes in the *New York Times* that he's still puzzling over his reaction: "Though the grief feels deep, its object remains a mystery."

The editor of the tabloid *Star* confesses to Liz Smith that he wept while assembling the magazine's special tribute. "I found myself crying as I haven't since November 1963."

"I always liked Jackie for years and years," says a woman who was just a little girl at the time of the assassination. "And now you won't see her in the news pictures anymore, just in memories."

"I can't think of a woman who influenced women of my generation as much," says a forty-two-year-old who had named her daughter Jacqueline.

In New York, a doctor lays a single peony in front of 1040 Fifth and muses to a reporter that "There was something she gave to us that was very magical. I felt I loved her in some way I don't understand."

Press coverage emphasizes her manners. As Frank Rich observes, during that week, "four words were called upon again and again to define her, as if they were a mantra: grace, dignity, style, class." Those are the words on the television and in the papers, but there's also another vocabulary in use: love, memories, magic.

"We are not allowed to believe in fairy tales anymore," Sarah Crichton writes in *Newsweek*, and "no one woman can ever embody all our dreams" as Jackie once did "in a simpler time": "When we wanted to grow up to be princesses, she was our princess. And later, when we wanted to be independent, she was independent. And she was always one step ahead, and one step better. She made it all look so easy, when for the rest of women it always seemed so hard." She "seemed the embodiment of romantic myths and fairy tales," Suzanne Fields surmises in the *Washington Times*, reflecting on how, "More so than others, this First Lady was a Rorschach test, especially for women, the inkblot in which we see what we want to see, interpreting our own wishes and desires."

It's personal: "we want," "we demand," "we fell in love," "we see," "we shared." A mystical, deeply felt bond connects them to her. And this goes for both women and men.

"Jackie was your creation," Henry Allen writes in the *Washington Post*. A "figment of an undying American psyche that took pride in presuming that it deserved her . . . pieced together from women's magazines who understood her power, and from the dingy snow of pre-color television, newspapers, Life magazine." She was always provisional at best, the Jackie of the moment serving as a stand-in until the real Jackie could be deciphered, hence "the feeling yesterday that she'd died young and deprived of a future she deserved, though of course the future was ours."

"She was the embodiment of everything we hoped would turn out in this society and hasn't," Sander Vanocur tells viewers of *The Today Show* on May 23, as the car carrying her casket makes the turn down Park Avenue and the cameras pan out to show the mourners crammed outside St. Ignatius Loyola. "People are saying goodbye to a lot today."

"We were many and restless, a crowd stirred by vague emotions," writes Wayne Koestenbaum, who was standing outside the church.

> When Jackie's casket appeared, carried up the church steps, our motley congregation applauded. . . . I clapped instinctively; I wished to exclaim, to shout, to turn grief into noise. . . . About these feelings there was nothing to do, nothing to say. . . . And so we applauded, as if the funeral were a performance, and Jackie's casket were a final, astounding coup de théâtre.

As the casket is lifted into the hearse, a thirty-four-year-old cook at the World Trade Center's restaurant raises a sign reading "Camelot Will Be Reunited in Heaven" while a woman nearby tries to explain to her grandson why they are there and who Jackie was.

Claude du Granrut, the daughter of the French family she'd stayed with during her year abroad in 1949, comes out of the church behind the casket. As she walks back to her hotel, seeing she is in black, people keep approaching her to inquire: *Did you know her? How do you feel? What was she like?*

*What must she have been like?* I wonder, watching Anderson Cooper's TV report during homeroom. I don't know what it means, what she means, but I wonder. I remember those books up there on the shelves next to the sequel to *Gone with the Wind*. That night, I go home and write in my diary that I cannot stop thinking about Jacqueline Kennedy.

Twenty years later, Claude du Granrut tells me, "I think the people make her what they want."

AT HER FUNERAL, HER LOVER READ C.P. CAVAFY'S "ITHAKA": a poem about adventure, discovery, voyages, pleasures, wisdom, and joy. It was a tantalizing, exotic note in a service where the name Aristotle Onassis was not mentioned. Already, the story you have just read was being wiped away.

Newscasters called her "Mrs. Kennedy." Most of the magazine tributes featured photographs from 1961, '62, '63. There was, Wayne Koestenbaum noticed, "a revision—a rehabilitation—of Jacqueline Onassis, restoring her to sainthood . . . her marriage to Onassis was erased with the absoluteness of Soviet regimes banishing dissidents from the historical record." Just a few years later, a biographer wrote of this period that, had she not lived another twenty years and gotten a job and "moved into her final years with purpose," the story you've just read would have been "a sad, inept coda to a life of dignity and accomplishment."

The years between her husbands' deaths were rewritten: as an embarrassment, a waste of time, rather than both a crucially important part of the story that connected her to all those people watching and also a huge part of the adventure that was her life. A time of much sadness and disappointment and struggle, it was also one of discovery and exploration and risk, all of it necessary to where she wound up, part of who she was and why people cared.

In the beginning, she wanted to escape and stay on the surface of things. By the mid-1970s, it was about possibilities and being present. At a dinner party, the poet Stephen Spender asked what she considered her biggest accomplishment. She told him it was that, after a rather difficult time, she remained "comparatively sane."

An understatement, for she wasn't just sane, she was triumphant. Her friend Vivian Crespi recalled the pair of them lying on a beach in bikinis, sipping rosé. And she remembered Jackie turning to her and saying, "Do you realize how lucky we are? To have gotten out of that world we came from. That narrow world of Newport. . . . You and I have taken such a big bite out of life."

"You must take it all together," she told the reporter in Tehran. "That is life." That is *a* life.

•

It's a story that goes on and on, beyond her and them and you and me, beyond the past and present, hurtling always ahead. Constantly changing, on the story goes, slipping from us, quick quick. Because we can never *really* know her, no matter how we'd like to think it. No matter how we keep reading and writing and reaching, through all these words from the last half-century and all the words not yet written, to find her.

We reach for someone who, even when she was alive, was already lost to us. Someone who was *something*: a story, a star, a ruin of an America in which we wish we lived and still want to believe in, even if it does not yet exist.

Jackie: she is always just beyond, her name electric on the air. However much we clamor, still she runs ahead. She flees us. And so she exists as possibilities: a life so well known but inevitably unknowable, a hodgepodge of guesses and tales we tell ourselves.

After our interview, when she hugs me goodbye, Gloria Steinem says, "If someone had to write about her, she probably would've been glad it was you." Her stepbrother tells me, "She would have liked that you're doing this."

That these statements are true is a story I let myself believe.

"Sometimes people ask . . ." said the photographer Henri Cartier-Bresson, in an audio clip that played over a loudspeaker as she sat on a folding chair alone in the darkened library of the not yet opened International Center for Photography in the autumn of 1974. An audio clip that held enough resonance for her to use a significant portion of the 1,500 words allotted, and quote it at length, in the final paragraph of the only article she ever wrote for the *New Yorker*.

His words as she heard them:

*Sometimes people ask, "How many pictures do you take?" . . . Well, there is no rule. Sometimes, like in this picture in Greece, well, I saw the frame of the whole thing and I waited for somebody to pass. . . . That is why it develops a great anxiety in this profession . . . always waiting. What is going to happen? . . . Quick, quick, quick, quick, like an animal and a prey. . . . I'm extremely impulsive . . . a bunch of nerves, but I take advantage of it. . . . You have to be yourself and you have to forget yourself. . . . And poetry is the essence of every- thing. . . . The world is being created every minute and the world is falling to pieces every minute. . . . It is these tensions I am always moved by. . . . I love life. I love human beings. I hate people also. . . . I enjoy shooting a picture, being present. It's a way of saying, "Yes! Yes! Yes!" . . . .And there's no maybe.*

# INDEX

# NOTES AND BIBLIOGRAPHY

# ABOUT THE AUTHOR

A scholar of biographical writing and a writer of creative nonfiction, Oline Eaton examines the intersections of celebrity, feelings, feminism, language, and trauma in her work. She holds degrees from Mississippi State University, the University of Chicago, and King's College London, and currently teaches first-year writing as a contingent, non-tenure-track lecturer at Howard University. Previously, she taught journalism as an instructor at The School of the New York Times, and first-year college writing as an adjunct at the University of Memphis, Trinity Washington University, American University, and New York University (D.C., NYC, and Shanghai). She lives in Washington, D.C., with her cats, Claude and Marcel.